Charles H Brigham.
April 1st 1878.

Saml. J. May

MEMOIR

OF

Samuel Joseph May.

BOSTON:
ROBERTS BROTHERS.
1873.

CAMBRIDGE:
PRESS OF JOHN WILSON AND SON.

THIS BRIEF

LIFE OF SAMUEL JOSEPH MAY

Is Dedicated

To the memory of his father, JOSEPH MAY, the faithful guide of his childhood; to JOHN THORNTON KIRKLAND, HENRY WARE, NOAH WORCESTER, and WILLIAM ELLERY CHANNING, the guides of his youth and early manhood;

AND

To all those, living or departed, who aided in or sympathized with his devoted labors in the cause of liberty, peace, temperance, education, and the advancement of the Gospel of JESUS CHRIST.

PREFACE.

IN July, 1871, Mr. May's family asked GEORGE B. EMERSON, SAMUEL MAY, and THOMAS J. MUMFORD to attend to the preparation of a suitable Memoir; and this committee intrusted the editing of the work to its youngest member.

A considerable portion of the volume consists of a partial autobiography. To this is added some extracts from a diary. The succeeding chapters have been furnished by members of the committee, assisted by many kind friends, including Messrs. C. D. B. Mills, Joseph A. Allen, William Lloyd Garrison, A. Bronson Alcott, W. P. Tilden, G. W. Hosmer, Edgar Buckingham, T. W. Higginson, and Joseph May.

The story of Mr. May's antislavery career is now presented in a condensed form, because it was given to the public some years ago in his "Recollections of the Antislavery Conflict."

The chief purpose of the compilers of this book has been to impart such a truthful impression of its subject's character as shall make young men see the beauty and feel the power of a noble life.

CONTENTS.

SKETCH

OF THE

LIFE OF SAMUEL J. MAY.

CHAPTER I.

CHILDHOOD.

ANCESTORS. — DEATH OF HIS BROTHER EDWARD. — HEAVENLY VISIONS. — A COLORED PLAYMATE. — A KIND COLORED WOMAN.

I WAS born in Boston, Massachusetts, on the twelfth day of September, 1797.

My father was Joseph — widely known as Col. Joseph — May, who was the son of Samuel May of Boston, by his second wife Abigail Williams of Roxbury.[1]

[1] Joseph May was born in Boston, 1760, and died there, 1841, at the age of eighty-one. In his youth, the family were members of the Hollis Street Church and Society; but, owing to dissatisfaction with the ministry of Dr. Mather Byles, — or, more likely, with his political attitude, — they ceased attendance there for a season, and joined themselves to the Old South congregation, where Joseph, who to his latest day was a good singer and especially fond of sacred music, sang in the choir at the early age of twelve years. When the Old South people were driven from their house of worship by the British troops stationed in Boston, they met, for about five years, at King's Chapel, the use of which was granted to them. On their return to their own house in 1783, Mr. May, then in his twenty-third year, preferred to remain at the Chapel, of which church he continued an active and devoted mem-

My mother was Dorothy Sewall, daughter of Samuel Sewall of Boston, by his wife Elizabeth Quincy, niece

ber and officer (one of the wardens) during his life. In 1785 he was one of the twenty who voted to make those alterations in the Liturgy which separated King's Chapel from the Trinitarian communion and from the Episcopal Church; and in 1787 he was one of the small but resolved congregation who ordained Dr. James Freeman by their own authority to be their minister, — a relation which continued upwards of forty years with uninterrupted respect and benefit.* His later pastor, Dr. Greenwood, and his life-long associate and friend, William Minot, Esq., have both spoken in published notices of his character and worth. "He considered it," they say, "most unworthy of a rational and moral being to seek after riches as the *chief good*. . . . His integrity has never been questioned. Important trusts were confided to him, and held until advancing age warned him to resign them. . . . He might be traced through every quarter of the city by the footprints of his benefactions. . . . His piety was practical, his religion was life-religion. His belief in the sure mercies of God and promises of the Saviour was as firm and deeply rooted as the mountains. His faith in a future and better life was as sight. It was not his lot to influence the destinies of whole communities; but, in the duties of a peacemaker, in reforming guilt, in relieving suffering, in protecting the orphan, and in raising weakness from despondency, he was actively engaged during his whole life. . . . He proved that wealth and fashion are not essential to the highest respectability; and his friends will agree that they have rarely known his superior in virtue or wisdom." He was of a continually cheerful spirit, and of unusual social gifts; an easy and witty talker, with a fine sense of humor and a fund of personal anecdotes and illustrative stories, which he told with spirit, and always to the delight of listeners. He was a great reader, but not a miscellaneous one; having for his favorite authors the best English historians, such poets as Pope and Addison, and the theologians of most advanced thought, — Priestley especially.

On his mother's side, S. J. May was related to the Sewalls and

* Sermon on the Death of Joseph May, Esq. By F. W. P. Greenwood, D.D. Boston, 1841.

of Josiah Quincy of Revolutionary memory, and sister of Dorothy, the wife of John Hancock, for whom my mother was named.

Quincys, — families whose private worth and public eminence are well known, not in New England only, but far beyond its bounds. His great-grandfather was Rev. Dr. Joseph Sewall, of the Old South Church (born 1688, died 1769). His direct ancestor (the father of Rev. Dr. Sewall) was Chief Justice Samuel Sewall (born in England, 1652, died, Boston, 1730). He it was, who, having in middle life participated (as a junior judge) in the trial and condemnation to death, at Salem, of many persons accused of witchcraft, afterwards strove in so many ways to atone for that early wrong. "He observed annually, in private, a day of humiliation and prayer, during the remainder of his life, to keep fresh in his mind a sense of repentance and sorrow for the part he bore in those trials. On the day of the general fast, he rose in the place where he was accustomed to worship, — the Old South, in Boston, — and, in the presence of the great assembly, handed up to the pulpit a written confession, acknowledging the error into which he had been led, praying for the forgiveness of God and his people, and concluding with a request to all the congregation to unite with him in devout supplication, that it might not bring down the displeasure of the Most High upon his country, his family, or himself. He remained standing during the public reading of the paper. This was an act of true manliness and dignity of soul." * Whittier has commemorated in verse the "sad and touching tale"

> "Of the fast which the good man life-long kept
> With a haunting sorrow that never slept,"

and of his deep and yearning desire, for his country as well as himself,

> "That the sin of his ignorance, sorely rued,
> Might be washed away in the mingled flood
> Of his human sorrow and Christ's dear blood!"

Those who knew Samuel Joseph May will recognize, in these brief portraits of his ancestry, traits which had strong resemblances in him, and will see, as the common phrase is, that he came honestly

* Upham's History of Witchcraft, vol. ii. p. 442.

My name was to have been James Freeman, after the late Dr. Freeman, minister of King's Chapel, Boston, my father's pastor and very intimate friend. But, although my parents had lost two sons named Samuel Joseph, the second dying the week after my birth, yet the name was so comprehensive of the family names both on my father's and my mother's side, that they concluded to confer it upon me. Samuel was the name of my father's only brother, and of his father. It was also the name of my mother's oldest brother, the late Chief Justice of Massachusetts, Hon. Samuel Sewall; of their father, and of their great-grandfather, who was the Chief Justice in the time of the Salem witchcraft, and was among the first to suspect, and afterwards to expose, the delusion. Joseph was the name of my father, and of his mother's father, and her favorite brother. It was also the name of my mother's second brother, the late Joseph Sewall of Boston; and of their venerated grandfather, Dr. Joseph Sewall of the Old South Church, in whose family my mother lived a number of years.

Thus denominated, I started upon the journey of life, in a very frail body, which so continued until my twelfth or fourteenth year. I was a very puny boy. The joys and sorrows of my childhood were, I suppose, very similar to those of other boys. But there was one

by his genial and cheerful nature; by his freedom from concealment and pretence; by his promptness to avow his convictions; by his courage to stand for the right; and by his sympathy with all forms and cases of human suffering and wrong. S. M.

great grief that probably made the deepest religious impression that my soul ever received.

I had a brother, Edward, two years older than myself. He was a fair-haired boy, with blue eyes, bright, playful, affectionate, and particularly fond of me. We slept together, we ate together; and he taught me all the sports I was old enough to take part in. He had recently commenced going to school, and I every day awaited his return, in the assurance that he would bring me something to gratify or do something to amuse me. One day, when he was six years and eight months old, he came home at early noon, full of glee, and summoned me to the yard to partake of his sport. He climbed the fence against the barn, pretending to sweep chimney; and, when the imaginary work was done, he attempted to get down by resting his weight upon the slender post of a chair, the top of which was broken off. The post gave way, and its splintered point penetrated his body, several inches, under his arm. Screams from the servants, who were near by, brought our fond mother to the spot. She, not knowing what had happened, supposed he had fainted or been stunned by a blow, and ordered a warm bath. But on raising his arm to remove his clothes, blood gushed out and revealed the deadly wound. She fainted on the floor by his side. The servants ran for some physician; neighbors came in offering assistance; all was confusion and dismay. My father and the doctor arrived as soon as possible. But the dear, beautiful boy was dead. The agony of my parents, the crying of my elder brother and sisters, assured me that something dreadful had happened; and there my beloved Edward was, eyes shut, body cold, giving no replies to the tender things that were said to him, taking no notice of all that was being done to him or about him. I gave myself up to a passion of grief, knowing not what it was, — but that some strange, awful change had come over him. Then they put grave-clothes upon him, and laid him upon the mattress in the best chamber, and straightened out his limbs, and folded his beautiful hands upon his breast, and covered him only with the clean, cold, white sheet. I saw it all, — for they could not keep me away, — and when father and mother and the kind assisting friends had darkened the room, and were about to withdraw, I besought them to let me lie down with Edward. My importunity was so earnest, so passionate, that my parents were almost afraid, and quite too tender, to withstand it. When left alone with him, or rather it, I well remember how I kissed his cold cheek and lips, pulled open his eyelids, begged him to speak to me, and cried myself to sleep because he would not.

At tea-time I was carried to the table; but the weeping of all about me, added to my own dismay, destroyed my appetite. I ate but little, and only asked that I might be permitted to go back to the chamber and lie by the side of Edward. My request was granted; and there I lay, until my grief was forgotten again in sleep, when I must have been removed, for I found myself next morning in the bed where I had usually slept with my brother, in my mother's chamber. But I hurried back to the corpse of Edward; and kept with it almost all the time until I was taken from it forever. I saw my father put the body into the coffin, in order, as he told me, that it might be laid away in the ground, and then we should see Edward no more. But he and my mother, and my brother and sisters, continually assured me that Edward was still living, — that he had become an angel, and had gone to heaven, to dwell with the good and the happy in the presence of God and Christ.

Two days after the death, the house was filled with weeping relatives and friends, with whom Edward had been a particular favorite. Our good minister read the burial service. I could not understand it; but it was solemn, impressive, and I listened with awe.

Then we went slowly, in solemn procession, to the burial-ground: all was new, strange, awful, to me. But when the carriages stopped at the gate, and I saw them taking the coffin off towards the tomb, I insisted upon seeing what they were going to do with Edward. So my uncle, Samuel May, took me in his arms, descended with me into the family vault, and showed me where the sextons had put away my brother. Then he pointed out the little coffins in which were the remains of several of my brothers and sisters, who had lived and died before I was born, and the coffin in which my grandfather was buried eight years before. My kind uncle opened one of the coffins and let me see how decayed the body had become, told me that Edward's body was going to decay in like manner, and at last become like the dust of the earth. But he again most tenderly assured me that Edward was still living, that his spirit was not in the coffin, that it was clothed with another more beautiful, glorious body, and that he had gone to live in heaven with God and Christ and the angels. Then he lifted once more the lid of Edward's coffin, and let me kiss again and for the last time his cheek, his lips, his forehead. I went home in a sort of maze, crying, and asking questions which the wisdom of man could not answer.

My only brother, Charles, then a lad fourteen or fifteen years of age, tenderly took me up to his chamber, lay down with me on his bed, and tried to comfort me and himself by telling me all that he imagined to be true about heaven and God and angels, and assuring me again, as others had done, that Edward had gone to live in that blessed place, in that happy and glorious company. Of course I believed all that such dear, good friends told me.

When night came, I was put to bed in the room where I had so often lain and slept with Edward. Sleep soon came to relieve my young spirit wearied with grief and strange excitement. And I dreamt — dreamt of Edward. All that had been told me was proved true by what I saw and felt. The ceiling of the room opened, over where I was lying: a bright, glorious light burst in, and from the midst of it came down my lost brother, attended by a troop of little angels. They left him. He lay by me as he used to do, his head on my arm or my head on his. He told me how happy he was, what a beautiful place heaven was, how kind God and Christ were to him, and how all the angels loved one another. There he lay until morning, when the ceiling above opened again, and the troop of angels came to bear him back to heaven. He kissed me, sent messages of love to father and mother, brother and sisters, and gladly rejoined the celestial company.

So soon as I awoke and was dressed, I hurried down to tell the family what I had seen, and to give them the kisses and messages that dear Edward had sent them. All day long I thought and talked of what I had seen; often, as I have since been told, expressed impatience to have night come; and when it came, went eagerly to bed, in the confident expectation that the heavenly vision would be granted me again. And it was. The next night, and for several nights afterwards, I enjoyed the felt presence of my brother, and morning after morning came down with the same or slightly varied messages of love. Until by degrees my grief abated, the loss of my brother was in some measure supplied by other playmates, new things attracted my attention and occupied my thoughts. But I have never forgotten my Edward, and the events of his death and burial; and the scenes that I witnessed, and the heavenly vision that I had, are vivid in my memory, although most of my life for several years afterwards is very indistinct.

I have been thus particular in narrating this part of

my life, because I believe it had the greatest influence in awakening and fixing in my soul the full faith I have in the continuance of life after death. Indeed, it sometimes seems to me that I do not believe more fully in the life that now is than in the life that is to come, and, moreover, that the future existence commences immediately after the close of the present.

In the fall of 1852, I received a letter from Mrs. H. B. Stowe, requesting me to inform her how much and how intimately I had been acquainted with negroes; what incidents in my life had probably prepared me to embrace the cause of the colored people so early and so earnestly as I had done. Of course, her request impelled me to look back, with an eager, searching eye, through the whole of my life, especially the early part of it, when biases in one direction or another were most easily taken. I was surprised at the many things which no doubt have had some influence in predisposing me to perceive and abhor the great injustice and cruelty of our country towards those whose only peculiar fault is that they are "guilty of a skin not colored like our own." Two of these things I will record here.

It has been a benefit to me, through life, that when a little boy, from five to seven years of age, I attended a Ma'am school, kept by a good old lady, — Mrs. Wallcut, — in company with boys and girls of various condition of life, some from the richest and others from the poorer families in the neighborhood. I well remember that I sat upon the same bench, and recited in the same class, with a boy whose skin was as dark as a starless night, but whose spirit was as bright and joyous as a cloudless noon-day. He was certainly more witty, if not more wise, than any of my school-fellows, and therefore was the favorite of us all. He was as good as the best in reading, spelling, repeating the Catechism, and in counting, which was the extent of our literary exercises; and in all our plays few were his equals.

About the same time, when six or seven years of age, I was going on an errand for my mother. A dog sprang after me, I ran, often looking backward as I was going forward. I fell, struck my temple upon a stone, and lay senseless. On recovering my consciousness, I found myself in the arms of a large black woman. As soon as I opened my eyes, she said very soothingly, "Don't be afraid, little boy. I know who you are. I'll carry you to your mamma." On reaching home, — my face, bosom, and hand smeared with the blood which had flowed freely from the wound, — the sight of me filled the family with alarm. My mother was agonized with the fear that, like Edward, I had met with some fatal accident. In her concern for me, she forgot every thing else. She stripped off my bloody clothes, washed my face and my hands, examined carefully the gash upon my temple, and found the injury to be not so serious as she feared. Then she thought of the kind woman who had picked me up, and looked around gratefully to thank and to offer her some reward. But my benefactress had disappeared. She remained long enough to be satisfied that I had not sustained much harm, and then quietly withdrew, not lingering to be thanked, or to receive any compensation, as very many poor white women would have done. Nor did she ever come to the house to "get her pay." Nor could we find out where she lived, or who she was, though my mother made much inquiry, wishing to make some return for the good deed she had done.

CHAPTER II.

CHILDHOOD CONCLUDED.

Visit at Marblehead. — A Severe Master. — The Jews. — First Sin. — Loss of Eden. — Rev. Dr. Channing. — A Lesson of True Benevolence.

SOON after my recovery from this disaster, I was sent to Marblehead to stay several months in the family of my uncle, Chief Justice Sewall. My uncle, aunt, and the children were each and all devoutly religious persons. Three of his five sons — Samuel, Edmund, Charles Chauncy — became ministers of the Gospel. One of the other two, Joseph, — who died while in college, — meant to be a minister; and Henry D., who was a merchant, — first in Montreal, afterwards in New York, partner of Arthur Tappan, — ought to have been a minister. I never knew children so early and so deeply imbued with the spirit of piety. I well remember their morning and their evening prayers, their shrinking horror of every profane or obscene word, and their practical, active charity. I gratefully record my indebtedness to them and their pious parents.

My uncle thought it best for me to attend school with his boys. So I went to the Marblehead Academy, then kept by Master Cole. He was a severe man, — believed in the rod, promptly, and not sparingly, applied.

That was the doctrine of the day. But to his treatment of me I ascribe my early conversion to the methods of moral suasion.

I was a little boy, able to learn — it was then supposed — only to read and spell. Twice each half-day, I was exercised, five or ten minutes, in reading and spelling lessons. All the rest of the three hours I was required, with other little boys, to sit upright upon a hard bench, doing nothing but thinking how irksome it was, and wishing that I had something to do. At length, one day, I set myself to work. I got a thread four or five feet long, tied it to a pin which I bent into a hook; I tore up a paper into small pieces, which I rolled into forms that it pleased me to regard as fishes. These I scattered upon the floor; and then, throwing down my hook, attempted to catch them and draw them in. I had not captured more than two or three, when I received several smart boxes upon my ears, and heard from the voice of my master the sharp reproof, — "You naughty boy, I'll teach you to behave better in school time!" He taught me what he little intended to do. He taught me to regard and fear him as a harsh, cruel man. I felt (though I do not suppose I clothed the feeling in these words) that he ought to have given me something to do, or else let me occupy myself as best I could.

Marblehead was then a queerer place than it is now. The people were almost wholly engaged in the fisheries, and in other kinds of navigation. A very large proportion of the men were sailors or sea-captains or mates, often absent from home on long voyages; so that the women were left to take care of the children, and manage their own affairs. They consequently became very self-sustaining and independent; and the feminine graces were not much cultivated. Then, being ignorant and used to frequent excitements caused by tales of hardship and fearful catastrophes, they were superstitious. There were fortune-tellers, and several weird women amongst them. Several houses in the town were haunted, and stories of ghostly apparitions were often current. Of course these things had some effect upon the imaginations of my cousins and myself. We dreaded the influence of the moon, and preferred to see the new one for the first time over the right shoulder rather than the left. But their parents and mine were very careful to assure us that there were no beings, out of the body, who would or could injure good little boys, and that we need be afraid of *nothing but sin.*

If the children of my day were taught, among other foolish things, to dread, if not despise, Jews, a very different lesson was impressed upon my young heart. There was but one family of the despised children of the house of Israel resident in Boston, — the family of Moses Michael Hays: a man much respected, not only on account of his large wealth, but for his many personal virtues and the high culture and great excellence of his wife, his son Judah, and his daughters, — especially Catherine and Slowey. His house, far down in Hanover Street, then one of the fashionable streets of the town, was the abode of hospitality; and his family moved in what were then the first circles of society. He and his truly good wife were hospitable, not to the rich alone, but also to the poor. Many indigent families were fed pretty regularly from his table. They would come especially after his frequent dinner-parties, and were sure to be made welcome, not to the crumbs only, but to ampler portions of the food that might be left.

Always, on Saturday, he expected a number of friends to dine with him. A full-length table was always spread, and loaded with the luxuries of the season; and he loved to see it surrounded by a few regular visitors and others especially invited. My father was a favorite guest. He was regarded by Mr. Hays and his whole family as a particular friend, their chosen counsellor in times of perplexity, and their comforter in the days of their affliction. My father seldom failed to dine at Mr. Hays's on Saturday, and often took me with him; for he was sure I should meet refined company there.

Both Uncle and Aunt Hays (for so I called them) were fond of children, particularly of me; and I was permitted to stay with them several days, and even weeks, together. And I can never forget, not merely their kind, but their conscientious care of me. I was the child of Christian parents, and they took especial pains that I should lose nothing of religious training so long as I was permitted to abide with them. Every night, I was required, on going to bed, to repeat my

Christian hymns and prayers to them, or else to an excellent Christian servant woman who lived with them many years. I witnessed their religious exercises, — their fastings and their prayers, — and was made to feel that they worshipped the Unseen Almighty and All-merciful One. Of course I grew up without any prejudice against Jews, — or any other religionists, because they did not believe as my father and my mother believed.

I was accounted a good little boy, and well remember that I used to love to be so, and to be so considered. And, notwithstanding ill health, I was a very happy, joyous child. I had many friends, and was rather a favorite among them.

But, when I was eight or nine years old, an event happened that expelled me from Eden, and made me very wretched. I think my recollections of it have helped me to understand and to expound, as I do, the account in Genesis of the fall of our first parents.

I had a sister Eliza, a year and a half younger than myself, to whom I was much attached. One day I saw at a toy-shop a doll, which I was sure it would delight her to have; but I possessed not money enough to buy it. While I was pondering in my mind how I should raise the means to gratify her and myself, I went with my mother to spend the afternoon and take tea with an aunt. Going about the house in search of amusement, I chanced to find, in the chamber of the maid-servant, lying upon the table, just the little sum of money that I needed. The temptation was too strong for me. I took it, and got away from the house without detection. The next day, after school, I ran to the toy-shop, purchased the doll and carried it home, and gave it, somewhat clandestinely, to my sister. Of course it soon became known throughout the house that Eliza had a new doll, and that it was given to her by her loving brother. But then, alas! the question arose, how did he obtain it? It was bought at Mrs. ——— shop. But where did he get money enough to pay for it? I was able to answer the first inquirers so as to satisfy them for the moment. I soon found myself involved in the necessity of inventing other falsehoods to conceal the first. The predicament was a new one to me. My perplexity was most distressing. I avoided as much as possible the members of the family. I especially feared the faces of my parents. Their eyes seemed to penetrate my bosom and read the secret. When alone, I was not at ease; for I heard a voice saying, "Thief, you stole it." Nothing amused me, nothing beguiled me of myself. Even music, of which I was very fond, and which my older sisters made of the sweetest kind, failed to quiet my troubled spirit. Every thing about me was changed. Our pleasant little parlor was dreary, and home a dreadful place.

I endured my misery but a day or two. Then I went to my parents and confessed my crime, telling them the whole truth. They were astonished and grieved, but they commiserated me in my sorrow and shame and soothed me by their compassion, while they exposed fully the heinous nature of the crime I had committed, and showed me to what horrible consequences here and hereafter a thievish disposition would lead.

They gave me money enough, and required me to go to the servant-maid from whom I had stolen it, confess to her my fault, repay what I had taken from her, and ask her forgiveness. I did it all willingly, gladly, and was greatly relieved. The woman treated me kindly, and only admonished me that I should come to a dreadful end, if I should continue to be a thief; but graciously expressed the belief that I should never steal again. The recollection of the thoughts and feelings that I had in those days is almost as vivid as the consciousness of them was at the time. I shall never forget how guilt darkened the day, made the night dismal, changed the aspect of my home, and gave to the voices of my parents a tone at which I started in affright. I was driven out of Eden.

One of the greatest advantages I have enjoyed in life has been my acquaintance with Rev. Dr. Channing. It commenced at an early day, when I was quite a small boy, and continued until his decease. He lived in Federal Street, not far from my father's house, so that I could go alone to his study when I was not more than six or seven years of age. He would talk most kindly to me, and instruct me by pictures of objects in nature and art. I can distinctly remember only one of my visits to him at that time. As his treatment of me then made a salutary impression upon my mind as well as memory, I deem it worthy of preservation.

I had tarried with him as long as his engagements would permit me to stay. He had entertained and instructed me by some pictures, in which I was much interested; and, among his lessons, he had, as usual, pressed upon me the duty of kindness to the poor and unhappy, assuring me that I should always enjoy, all the more, the good things which my heavenly Father accorded to my lot in life, if I shared them with those who were less fortunate. He told me that he could not allow me to tarry with him any longer at that time, as he was then very busy. So he bade me good-by, giving me, at the moment, three nice cakes, one for myself, and one for each of my younger sisters. On my way home I met a poor, ragged boy, about my own size. He looked very wishfully at the sweet things I was carrying in my hands; perhaps he asked me for one of them. Anyhow, I gave him one, and ran back to tell Mr. Channing how promptly I had followed his instructions, not doubting that he would give me another cake to supply the place of that which I had bestowed upon the poor boy, and to reward me for my charitableness. To my surprise, then, he merely commended very highly what I had done, telling me it was much better for me that I had given the sweetmeat to the little beggar, who probably seldom, if ever, got any thing so nice to eat, whereas I had plenty of pleasant food every day; and sent me off again with only the cakes for my sisters. There was a heavenly wisdom in his dealing with me at that time which I have often thought of since, and for which I have always been grateful.

CHAPTER III.

SCHOOL DAYS.

Ma'am Schools. — Mr. Cummings. — Mr. Daniel Adams. — Rev. Dr. Richmond, at Stoughton. — First and only Punishment. — Taught to be Careful.

MY generous father, who thought the best patrimony he could give to his children was a good education, spared no expense that was needful to insure us the best instruction. So we were sent to the private schools in Boston that enjoyed the highest reputation. The public schools of that day, although good, were not what they now are and have been since the days of Horace Mann.

From five to eight years of age, I attended what were then called Ma'am schools, — the first one kept in Milk Street by a Mrs. Cazeneau and her daughter, the second in High Street, kept by Mrs. Wallcut and her daughter. My only recollection of the former (excepting the kind looks of the school-mistress and the daily routine of exercises) is the temporary loss of my youngest sister, Abby, — now Mrs. A. B. Alcott, — then about four years of age. Eliza and I had persuaded our mother to allow us to take our darling little sister along with us to school. We had led her there and home again safely for several days, and she had become so eager to accompany us that she became quite a regular attendant. At length, it was regarded as a matter of course that she was to go to school as we did. We were less anxious about her, less watchful of her, feeling less our responsibility for her safety. One afternoon, as we were returning home with a party of our fellows and playing by the way, Abby slipped off into a side street, and went to find something curious of which she had heard, she knew not what nor where. So soon as we missed her, we commenced a search, but it was in a direction different from that which she had taken. We became alarmed, and ran home to report that she was lost. Of course the whole family were put in requisition to find the wanderer, and we were left at home alone to bemoan our carelessness, and indulge our fears for the fate of our little sister. First one, then another, returned from a fruitless search, only to aggravate our alarm, and make more glaring the sin of our unfaithfulness to the trust committed to us. Not until late in the evening was our anxiety relieved, when a young man, a cousin, came leading her in, weary and frightened, from a distant part of the city, where he had found her.

The most distinct recollection that I have of Ma'am Wallcut's school, excepting of the black boy already mentioned, is of a conversation that I had with my little school-fellows about heaven, one noon when we were kept in the school-room during the intermission because it rained. Our reading-lesson that forenoon had been in the New Testament, something about heaven and its joys. I do not remember what particular passage it was. The question was raised by some one of the children, in what the happiness of heaven consisted. Various conjectures were offered: I do not remember what they were, excepting two. One little girl said she thought we should have plenty of burnt almonds there. I told them, I expected we should sit up at table and drink coffee. This low conception was undoubtedly suggested by the fact that I, with my sister Eliza, was required to *stand* at the breakfast-table and eat bread and milk, while my parents and older sisters and brother sat at table and regaled themselves upon coffee and toast.

The first man's school that I went to was kept by Mr. Cummings, the author of the Geography which for a number of years enjoyed a high reputation. He was considered a teacher of superior skill, and for a number of years his school was regarded as the best in Boston. It was kept in a pleasant, wooden building situated in a yard in the rear of the Federal Street (Dr. Channing's) Church, at the corner of Berry Street. Unfortunately for me, Mr. Cummings resigned his place soon after I had become his pupil. Mr. Lanceolet Lyon succeeded him, — an inferior, though still a successful teacher, who enjoyed a good reputation for fifteen or twenty years. I attended his school until I was ten or eleven years of age, and was then put to Mr. Daniel Adams, the author of the well-known Arithmetic, who had come to the city with considerable renown, and occupied rooms in Court Street. There I commenced the study of Latin; but made very little progress in that or any other branch of learning, for I was frequently interrupted by serious sicknesses, and more often by severe headaches. The rooms which we occupied were low; no attention was paid to ventilation, and the air became so impure that almost every day I was disabled by nausea, headache, or lassitude.

My health was so poor that it was thought indispensably necessary that I should go into the country to live. So I was sent to Stoughton to reside in the family of Rev. Edward Richmond, afterwards D.D. He was a good and a sensible man, but not much of a teacher. He had only four or six pupils, — no two pursuing precisely the same studies. There was no excitement in the school, but dulness reigned there. It was not intended that I should be kept very closely at my books. Health, rather than learning, was the object of my rustication. So I was allowed to keep out, much of the time, in the open air: to range the fields, ride horse to plough, drive the cows to and from the pasture, and work in my garden. But I was very homesick, though my health had improved in other respects.

At the expiration of about a year, I was taken home again, and put to school to Mr. Elisha Clap, who kept in a large room under the First Church in Chauncy Place. He was accounted a very thorough scholar, and a strict disciplinarian, severe withal. He had been for a number of years Principal of the Academy at Sandwich; and had come to Boston to take charge of a select school of only twenty-five boys, for whose instruction he was to be paid one hundred dollars a year for each. This was a higher sum than had ever been paid a teacher in that city before. Chief Justice Parsons, Judge Parker, Harrison Gray Otis, Samuel Eliot, William Gray, *et id omne genus*, were his patrons. It was a good school, though his methods of teaching would now be considered obsolete, and his plans of discipline not highly esteemed. Under his instruction I fitted for college, and was entered without conditions, after the Commencement vacation, September, 1813, when just sixteen years old. Before I remove to Cambridge, I will narrate the occurrence which alone I had in view when I commenced this chapter, and which suggested its title.

Throughout all my school-days, I had endeavored to be a good boy; partly because I dreaded punishment, and partly because I loved to be accounted a good boy and carry home to my parents every week a note of commendation.

Mr. Clap was very strict, and our parents liked him all the better for that. He not only allowed no whispering in study hours, no communications by letter or by signs, but he allowed no unnecessary noises, when in our desks, or while going to or from the place of recitation, or coming in or going out of the school-room. Letting fall a book or slate, or any thing that could be heard on striking the floor, he accounted an offence, and forbade it by special regulation. Every one who met with that accident was to be punished by one blow with a ferule upon his hand. Few escaped.

Four or five months before I left the school for college, — when intent upon completing well my preparation, — I was engaged one day in a Latin recitation with my class, standing against the front row of desks, upon which we were permitted to lay our grammars, to be used if needed. A question about the construction of a sentence arose between a classmate and myself. It was a nice point. The teacher was pleased, and allowed, as he often did, some brief debate between us. In order to justify the construction upon which I insisted, I turned hastily round to get my grammar, in which I knew I should find a note exactly to my purpose. Unluckily, I had laid the book upon the desk just so, that, in turning, my elbow hit it and knocked it off. It fell to the floor, with not a little noise. A cloud settled upon the brow of the master. I faintly hoped that the punishment would be remitted in consideration of my exemplary conduct throughout the nearly three years that I had been his pupil. But, alas! he was inexorable. The punishment was inflicted in presence of the whole school. I cared not for the pain it gave me; but the sense of injustice and of disgrace wounded me to the quick.

I rushed home, and unburthened my full heart to my affectionate mother. She accepted at once my view of the case. We came to the conclusion that I ought not to be allowed to return to the school, unless Mr. Clap would make ample amends. Soon after, my father came in to dinner. He perceived the perturbation, and was at once informed of the cause, — the outrage that had been committed upon me. To our astonishment, he did not seem to catch the flame of our indignation. After a few minutes, he said, tenderly, but very firmly: "You were careless, my son. Carelessness is not a venial offence: it often is the cause of a great deal of evil. If your teacher will so train you that you will never be careless, he will do that which will be a great blessing to you through the whole of your life. By all means go to school this afternoon, and hereafter as usual." I obeyed him; for happily I belonged to a generation of which the children were pretty generally taught obedience to their parents. I went reluctantly to school, concealing, as best I could, my grief and my resentment. The kindness of the master's manner assured me that he regretted the occurrence almost as much as I did.

In justice to my father, I should state that, several years afterwards, he recurred to this event in my life; assured me that at the time of it he deeply sympathized in my and my mother's feeling. He thought the rule a severe one and that its operation in my case was particularly hard. "But," said he, "we all have to endure hardness in this life, and sometimes to submit to injustice; and I thought you might as well begin then to learn the lesson. Besides, it would have been very unwise to take you away from so good an instructor, just as you were about to complete your preparation for college."

CHAPTER IV.

COLLEGE LIFE.

Unsatisfactory Freshman Year. — Bowdoin Prize. — Sophomore Year. — Junior Year. — Resolves to become a Minister. — Daniel Webster and the Pond Lilies. — George B. Emerson.

ALTHOUGH, as I soon found, I had not been thoroughly well prepared, I entered College without conditions, in September, 1813. Our country was then at war with England. Quite a number of young men, therefore, came to Cambridge, who were more inclined to business than to learning. The class was at first unusually large, the largest that had then ever entered the University. There were in the beginning eighty-seven of us. Soon after the return of peace, in 1815, several left College, and went into merchandise; others left for other reasons, and three died. So that only sixty-seven were graduated, at the Commencement in 1817. Of my classmates, a number have since become distinguished men, as may be seen by recurring to the Catalogue; and we considered ourselves, as a whole, a superior set of fellows. At a chance meeting of the Alumni in 1819 or 1820, a dispute arose as to the comparative excellence of our several classes. William H. Gardner, of the class of 1816, settled the question by insisting that his was not only the best class that ever had been in College, but the best that was ever expected.

My Freshman year was, on the whole, an unsuccessful and a very unhappy one. Unfortunately I presumed to prejudge some of the subjects prescribed in the college course, and to decide that they would never be of any use to me, and that I could spend some of my time to better purpose, than in preparing myself very thoroughly to recite some of the lessons given us. This is the mistake which many foolish young men make. They do not consider that the course of college studies is devised by learned and wise men, so as best to develop the various faculties of the mind and heart; and that no young man can know, until he shall have completed the course, what parts of it have been, or are likely to be, most useful to him. I accomplished very little during the first eight months of my college life: I fell to a very low place in my class, and became displeased with myself, and really miserable.

In February or March, 1814, the subjects for dissertations to be written for the Bowdoin Prizes were given out. Four prizes were offered: two of the first grade, thirty dollars each; and two of the second grade, twenty dollars each. At once I determined to try for a prize. No Freshman ever had gained one, if any had ever written for one. Nor was it expected that students of the Freshman Class would enter the lists. Nevertheless I determined to try. I knew success would lift me, at a bound, from my low standing, and give me at once a position among my fellows, from which I could more easily ascend to something like eminence in the class.

I chose for my subject, "The Causes of the Diversities of National Character." I kept my intention a profound secret; for I knew I should be ridiculed, without mercy, for thinking it possible that I could write a dissertation upon such a subject, worthy of a prize, unless by success I showed that I could do it. I was obliged to study my subject and write upon it stealthily, lest my chum should discover my intention and divulge it to the class. I read Kaime's Sketches of Man, Sidney on Government, Montesquieu on the Spirit of Laws, from all of which I derived invaluable hints, although I could not find in them any thing exactly to my purpose. I got all my materials ready, and several parts of the Dissertation written during the term that followed the announcement of the subjects; and in the spring vacation of two weeks, the last of May and first of June, I engrossed and carefully copied my virgin Essay.

It was signed "Juvenis of the Freshman Class," and was stealthily deposited in the appointed place, before the close of June. Never can I forget the almost sleepless anxiety with which I awaited the award. It was not given until two months afterwards, just before Commencement.

One morning, in the Chapel, after prayers, in the presence of the whole College, the President requested all to be seated, and hear the report of the committee appointed to examine the various Dissertations that had been given in for the Bowdoin Prizes. Thirty one or two, in all, had been read and compared by the impartial examiners, who knew not the author of any one. All of them were deemed meritorious, several of them were excellent; but the committee, after much deliberation, had given the preference to the four following: first one, by Mr. John Ware, resident graduate; the second, by ——, of the Senior Class; the third, by Justin W. Clarke, of the Sophomore; and the fourth, by Samuel J. May, of the Freshman Class. I felt at one moment like fainting or sinking through the floor, and then like exhaling. My personal friends crowded about me with their congratulations. But my cup of joy was not unmixed. Some contemptuous remarks came to my ears, and the cruel insinuation that it must have been written for me by another.

A few weeks after, the Dissertations were read aloud in the Chapel, each by its author, in presence of the Faculty and all the classes, and then fair copies of the same were deposited in the Library of the University.

This was the great event in my college life. From the hour of this success, I began to retrieve my reputation as a scholar, and received a full share of the honors which the Faculty could confer.

At the commencement of the Sophomore year, I began to chum with my cousin, Samuel E. Sewall, a most conscientious young man, a diligent student, and a distinguished scholar. With him I continued to live, in the same relation, to the close of our college life; and it was a very great advantage to me that I was so associated with him. We graduated at Commencement, 1817, he as seventh or eighth, and I as the thirteenth or fourteenth, in a class of sixty-seven. I was associated, at the Exhibition on that day, in a Colloquial Discussion on the Sabbath, Jewish and Christian, with Samuel A. Eliot, of Boston.

Early in my Junior year, I formed the determination to devote myself to the Christian ministry. I cannot now remember all the influences that led to nor the considerations that fixed me in this determination. But from that time I paid more particular attention to all those branches of study which had the most obvious bearing upon theological doctrines and moral principles.[1]

[1] At the time when Mr. May entered college, and while he was residing at Cambridge, the President and professors were men of marked talents and character, whose influence, direct and indirect, could not but have been very great.

Dr. Kirkland, the President, was a man of the most genial nature, of an unperturbed constancy and serenity, generous and warm-hearted, and showing a strong interest in all the students. His remarkable knowledge of character, and his power of penetrating into that of every person, were what he had earnestly prayed for, and which were fully granted. He felt and sympathized with whatever was excellent; he saw, almost instantly, what was wayward, false, or wanting; and he knew what allowance to make for inherited tendencies, for the influence of bad example, and for the faults of a perverted or neglected early education. He was always ready to help; and he did it so graciously that the kindness was never forgotten. His manners — though a part of his childhood was literally spent among savages, to whom his father was a missionary — were delicate and urbane, as of one who had passed his life in the best society. Such is the almost miraculous power of a devoted Christian mother. He had the persuasive

My most intimate friends in College were Robert Schuyler, Benjamin Fessenden, John Doane Wells,

eloquence — "the visible rhetoric" — of a spotless life and noble character.

John Farrar, professor of Natural Philosophy and Astronomy, was, in conversation, manners, and feelings, all we could ask for in a gentleman; and, as a lecturer, of unsurpassed ability. He was so clear and attractive, and interested his audience of Seniors and Juniors to such a degree, that they forgot every thing else; and the dinner-bell itself, though coming half an hour after the normal end of the lecture, was often an unwelcome surprise and interruption. Listening to this natural eloquence, one felt that it would be an easy thing to lecture well upon such subjects.

No person, well prepared in the classical department, could fail to be influenced by the purity and refinement of taste of Levi Frisbie, professor of Latin; who, though unable, from the weakness of his eyes, to read himself, showed others how to read; and who, in his class, when a good scholar hesitated for the best rendering of a word or sentence, threw out from underneath the handkerchief which almost constantly covered his face the most fitting word or phrase which the English language afforded. This could not happen often, and, indeed, happened only to those who were nice in translating. Professor Brazer, an excellent Latin scholar, pupil and successor of Mr. Frisbie, said, when he was himself a teacher, that nothing had ever done so much to raise his own standard of correct translation as these interjected words.

Probably no one, susceptible of the highest impressions, could remain unmoved by the elevation and purity of Mr. Frisbie's religious character, which shed about him an atmosphere of exalted feeling which almost imperceptibly elevated. The very presence of such a man is a purifying influence.

In those years, Andrews Norton was college librarian. This office often enabled him, in his modest way, to give an important turn to a scholar's reading. By a few words to a student going off to teach a winter school, he directed all the leisure hours of ten weeks in the country to the most profitable reading and study. During a part of Mr. May's time, while a student in theology, he occupied a room near to Mr. Norton's in the pleasant Appian Way;

Thomas Russel Sullivan, Samuel A. Eliot, Joseph Coolidge, Charles Henry Warren, Joseph H. Jones, and, above all, George B. Emerson.

Benjamin Fessenden was one of the most ingenuous,

and, attracted perhaps by his signal ability and the richness and suggestiveness of his conversation, sometimes visited him. Half an hour with Mr. Norton could not fail to awaken and encourage the highest thoughts and noblest purposes in a person as receptive of good as Mr. May.

Of the sincerity, the quiet wisdom, the calm sagacity, the faultless purity of life of the Christian veteran, the elder Henry Ware, Mr. May had reason to be made fully aware, on the occasion mentioned by himself. It was, doubtless, the perception of these rare qualities which attracted him.

Dr. McKean, professor of Rhetoric, came very little in contact with the students, and influenced them only by his lectures. Mr. May was introduced to him, visited him in his study, and felt and acknowledged his kindness.

The other professors and tutors were men of high character; and, together with those above mentioned, they had a power to influence young men in the formation of their character and their plans for life, such as has rarely been possessed by a college faculty. It cannot have been accidental that, from nearly every class that came under their instruction, so large a number embraced the profession which looks to a higher end than mere earthly success; that during Dr. Kirkland's presidency so many of the leading men in ability and scholarship, — such as A. Lamson and F. W. P. Greenwood; C. Francis and Jared Sparks; the brothers W. B. O. and O. W. B. Peabody; A. Cummings, S. J. May; E. S. Gannett, A. Young; A. Hill and G. W. Wells; F. Cunningham and J. Whitman; and many others still alive, — chose theology for their profession.

During the latter part of the time that Mr. May passed at Cambridge, Edward Everett and George Ticknor came to widen, by their eloquence and thorough scholarship, the course of instruction, and to inaugurate a change which is at this moment showing its ripe fruits. G. B. E.

kind-hearted persons I ever knew; and we were wedded to each other not only by a true friendship, but by our mutual love of song. Our voices harmonized perfectly; and we spent many, perhaps too many, hours together in singing.

John D. Wells was not at all distinguished as a college scholar; but he was sensible, and had a great deal of information on some scientific subjects, of which he was particularly fond. Then he was as pure as distilled water, and as affectionate as a woman. I sometimes felt really "in love with him." Unexpectedly to himself, quite as much as to anybody else, he rose more rapidly after leaving College than any of my classmates, and died suddenly, when about thirty-three years of age, one of the most popular anatomical and medical lecturers in our country. He was a professor in three medical schools at the same time, and killed himself by his undue exertions to discharge his official duties in each.

Thomas R. Sullivan, now also dead, was a grandson of Thomas Russel, one of the merchant princes of Boston, at the close of the last and for the first ten years of the present century. He was a young man of the most delicate sense of propriety, and of scrupulously courteous manners.

His father, the late John L. Sullivan, Esq., was a large owner, and the principal manager of the Middlesex Canal. Once or twice every summer for a number of years, he was wont to invite a party of friends to spend the day with him upon the Canal and on Woburn

Pond, one of its principal feeders. It was an occasion that always brought together as many of the *élite* of Boston as could be pleasantly accommodated in the largest canal-boat. The Sullivans, Amorys, Eliots, Otises, &c., were there; and his son was empowered to invite a suitable number of collegians, to insure to the party a due amount of fun and frolic. I was repeatedly invited.

On one of these parties, an incident happened by which I was very pleasantly introduced to the great Daniel Webster, who had then recently removed his residence from Portsmouth to Boston; and the addition of whose company to "the Canal Party" made all who had the honor to be invited the more eager to go.

On our return from Woburn, we stopped for a while at a beautiful point on the-shore of Spot Pond. So soon as the ladies came upon the margin of the little lake, they espied uncountable numbers of the lilies, whose fragrance is so refreshing. Each and all exclaimed how much they longed to have them. But, alas! they were too far off to be reached by any means but a boat or a raft. But where could the one be found, or the materials for the other be collected? The more the probability of getting them seemed to recede, the more earnest became the desires of the young ladies to be possessed of the beautiful flowers, and the more touching their expressions of disappointment. At length Mr. Webster exclaimed, "Oh that I were as young as I was a few years ago! I would ransack the shores of the Pond, until I found some boat or boards by which to reach and gather those lilies." No sooner were the words out of his mouth than the young men of the party bounded off at the top of their speed, to find what he had intimated ought to be sought after. Nearly all went. I stood very demurely, enduring as well as I could the glances of almost contemptuous surprise at my want of gallantry. I stood until my fellows were too far gone to see what I meant to do, when I waded out and collected all that I could bring in of the lovely tempters. Shouts of applause cheered me on; and when I reached the shore, soaked with water from my waistcoat pockets downwards, and presented to each of the ladies one or more of the flowers they had so much desired, their thanks were profuse, and to me quite as grateful as the fragrance of the lilies, mixed as they were with tender expressions of anxiety lest my gallantry should cost me some severe sickness. The gentlemen were not backward in commending the exploit, and Mr. Webster was louder than all of them in my praise. "Ah, sir," said I, "the ladies owe these lilies less to my gallantry than to your eloquence. I could not stand unmoved by your appeal." "Never before," he exclaimed, — "never before have I gained a lily by my eloquence." "No, sir," I rejoined, "but it has often been crowned with laurels." All this of course prolonged somewhat the merriment, until we saw the young men returning along the shore of the lake, dragging an old dory which they had found about a quarter of a mile off. Immediately all the company arranged themselves to welcome the poor fellows, every lady with a lily in her bosom, or on her head, and every gentleman swinging one in his hand. So soon as my comrades got near enough to espy the flowers, they dropped the rope of the boat, and pushed forward to be assured that the appearance was a reality. And when they saw that the lilies had indeed been taken from the pond, and found that they had "gotten only their labor for their pains," while they in their hearts generously exulted with me in my triumph, they threatened me with all sorts of retaliations if I were not protected by the presence of the fair sex.

After this pleasant introduction to the great orator, he always graciously recognized me wherever we met, until his fearful recreancy to the cause of liberty impelled me to lift my voice on the 4th of July, 1838, in earnest condemnation of one whom I had once so profoundly respected and ardently admired.

The last named in the foregoing list of my most intimate college friends — George B. Emerson — was one of our prominent scholars. But, better than that, he was a sensible, staid young man, right in all his purposes of life, correct in all his habits. The class called him "Pater." I respected and loved him more than any one of my fellows; and my acquaintance with him has been one of the great blessings of my life. After we had been intimate a year or more, we found that we were of the same age precisely, — to a day, as our family records showed; to an hour, so far as our mothers could remember. This, no doubt, helped to cement our friendship. He was less convivial than myself, more studious, and consequently a much better scholar. He was often vexed with me that I did no better; and his faithful, affectionate admonitions roused me to exertion, and kept me from falling to a lower grade.[1]

[1] Of the feelings entertained toward Mr. May by those of his classmates who knew him best, the following extracts from letters give evidence.

One of them, Fessenden, with whom he was intimate till the end of their theological studies, says: —

"All my recollections of May are pleasant. I never heard an angry or unkind expression from his lips. He could vent his righteous indignation at wrong in no measured terms; but, while he condemned, he pitied and forgave. His heart always overflowed with the milk of human kindness, and his whole aim and desire was to make his fellow-men better and happier. You and I knew that splendid man, his father. Sam inherited his noble qualities, and an anecdote of the father will illustrate the character of both.

"It was said that the Colonel, while travelling on the road, would alight and remove a stone or other obstruction that might jolt or incommode the traveller. So Sam's whole life was, I think, spent in efforts to remove obstacles in the way to the happiness and peace of his fellows. He is to-day reaping his reward."

Another, S. E. Sewall, writes thus: —

"I am sorry that I remember so little about S. J. May's life in college. Our college life seems to me like a pleasant dream, of which I retain a vivid recollection of only a few particulars.

"I felt then, as I have ever since, the charm of his character. Always affectionate, always sympathetic, always conscientious, with a delightful voice and agreeable manners, — every one who met him was drawn towards him. I did not realize then, as I have since, the full excellence of his character, and his great power of acting on individuals and society, — a power which he always exercised for good purposes. In truth, my admiration of his character has been steadily growing, till now, when he is gone from us, I see its nearness to perfection."

Another says: —

"Mr. May was always a modest man, but he was sincere and conscientious; and, embracing the truth which offered itself to him as if it came from the Source of all truth, he could not easily be moved from his conclusions. He listened patiently, and with perfect fairness and honesty, to all that was said; but yielded only to what seemed to him a higher view of truth. It is remarkable in how many instances he embraced truths of the highest importance, though, to hold them, he was obliged to stand out against those for whom he had the greatest affection and respect."

CHAPTER V.

PREPARATION FOR THE MINISTRY.

TEACHER AT HINGHAM. — RESIDENT GRADUATE AT CAMBRIDGE. — STATE OF THEOLOGICAL LEARNING. — PAINFUL DOUBTS. — NOBLE COURSE OF REV. DR. WARE. — NOAH WORCESTER AND THE PEACE SOCIETY. — TEACHER AT BEVERLY.

EARLY in October, 1817, I removed to Hingham, on an engagement with the Rev. Henry Colman, to study theology under his direction, and assist him in teaching a small classical school, comprising, if I remember correctly, six or eight boys from Boston, and his three children, Anna, Sarah, and James Freeman.

The arrangement was that we should keep the school, each alone, a week alternately. I did not like it. I could neither pursue any course of study as I wished to, nor could I conduct the school in a manner satisfactory to myself. On the first of the following May, therefore, I was generously released by Mr. Colman from my engagement; and my classmate and friend, Robert F. Walcutt, succeeded me.

But my short residence in Hingham was by no means an unimportant portion of my early life. It not only instituted a friendship between myself and Mr. Colman, which continued with unabated warmth as long as he lived, but it introduced me to the acquaintance of a number of remarkable and interesting persons. I would particularly mention the Rev. Dr. Allyn, of Duxbury, — a very eccentric but a very wise man; and his admirable daughter, Abby Allyn, afterwards the wife of the late Professor Convers Francis, of the Divinity School, Cambridge. To Mr. Colman I am indebted for the honor and pleasure I enjoyed of being introduced, in the spring of 1818, to the venerable John Adams and wife. Mr. Adams was quite a theologian, and devoted much of his time during the last years of his life to the study of theology. He loved to converse with sensible, learned ministers. Mr. Colman seemed to be one of his favorites. And on one occasion, when going to visit the venerable ex-president, he was so kind as to take me with him. Both Mr. and Mrs. A. appeared to be in excellent health, excepting only some of the infirmities of old age. They conversed with much animation on the subjects which were at that day most interesting; and I listened to them for hours, with admiration of them, not only for what they had been, but what they then were.

Immediately after the short spring vacation in May, I removed to Cambridge, and took a room next to the house in which Professor Andrews Norton (then the librarian) lodged. My classmates and friends, Samuel A. Eliot, Benjamin Fessenden, and Thomas R. Sullivan, — all of them engaged in the study of Divinity, — occupied rooms in the same street.

From the Dana House I removed to the Appian Way. There I lived, if I remember correctly, a year; enjoying the society of the above-named classmates, and occasionally of Professor Norton. The Divinity School was then hardly organized. We obtained what advice and direction we sought from Dr. Ware, Professor Norton, and Professor Frisbie. We attended any of the College Lectures that we pleased, and had some special lectures given to us, by Professor Frisbie, on Moral Philosophy; by Professor Norton, on Biblical Interpretation; and by Dr. Ware, on Dogmatic History. We also received some instruction in Hebrew from Professor Willard; and, towards the last of our course, from Professor Edward Everett, on Greek Literature. But, for the most part, we were left to ourselves to pursue our studies as we might, receiving no thorough training in any department.

We formed a society for mutual religious improvement. At our meetings, one of our number offered prayer, and preached a sermon, which we criticised. Some one or two of the professors usually attended these meetings, and favored us with their criticisms. Professor Everett kindly invited us to meet him for exercises in elocution, and we did so a few times.

Now, when I look back upon the course of study we pursued, it seems meagre indeed. Most of the best books which are now studied by the young men in the Divinity School have come into existence, or been introduced from Germany, since our day.

Soon after the commencement of my studies at Cambridge, an incident happened, so honorable to another, and so important in its influence upon myself, that I ought to preserve the memory of it. Before beginning the study of Theology, I had never thought much on the subject. My religious affections had been quickened and cultivated by my parents and other religious friends, and by some of the circumstances in which I had been placed. But as to the doctrines of the Gospel, I had accepted reverently, without questioning, such as were current among Unitarians in the days of my youth. As soon, however, as I set about preparing for the ministry, I felt it to be my duty to study the subject, and look into the mysteries of our Faith, so far as it may be given us to know them. The New England Unitarian Controversy had commenced, having been started in 1815, by Dr. Morse, of Charlestown, in "The Panoplist," by an attack upon the liberal ministers of Boston. I had, however, been too much engrossed with college matters to pay any careful attention to it. Nor had it advanced far when I entered the Divinity School.

Of course I commenced, in good earnest, the study of the Sacred Scriptures. And it was not long before doubts of their plenary inspiration arose in my mind; and then a disbelief of the miraculous conception of Jesus Christ. I was alarmed, distressed. It seemed as if the very foundation was falling away from under me. I feared that there might be some fatal defect in my mind, that would unfit me for the Christian ministry. My concern became so serious and oppressive, that I felt obliged to reveal my spiritual condition to the Father of the Divinity School, and ask his counsel. So, in great perturbation, I went to Dr. Ware's study.

He received me kindly, as he was wont to do. I looked anxiously around, to be sure that no other person was in hearing, and then asked him if he was willing to receive an important communication from me. He encouraged me to unbosom myself with perfect frankness. I was much agitated; for I feared that I was about to shock him, and reveal to him a condition that he would deem hopeless. However, I had resolved that I ought to do it, and so I did. I told him of the doubts that had arisen to trouble me, and, as I feared, to debar my progress in the course of life which I had chosen. I kept no secret of my heart on the subject undisclosed. When I had finished, — the Doctor had listened so silently and thoughtfully that I felt like a convicted criminal, in the presence of his judge, about to receive sentence, — it seemed a long while before he spoke. But when he did, it was in the tenderest accents. "My young friend," said he, "I am glad to find that you have arrived at a doubt. I perceive that you have begun *to think* on the great subjects to which you have turned your attention, — that you have entered upon the study of Theology in good earnest." After a long breath of surprise and relief, I replied: "I thank you, sir, for your kindness; but will you tell me how these doubts are to be resolved?" He answered: "Mr. May, I cannot resolve your doubts for you if I would; and I would not resolve them for you if I could. When finite minds turn to the contemplation of the nature, character, providence, and word of the Infinite, it is to be expected that some things will appear difficult to be understood, that doubts will arise. These are adapted to stimulate us to further and more careful inquiry. The All-wise Father has not vouchsafed to us a full and exact statement of all the truths we are eager to know respecting Himself, His beloved Son, our own nature and destiny. We are left to seek after, if happily we may find, what we desire to know. This is a part of our trial, of our discipline. You have just entered upon the grand inquiries. You should not wonder that you are perplexed by some queries that have suggested themselves. Go on diligently in your search after the truth. These doubts will be removed; other doubts will perhaps arise. And they will stimulate you to further and profounder researches. I have had my doubts; I have some still, and expect to have them until faith is turned to sight." "But, sir," said I, "what are the essential truths,—truths that I must believe?" "All truth," he replied, "is essential. You are bound to believe whatever, at any time, shall appear to you to be true; and you are bound to believe it until you shall cease to be satisfied that it is true." I still insisted, "How shall I know, sir, that what I believe at any time is true?" "If you sincerely desire and long for the truth," the Doctor added, "the Father of your spirit will not permit you to remain satisfied in error. And if what you believe, at any time, leads you to reverence God and keep his commandments, to love your fellow-beings and delight to do them good, it cannot be a dangerous error."

This conversation not only comforted and strengthened me at the time, but has had an effect upon the conduct and character of my life ever since. I have never been afraid to pursue any inquiry after truth, however it might seem to endanger long-cherished opinions.

During the last years of my college life, I became acquainted with the venerable Noah Worcester, D.D., author of a somewhat remarkable book, in its day, entitled, "Bible News of the Father, Son, and Holy Spirit;" but most widely known, and to be longest remembered, as "the Apostle of Peace." Having bestowed much attention upon this subject, in 1814 he published his "Solemn Review of the Custom of War," — the most impressive and efficient pamphlet that has ever been published, so far as my acquaintance with such things extends.

This tract produced a powerful effect on my mind. I sought the acquaintance of the venerable author, and record it as one of the blessings of my life that, from 1819 to the time of his death, I enjoyed his friendship, and was permitted to hold some correspondence with him. He was the most holy man I ever knew.

The first great Christian reform that I ever embraced was thus the one inaugurated by him, — the attempt to abolish the custom of war.

In the winter of 1818 and 1819, I kept a district school for two or three months, in the town of Beverly. This was my second experience as a pedagogue, having taught a school in the town of Concord, in the winter of 1816 and 1817. Nothing remarkable happened in my experience as a school-teacher, excepting that I peremptorily and persistently refused to prepare my pupils for the examination, by the special assignment to each one of the questions to be answered by him or her, and the passages to be recited in presence of the committee. Such, I was told, had been the custom of my predecessors; and my refusal to comply with it excited not a little commotion throughout the district. But when, in the end, my pupils appeared so well that the school was pronounced by the committee one of the three best in the town, the parents and children were more than satisfied.

CHAPTER VI.

HORSEBACK JOURNEY TO WHITE MOUNTAINS.

COMPANIONS. — ASCENT OF MT. WASHINGTON. — MOUNTAIN CRANBERRIES. — "OLD CRAWFORD." — THE FORGOTTEN FLASK. — SUSPICIOUS CHARACTERS. — GREAT DEMAND FOR MILK. — THE BEST BEHAVED.

AT the time we were leaving College, the dysentery prevailed in Cambridge. Many of the students were sick, and several died. Emerson had it. He was barely able to stand upon the stage on Commencement Day long enough to deliver his dissertation. So soon as the exercises of Commencement were over, I took him to my father's house, where my mother and sisters nursed him for more than a week. When he had recovered sufficiently to travel, I went with him to his home in Wells, now Kennebunk, Maine, and spent several weeks with him. His father, Dr. Samuel Emerson, was a good scholar and excellent physician, a most genial man, and a fine musician. I enjoyed every moment that I remained under his roof. He embraced me as a son, and our friendship continued until his death.

Two years after this, while I was making a visit at Emerson's, our classmates, Samuel E. Sewall, Caleb Cushing, and Joseph Coolidge, with William Ware of the class before us, came, according to agreement made at Cambridge and at Emerson's invitation, to go with us to the White Hills and Mount Washington, their summit, in New Hampshire. We were joined by Joseph G. Moody, of Kennebunk, a cousin of Emerson's, a graduate of Bowdoin; and, on the fifth or sixth day of September, we set off on our excursion, — six on horseback, one in a wagon, to carry our baggage and give to the inexperienced horsemen of the party an occasional respite. This proved to be a wise precaution; for several of us had never before ridden on horseback ten miles at a time.

The incidents of this journey were all so pleasant and some so amusing that I cannot resist the temptation to record them. We left our horses at the Willey House[1] at 12 M. on the 9th of September, walked to the highest point of the Gap, and there, after resting awhile and admiring the bold, sublime features of the scene, we stepped over one of the little brooks that was hastening on to contribute itself to the Saco, and commenced the ascent of Mount Washington, the peak of which was four or five miles off. We toiled up about half way to a spot where we were told it would be best for us to spend the night, and where there was a rough bark shed about twelve feet long and eight feet deep, open in front. "Old Crawford" was our guide and instructor in all that we needed to know of "camp life upon the mountains." Under his direction we gathered about a cord of dry wood, enough to keep

[1] The dwellers in which were afterwards overwhelmed by an avalanche

a good fire all night burning in front of our shed. We then covered the floor of the shed with enough of the small boughs of the hemlock to make us a soft bed; and after eating a hearty supper of the good things we had carried in our knapsacks, and talking awhile of our adventures thus far on the journey, we bestowed ourselves at an early hour upon our leafy couch, side by side, for a long night's rest, that we might be well prepared for the fatigues of the next day. Our good old guide reclined himself at our feet, intending, as he assured us, to keep one eye open, so that the fire should not go out nor any harm befall us. We slept soundly, and awoke just as the sunlight was gilding the tops of the trees. We made our toilette as well as was possible under the circumstances; did justice to the breakfast which our guide helped us to prepare, and which we all pronounced excellent; and by seven o'clock took up our line of march. The path was narrow, so that much of the way we were obliged to follow our leader in single file. It was obscure, often determined only by marked trees, some of which "Old Crawford" alone could discover. But he confidently assured us he knew the way. About nine o'clock, however, a dense fog settled upon the side of the mountain. Our guide was perplexed, and, bidding us stay where we were, went off to explore. It was so cold that we made up a good fire, and waited as patiently as we could for his return. He got back in less than an hour. He had found what he was sure he had not lost, — his way. The cloud passed off; we started forward with renewed alacrity, and soon reached the summit of Mount Adams. From that elevation we could see what remained to be accomplished, — a descent of several hundred feet into the valley between, and then the ascent to the summit of Mount Washington, three or four hundred feet higher than we had yet climbed. Nothing daunted, we shouted and sang to wake up all our energies, and then pressed on. The mountain cranberries were in perfection, and we regaled ourselves upon them freely. Just as we reached the top of a steep hill over which our path lay, we came upon an extensive bed of them; and William Ware threw himself prostrate into their midst, crying out, "Come, boys, let us browse." This future author of "Zenobia," "Julian," and their kindred works, was rather the merriest and wittiest of us all. We needed not a second call, but instantly were lying as low as he, and eating as freely of the not forbidden fruit; for, though we had never tasted them before, "Old Crawford" assured us mountain cranberries were wholesome.

About twelve we reached the little crystal lake that wells up at the foot of the last ascent. It was then called "Washington's punch-bowl;" but we found it filled only with "Adam's ale." We drank freely of the beverage without adulterating it; for, though none of us were then pledged to total abstinence, we cared so little for "eau de vie," that the single bottle of it which we had brought with us had not been uncorked, and was carelessly left behind us on the top of Mount Adams.

After refreshing ourselves with such food as we had and the cool water from the aforesaid punch-bowl, we commenced the ascent of the Peak. It was much steeper and more difficult than any we had yet attempted; but we accomplished it in less than an hour, for at one o'clock we stood upon the summit of Mount Washington. There was no shelter there then. Few adventurers had scaled that height before our day. The road has been made and the Mountain House built long since we were there. We found a few names and more initials engraven upon the rocks, and one brass plate, on which were the names of a small party that had visited the spot the year before. We found it quite cold, and a good deal of ice there; but we were loath to quit the height we had reached with so much toil. When we were about half way up from our last stopping-place, an eagle of the largest size sailed haughtily away from her lonely aerie, as if indignant at our intrusion. I felt like making an apology, for it did seem as if none but winged bipeds had any right there. But we were amply repaid for our presumption. We had risen to a region above all mists and clouds. There they lay far below us; and as the rays of the sun struck upon their upper surfaces, they looked just like banks of the whitest snow.

About two o'clock we reluctantly began our descent, and between five and six reached the shed where we lodged the night before. Two or three of our party — Cushing and Coolidge and Emerson — pressed on to the Willey House. The rest of us, with the old guide, were too much fatigued to go any further; so we passed a second night upon the mountain.

The next morning, by nine o'clock, we rejoined our companions; and, mounting our horses, were in due time back at "Old Crawford's" House.

Our return journey was even more pleasant than the outward. We came by the way of Red Hill, Winnipiseogee Lake, and Smith's Pond. We stopped at an inn in the small village of Centre Harbor. We ascended Red Hill, which would be called a mountain if it were not in the region of those that are so much more lofty. From the summit, the prospect was most enchanting.

Smith's Pond we reached with some difficulty, owing to the bad condition of the road, much of which was "corduroy." But we found it an exceedingly beautiful sheet of water, and concurred in approving the taste of one of the old royal governors of the State, — Wentworth, I believe, — in placing his summer residence upon the shore of it.

We did not hurry homeward, seldom travelling more than twenty miles a day. Often we passed through unfrequented roads; and, as there were six of us on horseback, rather shabbily dressed, and two carried fowling-pieces, and one a travelling barometer, we made a somewhat formidable, and perhaps suspicious, appearance. Suffice it to say, the inhabitants of one small hamlet of two or three houses were so much alarmed that they fled at our approach.

One day — I think it was as we were going out — we passed a man on horseback. Wishing to learn something about the country through which we were travelling, I dropped behind my party and essayed to join him. It was evident he did not incline to my company. After putting various questions to him, which he answered very shortly, I said to him, "Pray, sir, what is the name of that tree?" pointing to a large one on his side of the road. He replied, very gruffly, "There is no need of your asking that question." "Why, sir," I rejoined, "I surely should not have asked you the question unless I had desired to know." "Ah!" he said, with all the determination of manner that he could command, "I can see through folks as well as most men." This revealed to me his distrust of us, and his fear. Laughingly, I said, "Who do you take us to be?" and, not waiting for his answer, "On the whole, I do not wonder much that you are suspicious of us. We are rather an ill-dressed, shabby-looking set of fellows, but you need not be afraid of us. We are a party of collegians, just graduated at the University, and are off on an excursion to Mount Washington. Knowing that we shall have to make our way through tangled woods and bushes, and sleep upon the ground, we have put on our poorer instead of our better clothes. We have brought with us those fowling pieces, that we may hear the reverberations of their reports in the Gap, and perhaps shoot a few partridges or rabbits. The other thing, which that young man [pointing to Caleb Cushing] has in his hand, and which, at a distance, may look like a gun, is a travelling barometer. We are taking that with us in order to ascertain the heights of the several mountains over which we shall climb." This account of ourselves seemed to satisfy him that we were not banditti; and he told me the name of the tree we had passed.

On one of the retired roads over which we passed, we came to a small, neat house, around which were the indications of a large dairy. So the purveyor of our party went to the door, and inquired if we could have some refreshment, telling the woman of the house that bread and milk would be all we should desire to have. The good woman, a little flustered at seeing six highwaymen at her gate, replied hurriedly, "Oh, yes, sir! oh, yes! come in, you can have that." So we all went in, and took possession of her largest room. She soon brought us bowls of the delicious beverage, with bread that was equally good. We quickly emptied the first bowls, and called for more; and despatched their contents with little less delay. But when we asked a third time for an equal portion, she seemed surprised; and, placing it upon the table, she burst into a laugh, exclaiming,—"Young gentlemen, I should think you had never been weaned!" We enjoyed the joke as much as she did, and willingly paid her three times as much as she asked for her milk.

Our excursion occupied just a fortnight. On the last day we dined at an inn, somewhere within five or six miles of Kennebunk. We sat awhile after dinner, recounting the various incidents of our journey, and discussing anew some questions upon which our opinions had been divided. At length the question was raised, Which one of the seven had borne with most patience and good-humor the discomforts with which our pleasures had been slightly intermixed, — the joltings, the chafings which the inexperienced riders had had to endure, and the repeated wettings that we all had suffered? Each one put in his own claim for the meed of praise, and defended it stoutly. The discussion was spirited, and continued until we were obliged to start for home, when the question was put to vote, and decided in favor of William Ware, *nem. con.* We then soothed ourselves and each other, by passing unanimously the resolution, to wit: "That we seven were the best behaved, most patient, courteous, good-natured set of fellows that ever came together, though William Ware was rather the best of the whole."

We were most cordially welcomed by our friends in Kennebunk, especially by Dr. and Mrs. Emerson: we spent the evening at their house, enjoying a feast of music and a flow of soul. The next morning, Ware, Cushing, Sewall, and Coolidge started for their homes. I remained a day or two longer, and then joined Mr. Benjamin Willis, Jr., of Portland, who called for me on his way to Boston, whither he was going to be married to my sister Eliza. Their union was consummated on the 19th of September. She was a bright, beautiful, affectionate girl, and her departure from the old home left us all feeling very sad.

CHAPTER VII.

BEGINS TO PREACH, AND TAKES A SOUTHERN JOURNEY.

Teaches at Nahant. — Motley, the Historian, taught to read. — First Preaching. — "Approbated." — Brooklyn, Conn. — Preaches in New York. — Prejudice against Unitarianism. — Visits the South. — Rev. Jared Sparks, at Baltimore. — Washington and Richmond. — First Sight of Slavery. — Preaches in New York again. — Assists Rev. Dr. Channing. — Thinks of Preaching in Richmond, Va.

DURING the summer of 1820, at the invitation of several gentlemen of Boston, I accompanied them to Nahant, which had then become a favorite resort in the hot season, and spent three months. I instructed their children during the week, and conducted the exercises of public worship each Sunday morning. I remember that I enjoyed my little school, and that, among my pupils, were some boys who have since become distinguished men, — especially the Rev. Robert C. Waterston, and the historian, John Lothrop Motley. The last-named gentleman I met repeatedly in Rome, in the spring of 1859. One evening I said to him, "Mr. Motley, I think I am entitled to some share of your great reputation." "Well," said he, "you may have all you can justly claim; prove property and take it away." "Why," I continued, "have you forgotten that I taught you to read?" "Did you?" he rejoined with great hilarity; "you must have done it well, for I have known how ever since."

As to my Sunday services, I presume they were more beneficial to myself than to anybody else. It was a good opportunity for me to practise. My audience was not large, seldom more than thirty or forty in number, for Nahant was not then what it has since become; but they were, for the most part, individuals of refinement, and my personal friends. I usually read a sermon of some one of the popular preachers who had then published volumes of their discourses. I took pains, of course, to select, each Sunday, such a one as I supposed would be edifying to my hearers, and prepared myself, as well as I could, to deliver it acceptably and impressively. This was the principal training that I had for the pulpit. Three or four times I ventured to deliver sermons of my own, and was greatly encouraged and benefited by the friendly criticisms that they elicited.

Early in the following December, I applied to the Boston Association for their "approbation" of me as a preacher. They assigned me Ephesians, ii. 18, "Through him we both have access by one spirit unto the Father," as the text of a sermon they wished me to write, and read to them at their next meeting, a fortnight afterwards. I did as they required. The next meeting was held at the house of Dr. Channing. I read my sermon, and received a certificate of the clerk of the Association, and the kind congratulations of the fathers and brothers in the ministry.

My first sermon as an "approbated" minister of the Gospel was delivered in Springfield, from the pulpit of my particular friend, the late Dr. William B. O. Peabody. I started from Boston the day after I had received the approval of the Boston Association. I rode to Springfield in a chaise with my friend, the late Mr. Henry Sterns, then a merchant in that town; and we were nearly three days in accomplishing the journey, as his horse was young, and he was unwilling to drive him more than thirty-five miles a day.

Soon after my return to Cambridge, I was requested to supply the pulpit in Brooklyn, Conn., for a few weeks. The first Unitarian Church in Connecticut was there established. It was composed of the majority of the "First Ecclesiastical Society" in that town, which, under the preaching of the Rev. Luther Willson, had, a few years before, renounced the Orthodox creed and the authority of the Consociation; and, after Mr. Willson left them, had sent to Cambridge for a preacher of the Gospel as it was understood and expounded by Drs. Channing, Ware, Worcester, and others. The minority had seceded, and met for worship in a hall fitted up for their use. I had first heard of this little Church, in Hingham, while studying with Mr. Colman. He was one of the council called, in the fall of 1817, to advise and comfort this Church and their pastor, Mr. Willson, under the persecution which they endured for a while because of their defection from the faith of the Consociated Churches of Connecticut. On his return, Mr. Colman gave me a full and very interesting account of the trials of this Church and their minister, and awakened in my heart a strong *presentiment* that it would be given to me to serve them in the Gospel ministry. So when the summons came, in the winter of 1821, I did not hesitate to obey it.

I went to Brooklyn in the latter part of March, and preached to the people five or six Sundays. Their zeal in behalf of the new faith which they had embraced, and were endeavoring to maintain, awakened a lively interest in their cause; and I found amongst them a large proportion of very intelligent and conscientious Christians. At the end of my engagement, the Church and Society gave me a unanimous invitation to settle with them for life. I could not at once and peremptorily decline their invitation, and yet dared not accept it without consideration and the advice of friends. So I left them with the promise to give them an answer in the course of a few weeks. On my return to Boston and Cambridge, all whom I consulted concurred with me in the opinion that it would be inexpedient for one so young and inexperienced to undertake the ministry in a State where I should have the influence of all the churches and ministers against me, and where I should have no brethren of my own faith near to encourage and help. Accordingly, I addressed a letter to the Church in Brooklyn, tenderly, but very decidedly, refusing to become their pastor. When I had deposited my letter in the post-office, I said within myself, "How little reliance is to be placed upon presentiments!"

On the 17th day of April, while I was staying in Brooklyn, there fell the largest amount of snow I had ever seen. The roads were literally filled with it, the stone walls in many places being covered, out of sight. The next day I was upset five times in going two and a half miles out from the village to visit and comfort that excellent man, Deacon Roger W. Williams. He was declining slowly and sorrowfully to the grave; his heart having been broken by the harsh denunciations and severe treatment he had received from the original Church in Brooklyn, of which he had been for many years a deacon, and from the Consociation of Windham County, with which that church was connected.

I returned to my rooms in Cambridge, and there continued five or six weeks, — studying, writing sermons, and preaching every Sunday at Salem, Lynn, or elsewhere.

Early in June, a message came from Dr. Channing to Dr. Ware or to Stephen Higginson, Esq., the College Treasurer, — who took so lively and active an interest in the well-being of the churches and the well-doing of the Cambridge divinity students, that we called him "*the Town Clerk of Zion*," — a message came to one or the other of those excellent men from Dr. Channing, that he found himself unable, because of ill health, to fulfil his engagement to preach three or four Sundays to the First Unitarian Church in New York City, then recently founded; and that he wished one of the divinity students to be sent thither in his stead. I was called upon to go. I shrank from encountering the disappointment which I knew the people of the New York Church would feel on seeing any one — especially a stripling like myself — in the pulpit, instead of Dr. Channing. But there was no one else who could or would go, and so I went. We encountered a fearful storm upon the Sound, by which we were driven back, and delayed ten or twelve hours. However, I reached the city in time, early Sunday morning, to prepare myself for the services of the day; and then first saw, and preached in, the neat little chapel in Chambers Street.

I remained in New York four weeks or longer, supplying the pulpit, and performing parochial duties as well as I was able. It was my happiness to be domiciled, the while, in the family of my cousin, Henry D. Sewall, Esq., who lived in Franklin Street, then "far up town." Broome and Grand Streets were then the uppermost streets; Canal Street was not compactly built up, and there were no omnibuses, nor gas-lights, nor telegraphs, nor rail-roads. Steam-boats had only recently been invented, and "The Chancellor Livingston" was the admiration of all men.

Mr. Sewall, one of the founders of the church, was a man of much literary taste and culture, and, better still, of deep religious sensibility. He gave his time and his heart and soul to the cause of rational and liberal Christianity. He prepared a hymn-book for the use of the worshippers at the chapel, and it was a collection vastly superior to any that was extant, until Dr. Greenwood published his, which was scarcely, if anywise, better. Mr. Sewall was encouraged by the sympathy of his excellent wife; and he was blessed by the co-operation of numbers of rare men and women. There were the Hon. Henry Wheaton, afterwards United States Minister to Holland, and author of some important works on law; William C. Bryant, the poet, and since chief-editor of the "Evening Post;" Messrs. Henry D. and Robert H. Sedgwick; and the Hon. Roger G. Van Polanen, a Dutch gentleman of learning and refinement, and formerly a high official under the government of his own country. Besides these gentlemen and their wives, there was Mrs. Philip Schuyler, one of the most dignified, intelligent, and fascinating women in the city. She spent the larger part of every winter in New York, and was a confessor of Unitarianism. Still, although the church comprised these and many other very respectable and excellent people, the prejudice against the so-called new heresy was so strong and bitter that it required no little determination and moral courage to stand up against it. The strangest stories were afloat respecting our belief and our unbelief. I went one day with Mr. Sewall to show our chapel to an intelligent lady of his acquaintance. She was pleased with the building, which was really quite appropriate and tasteful. After examining the pulpit, outside and in, "May I look at your Bible?" said she.

"Oh, certainly, Madam," was the reply. She turned over the leaves; read a little here, and a little there. Then she examined carefully the title-page. "Why," she exclaimed, with great surprise, "it is the same as ours." "Certainly," we answered, "and not only may all the articles of our faith be found in this volume, but adequately expressed in the very words of Christ and his Apostles, as they used them; which can be said of the distinctive doctrines of no other Christian sect that we are acquainted with."

Another day I was walking down Broadway, and at a bookstore window, near the Park, saw a large number of persons gazing eagerly at a large sheet of paper. I pressed towards it, and, when near enough, found that it was an elaborately and elegantly printed list of all the churches and places of worship in the city. The Christian churches were named first, but ours not among them. Then came, under the head of synagogues, first the two or three Jewish; after which, at the bottom of the list, was *The Unitarian Chapel.* This little incident affected me much at the time, though I smile at it now; for it disclosed the misapprehension, prejudice, and hostility, against which, as a minister of Unitarian Christianity, I should have to contend.

At the expiration of my term of service,— another gentleman, Mr. James Hayward, having been engaged to preach to the church as a candidate for settlement,— I left New York, in company with my sister Louisa, on a journey southward, for the purpose of seeing more of our country and of visiting friends in Baltimore, Washington, Alexandria, and Richmond. If I remember correctly, we went by steamer to New Brunswick, thence by stage-coach to Trenton, and by steamer again down the Delaware river to Philadelphia. We were the whole day in accomplishing the trip. Six coaches were employed in taking the boat's company of travellers across New Jersey. We were so fortunate as to be put into the foremost coach, in company with five or six ladies and the venerable Samuel Coates, then prominent amongst the patrons and directors of the Philadelphia Hospital. It was precisely in the midst of the season of flowers, when the high laurels, and the magnolia, and tulip-trees were in full blossom. The woods, through patches of which the road frequently passed, were brilliant with their hues and fragrant with their perfume. I alighted twice from the coach and gathered a profusion of the magnolias and the laurels to fill the laps of my fellow-travellers.

We tarried in Philadelphia until after the following Sunday, and visited the Water-works, the Market, the Hospital, and other objects of special interest. I preached on Sunday forenoon and evening for Mr. Taylor, and dined and spent several hours with him. I found him to be a Scotch gentleman, a stern religionist, an earnest and somewhat dogmatic Unitarian.

Early in the following week we proceeded to Baltimore. There we were most cordially welcomed at the house of Mr. Amos Williams, one of six brothers, sons of Capt. Joseph Williams, of Roxbury, cousins of my father, who, settled in Baltimore when young men, had done much to promote the growth of the city, had gained wealth and social distinction there, and were among the principal founders and supporters of the Unitarian Church.

Rev. Jared Sparks was then the minister of the new church, and an inmate of the family of Mr. Williams. I passed a week there with him, and learnt how diligent and faithful a student he was, and how active and able a champion of the Unitarian cause. He was then publishing "The Unitarian Miscellany," a monthly periodical of great value in its day, which was continued through six volumes, and the greater part of its contents furnished by his pen. While staying with him, I wrote an article on "A New Translation of the Scriptures," which he published in his second volume. It is worthy of note only as being the first composition I ever committed to the press, excepting only, I believe, a brief article on "Christian Liberality," published while with Mr. Peabody, in the "Springfield Recorder."

I stayed long enough to supply Mr. Sparks's pulpit one Sunday. The church, then recently built, was peculiar in its structure, very expensive, and, after all, not well adapted to its purpose. The pulpit was surmounted by a dome, which seemed to swallow the voice of the speaker, and then pour it down again upon his own head. To me the effect was very peculiar and perplexing. It seemed as if the words I had just pronounced fell back about my ears like water from a shower-bath.

I could not be sure when I had uttered the sentence before me. Fortunately, my first attempt was in reading the introductory hymn. I kept my eyes upon the book, and diligently read aloud each line, giving as little heed to the sound of my voice as possible. When I next rose, which was to offer the prayer, sensible that I could neither hear myself nor be heard by others, if I should speak as before, I took a new pitch, spoke in my lowest tone. It happened to be just adapted to the house, and I went through all the services in that tone, with little difficulty to myself and apparently to the acceptance of my audience.

Early in the following week, my sister and I left our hospitable relatives in Baltimore, for the city of Washington, distant thirty-five or forty miles. We travelled in the public stage-coach, a clumsy, lumbering vehicle, and took the middle seat that we might avail ourselves of the windows over the doors to see as much as possible of the country. I do not remember any thing in particular that attracted our attention, excepting one sight that moved us deeply and first awakened thoughts and feelings that a few years afterwards took shape and gave direction to the whole course of my life. We saw, standing by the road-side, a row of negro men, twenty or thirty in number, and soon perceived that they all were handcuffed, and that the irons about their wrists were fastened around a very heavy chain that was passed between them and attached to the tail of a large wagon, in which were bundles, apparently of clothes, and some young children lying upon straw.

Four or five black women were passing along the line and giving to each of the men a thick slice of coarse bread. My first thought was that they were prisoners. "Look," I cried to my sister, "see these prisoners! What can they have been guilty of, so many of them?" Scarcely had I uttered the words, when the truth flashed upon my mind. "Oh, no! Louisa, they are slaves. They have probably been bought up by some slave-dealer, and he is taking them in this way on to some more southern market." We had heard of the abomination of slavery and the internal slave trade, but had not seen it before. The house-slaves in our kinsmen's families in Baltimore seemed to us like any other domestic servants, and had excited no remark. But here the monstrous wrong stood palpably before us. My sister gave way to the expression of her feelings of horror and indignation, and I responded with all my heart. "I reckon," said one of our fellow-passengers, "that you and the lady are from New England." "Yes, sir," I replied, "and I never before felt so grateful as I do now that I was not born where human beings can be bought and sold, and treated like cattle; and that my eyes have not been accustomed to such sights as that. I am ashamed of my country and of my race." My earnest manner of speaking, and yet more the deep emotions of my sister, evidently touched the chords of a common humanity in the hearts of our fellow-travellers. There was silence for a few minutes, when the gentleman said, "I do not wonder you feel so. It is bad. It is shameful. But it was entailed upon us. What can we do?" I did not then know how to answer the question. So we said little more upon the subject. And we jogged on, in saddened mood, to the Capital of our Republic.

Here, too, were resident several of our relatives — Dr. Frederick May and Dr. George W. May. The former, at whose house we were cordially invited to stay, was a physician of eminence; the latter, a much younger man, just getting into a good practice.

We tarried there a week, visiting our friends and the public buildings, which were then fewer and much smaller than they are now; and, of course, Mount Vernon, which was then in a very much better state of preservation than when I last was there, in 1856.

A small body of Unitarians had recently gathered themselves into a church, and had fitted up a hall, capable of holding three hundred people, over the public baths, for their place of meeting. I was invited to preach to them, and did so one Sunday. Just after I had taken my seat in the pulpit, I was surprised and delighted to see the Hon. John Quincy Adams walk modestly up the aisle, and take a seat in a conspicuous place. I was told he seldom failed to be there. He was at the time Secretary of State, and an aspirant to the Presidency. Yet he shunned not to declare his faith in the doctrines of Unitarian Christianity, then "everywhere spoken against," and after the way which most men call heresy he publicly worshipped the God of his fathers. I record this to his praise, as his conduct in this respect contrasted most honorably with that of too many of the prominent men of that day, who were Unitarians in New England, but avoided the odium of that sect in Washington, by attending one or the other of the fashionable churches.

The next day, Louisa and myself proceeded to Alexandria, there to visit a very dear friend, since dead. I tarried only until Thursday; and then, leaving my sister to divide the time of my absence between our friends in Alexandria and Washington, I went on by stage coach to Richmond, there to see the remnants of the Jewish family, spoken of in the early part of my memoirs, my excellent friends Catherine and Slowey Hays.

My stay in Richmond was short, not exceeding a week; and I returned to Washington in the same way that I went. My stage companion for the first few hours, or the only one whom I remember, was Judge Brock. He did not seem much inclined to conversation. Once, as we were passing by a large cornfield, I observed a black woman hoeing. She was wretchedly clad, and looked squalid and woe-begone. Involuntarily I expressed the offence that the sight gave me, adding that I was thankful I lived in a part of the country where such sights of enforced degradation were not to be seen. "Sir," said he, with considerable severity of manner, "northern men will not be permitted to speak so freely and reproachfully of our institutions, about which they know so little." Of course I waived the subject, for he was a much older man than myself; and we talked but little to each other afterwards.

Before reaching New York on my return, I accepted an invitation from the committee of the Unitarian Church to preach to them again, three or four Sundays. I was entertained during my stay at the house of Mr. Henry D. Sedgwick, who then resided in Cedar Street. His excellent wife was Miss Jane Minot, whom I had known from my early childhood. She was the only daughter of Judge Minot, of Boston, whose pew at the King's Chapel was very near my father's. I resided in their family three weeks or more, and have every reason to remember it with pleasure. While there, I became somewhat acquainted with Miss Catherine Sedgwick, who has since attained so high a place amongst American authors. She had just then published her first work, "The New England Tale;" and I well remember with what intense interest her brothers, Henry and Robert, awaited its reception by the public.

On my return to Boston, I gave up my room in Cambridge, and removed my books and study furniture to my father's house in Federal Court. After preaching a few weeks at Salem, Lynn, and elsewhere, I was invited by the committee of the Church in Federal Street to assist Dr. Channing, whose health was very feeble, one month. At the close of the first engagement, I was requested to renew it for three months more, which I did. The arrangement was, that I should supply the pulpit half of each Sunday, and hold myself in readiness to take the Doctor's place at any time when he should feel too feeble to preach. It was, as I found, a trying situation; for in several instances the people came to hear Dr. Channing, then at the height of his fame as a preacher, and were put off with the best that I could do in his stead. Nevertheless, this engagement brought me into an intimate relation to the man, whom I venerated as much as any one I had then known. I remember him and his great kindness to me with unfeigned respect and gratitude. His wise and friendly criticisms of my sermons and prayers were invaluable to me. And he did much to improve my manner of reading hymns, in which he himself excelled.

There was at that time an association of the leading men of his church, which met once a week for mutual religious improvement, and to consult together about plans of usefulness. It was my privilege to meet with them, and listen to their conversations, which were always upon high themes, and often called from the Doctor his happiest and most precious utterances. I remember it was at one of these meetings, after theatres and public amusements had been the subject under consideration for several evenings, that the question was raised whether popular lectures upon literary and scientific subjects might not be made very attractive, as well as useful, to very many who frequented the theatre and balls for the want of some better occasions for social enjoyment. Several doubted whether such lectures would be largely attended, but the majority believed that a great many people would be eager to avail themselves of such opportunities to acquire useful and entertaining knowledge. If I am not mistaken, this was one of the earliest movements that led to the institution of courses of public lectures, — the Lyceum and the Lowell Institute.

At the close of my term of service as Dr. Channing's temporary assistant, some time in the winter of 1822, Rev. Orville Dewey was invited to take the same position.

While in Baltimore after my return from Richmond, in July, 1821, I conferred with Mr. Sparks upon the practicability of gathering a Unitarian Church in that city. In January of 1822 I received a letter from him, proposing that we should soon commence the enterprise. We entered into an arrangement that, soon after the close of the session of Congress, of which he was then one of the chaplains, I should come to Baltimore and supply his pulpit two or three Sundays, that he might go to Richmond, make a reconnoissance, and ascertain whether there were persons enough there, favorably disposed, to warrant my following him and commencing the foundation of a Church. How different might have been my course in life, if this plan had been carried into operation! It does not seem possible; but I might have become reconciled to slavery, or so overborne by the influence of slaveholders as to have been awed into silence respecting the great abomination, "the sum of all villanies." On the whole, I am grateful to the Sovereign Disposer of events that I was withheld from the great temptation.

CHAPTER VIII.

BROOKLYN, CONN.

HIS REASONS FOR GOING TO BROOKLYN. — ORDAINED IN BOSTON. — BROOKLYN AND THE PARISH. — INSTALLED. — A CHILD'S PROTEST AGAINST REV. DR. FREEMAN'S CHARGE. — PROBABLE ROBBER. — SCHOOLS OF CONNECTICUT. — MARRIES. — ECCLESIASTICAL USAGES. — VIEWS OF SUNDAY. — HIS ONLY SILK GOWN AND BANDS. — THE LORD'S SUPPER. — IMMERSION. — THE TRINITARIAN CHURCH. — REFUSES CHAPLAINCY OF A REGIMENT. — DECLINES TO PRAY AT A HANGING.

JUST after the above arrangement was made, about the middle of the month of February, I was coming out of my father's house, on the way to the post-office with a letter to Mr. Sparks upon the subject, when lo! at the door I met Mr. John Parish and Mr. Herbert Williams, a committee from the Church in Brooklyn, Conn., sent to insist upon my becoming their minister. They were so earnest, so importunate, said so much about the importance of maintaining the first Unitarian Church in Connecticut, about the critical position of their little band, and of the unanimity of their choice of me to be their pastor, that I could not but feel that theirs was indeed a loud call to me, in the providence of God, to undertake the work of an evangelist in the most "Orthodox" State in New England. The above-named good men waited a day or two for my answer.

I spent the greater part of the night in revolving the question in my mind, arguing *pro* and *con* in the court of conscience. My father and mother strenuously opposed my accepting the invitation to Brooklyn. They could see only conflict, hard work and poverty, before me there. All the friends whom I consulted concurred with them in advising me to refuse. Even Mr. George Cabot, whose opinion I greatly respected, argued and urged to the same effect. Still, I could not dispel from my heart the conviction that it was my duty to take up the work which seemed to be given me to do. I remembered the principle which I had always insisted, in conversations with my fellow-students, ought to govern a young minister in the selection of his field of labor. I had often denounced the too common saying, that the loudest call came from the city churches, or from those which would pay the largest salaries. So, after earnest and prayerful consideration, I determined to accept the invitation from Brooklyn, and informed the committee that I would make the trial for a year.

In order that I might exercise at once all the functions of a pastor, — administer the ordinances, as well as conduct the services of public worship, — it was thought advisable that I should receive ordination before leaving Boston. Accordingly I applied to the Churches of the Boston Association, to be ordained by them. My request was promptly granted; and the 14th day of March, at Thursday Lecture, was appointed to be the time for the customary services.

On the 5th of March, our family were plunged into a deep affliction. My sister, Eliza Sewall, — then the wife of Mr. Benjamin Willis, of Portland, — who had been sick several weeks, suddenly died, leaving a son and a daughter, both less than five years of age. On the same day, my father's venerable and excellent uncle, Joseph Williams, of Roxbury, departed, in a good old age. I had spent many happy days and weeks in his family; and, though to him the event was a release from the burdens of life, to us it left a sad void. These bereavements, especially the loss of my sister, made us all the more sad as we went on with the preparations for my removal to what was then a long distance, eighty miles by stage-coaches, from the old home.

My mother got home from Portland on the 13th, just in time to witness my ordination as an evangelist, in Chauncy Place Church. Rev. Dr. Freeman preached the sermon, President Kirkland gave the Charge, and Rev. Henry Ware, Jr., gave the Right Hand of Fellowship.

The next day I left home for Brooklyn, *via* Providence, and reached there Saturday afternoon. On Sunday, the 17th, I commenced my labors as minister of "the First Ecclesiastical Society of Brooklyn, Connecticut."

I found the Society, comprising about forty families, made up of some of the most sensible and respectable people in the town. All but half a dozen were plain farmers, living on good farms, some of which their grandfathers, or remoter ancestors, had purchased of the Indians, and reclaimed from the forest.

The village of Brooklyn was rather a pretty one. A few years before, it had been made the county seat; so that there were the court-house and jail, and sundry hotels and stores, and a printing-office. It was the residence formerly of General Israel Putnam, of Revolutionary fame, and had been beautified somewhat by his taste, or the taste of some of his family, who had set out rows of elm and maple trees on either side of the principal street, which, when I went there, were well grown, so as to cover the road with their shade. The general's house was still standing; and the arm, from which used to swing his tavern-sign, remained in the crotch of the principal tree in front, and directly opposite the steeple end of our meeting-house. That structure was becoming venerable. It had been standing more than fifty years, and was built after the New England fashion of that day, — a tall, slender spire, and, as it seemed to me, more than commonly graceful, surmounted by a weather-cock, that once was gilded.

Although I engaged only for a year, I soon came to feel that Brooklyn was probably to be my field of labor for life, and I reconciled myself to it. I set about earnestly and prayerfully the work that was given me to do. In addition to the regular services of each Sunday, for which I was left to provide alone, with very seldom the relief of an exchange, I instituted a weekly meeting at the houses of my parishioners, where we conversed for an hour or two on the fundamental doctrines and duties of Christianity, and I read to them selections on the subjects under consideration, from the writings of our best authors.

The opposition of my Orthodox neighbors was less violent and unfair than I expected. Still, there were busily circulated throughout the community grievous misrepresentations of the faith and the spirit of Unitarians. I perceived that these could not be overtaken and corrected merely by my preaching to those who would come to hear me. Accordingly, early in January, 1823, I commenced the publication of a small paper, entitled "The Liberal Christian," which was published somewhat more than a year, once a fortnight, eight pages small quarto. Upon the pages of this periodical I spread out before my neighbors throughout that region explicit statements of our doctrines, and arguments in support of them. My labor was not for naught. I received assurances and proofs that it did good; and it brought to my acquaintance numbers of persons living in different parts of the county and the State, some of whom embraced the doctrines of Unitarians, and all of whom were disposed to encourage religious inquiry, and maintain their freedom.

I had not been preaching many weeks, before my attention was arrested by a staid, sensible-looking gentleman and lady, who came to church several Sundays, and whose countenances were radiant with the interest they took in what they heard. Very soon, they were introduced to me as Squire Sharpe and his wife, of Abington, a part of Pomfret, — the Hon. George Sharpe, lately a member of the Senate of Connecticut. I confess to not a little exultation at seeing frequently in my audience these persons from a neighboring town, who were acknowledged of all men to be persons of very sound sense and of elevated moral character. And when they "took a pew," and actually joined the Society, it was considered a great acquisition. They became my parishioners, and cordially invited me to visit them, which it became my official duty, as well as pleasure, to do.

Soon after, I was walking one afternoon towards that quarter of Brooklyn which adjoined Abington, when I saw, descending a long hill, a large charcoal-cart, driven by a man whose contour and gait seemed to be that of my new friend, the Hon. Mr. Sharpe. I could not think it possible; for I was a city boy, and had not been accustomed to seeing gentlemen — members of the Legislature, honorable senators — dressed in frocks, working like day-laborers, especially as colliers, upon whom in Boston I had been wont to look as a very low class. But the nearer we drew to each other, the more evident it became that my new and honorable friend was the collier before me. I remembered Burns's poem, "a man's a man for a' that," and braced myself up for the occasion. When near enough, we saluted each other, and I drew off my glove to shake hands with him. "Oh, no!" said he, with a hearty smile, "I never give my hand to a friend, when it is so dirty. My brother and I wish to clear up a four-acre wood-lot, that we may plant it. The best way to dispose of the wood is to reduce it to coal: and we long since learnt the wisdom of Dr. Franklin's maxim, 'If you would have any thing done well, you must do it yourself;' so we have gone into it. It is a dirty job, but we shall get through in three or four weeks, and then you must come and visit us." We parted, I a wiser and stronger man; having learnt that no labor is degrading, and that it is not the exterior that makes the man.

The members of the Society, though assured of my willingness to remain permanently with them, were desirous of putting an end to the rumor often sent through the community, "Mr. May is about to leave the Brooklyn Church." Moreover, they were confident that the services of an installation, conducted by some of the most distinguished men of our denomination, would make a salutary impression upon the public mind. I therefore yielded to their wishes.

The installation took place on the 5th of November, 1823. Rev. Dr. Bancroft, of Worcester, was the moderator of the council; Rev. Dr. Lowell, of Boston, was the scribe. Rev. Luther Willson, of Petersham, the former pastor, offered the introductory prayer; Rev. James Walker, of Charlestown, preached the sermon; Rev. Dr. Freeman gave the Charge; Rev. William B. O. Peabody, of Springfield, gave the Right Hand of Fellowship; Rev. Dr. Thayer, of Lancaster, addressed the people; and Dr. Parkman, of Boston, offered the concluding prayer.

The audience was as large as the meeting-house

would comfortably hold, and the impression made upon them was obviously favorable and strong. Historical truth requires me to make one exception. A little girl about six years old, who was very fond of me, and one of my pets, was much offended at the Charge. Dr. Freeman's manner was solemn and earnest. She was very intent upon him for a few minutes, then, bursting into tears, she rushed out of the house, crying quite aloud, "That old man is scolding my dear Mr. May, and I won't hear him any more."

With the new impetus thus given me, I pressed forward in the way of my duty. Regarding Jesus of Nazareth as the best teacher of Christianity, I determined to make his words and his character the standard of my faith and practice.

Dr. Noah Worcester had fixed my attention upon the teachings and example of Christ, in respect to evil-doers, violent, injurious persons, and personal enemies. His "Solemn Review of the Custom of War," and his articles in the "Friend of Peace," had convinced me that the precepts, spirit, and example of Jesus gave no warrant to the violent, bloody resistance of evil; that wrong could be effectually overcome only by right, hatred by love, violence by gentleness, evil of any kind only by its opposite good. I preached this as one of the cardinal doctrines of the Gospel, and endeavored especially to show the wickedness and folly of the custom of war.

An incident occurred which enabled me to put in practice this principle. As some uncertainty hangs over it, I should not record it, were it not that the story has been often told by others, sometimes even from the pulpit, and published, with more or less exaggeration. I shall now therefore state the facts, exactly as I have always stated them, and leave others to make out of them whatever may seem probable.

Early in the summer of 1824 I went to Springfield, to visit my friends there, and to exchange with my friend Peabody. I travelled by Mr. Herbert Williams's horse and chaise, and had brought his wife or his sisters, on the way, to visit their relatives in Leicester. On my return, wishing to travel from Springfield to Leicester (about fifty miles) in the course of the day, without tasking my borrowed horse too severely, I started before four o'clock, A.M. When about half-way across Wilbraham Plain, — three or four miles from any inhabitants, and near the spot where a Mr. Lyon had been robbed and murdered a few months before, — I espied a man in the road before me, whose appearance and manners I did not like, and who seemed to be a less desirable acquaintance the nearer I drew to him. He was ill-dressed, and his clothes looked as if he had slept upon the ground. He carried in his hand a short, heavy stick, or bludgeon, and was lingering, or walking very slowly, through a patch of dense woods. He looked round at me occasionally, as if waiting for me to come up. My apprehension was that he intended to strike down my horse, and then attack me. The fear may have been wholly without foundation, but I acted as if that were really his intention. Just before my horse's head came within reach of his bludgeon, I stopped and said, "Friend, you are going my way: will you not ride with me?" He hesitated, was embarrassed, and then replied, "Don't care if I do." "Well, then," I continued, "come round on this side and get into the chaise." He did so, and we jogged on together. It was some time before I could get any thing out of him. He looked like a bad man, but did not seem like a very ignorant one. He was a Scotchman, or from the north of England. Whither he was going, what was the object of his journey, — I could not learn. So I talked to him on various subjects, suggested by the objects that we passed, until at length he became more easy and communicative. About eleven o'clock I stopped, intending to give my horse a long rest, and in due time to get some dinner. I invited my fellow-traveller into the hotel with me, and said he should be welcome to dine with me if he would. He declined, slunk away, and kept out of sight, until at one o'clock, when I came out, he was there, and resumed his seat by my side. The afternoon ride passed very much as the morning had done. My suspicions of his ill intention toward me faded from my mind, and I rested in the conclusion that he was only a poor, unfortunate man who did not choose to make a confidant of a stranger, and so held himself in reserve. Between five and six, P.M., we reached the village of Leicester. Pointing to Dr. Nelson's house, half a mile off to the left, I said to my companion, "Well, sir, we must part here, for I am going to stay at that place to-night." If he had only replied in some common way, — if he had said, "Thank you, sir," or "I am much obliged to you, you have done me a great kindness," — I should never have thought more of the occurrence than that I had helped a poor, wayfaring man some forty-five or fifty miles over his road. But he got out of the chaise, took hold of the handle of the dasher, and, looking earnestly at me, said, with emphasis and emotion, "Thank you, sir: you probably never will know the benefit you have conferred upon me to-day." Instantly, the impression his first appearance in the morning made upon me was revived. I felt sure that he had intended me harm, and that I had averted his evil purpose. He turned off into an opposite road, and walked rapidly away. I longed to ask him what he meant by his peculiar words and emphasis, but I was withheld. So he went away, carrying his secret with him.

I had heard much of the common schools of Connecticut, and of the large fund by which they were supported. So I went to reside in that State, expecting to find the system of public instruction there the best, as well as the most popular, of any in our country. I very soon began to pay attention to the education of the young; and soon after my installation, by which the people were assured that I had become a permanent resident amongst them, they elected me to be one of the town school committee. In that office I continued so long as I lived in Connecticut, for it was customary in that, as in all the New England States, to commit the care of the schools to the ministers of religion.

I determined to do my duty as well as I knew how. So I informed myself thoroughly of the condition of the schools, — the houses, furniture, books, and, above all, the qualifications of the teachers. In all respects I was disappointed, and did not conceal my feeling of dissatisfaction; and even ventured to express the opinion that the School Fund was not operating to increase, but rather to diminish, the popular interest in the schools.

My associates upon the committee were anxious to improve the character of the schools in Brooklyn. In the first place, we proposed to make the examination of candidates for the office of teachers more thorough and real, so as to keep out all such as were undoubtedly incompetent. The first winter we rejected six who offered themselves, so that we examined fifteen teachers to supply our nine schools. The next year we rejected four. This brought upon the school committee the reputation of being "mighty strict," and kept away many who were conscious of their incompetency.

On the 1st of June, 1825, I was married to Lucretia Flagge Coffin, second daughter of Peter Coffin, Esq., of Boston. She was born in Portsmouth, N.H., where her father was a merchant until 1810 or 1812, when he removed to Boston. Her mother was Anne Martin, a daughter of Thomas Martin, whose father was a Huguenot. We lived in a hired house upon Brooklyn Green, until the fall of 1828, when the house was sold, and we returned to board in the family of Mr. John Parish.

I sought to learn the whole "Truth as it is in Jesus," from the words and the life of the Teacher himself.

It soon seemed to me that Christianity had been encumbered with many dogmas that really had nothing to do with it, and that, notwithstanding Christ's reproofs of pharisaism, the Church still cared more for "the mint, anise, and cummin" of ceremonial observances than for "the weightier matters of the Law,"—the keeping holy the Sabbath day, partaking of the Lord's Supper, and submitting to the ordinance of baptism, more than doing justly, loving mercy, and walking humbly. I conformed for a year or two to "the usages of the Church," without questioning any of them. I saw them to be good in themselves, or that they might be so, as means and instruments of spiritual culture; but mischievous, worthless, when regarded, as they too generally seemed to be, as the *essentials* of religion.

I valued the Sabbath as a day of rest from the ordinary cares of life; of sacred leisure secured to us by the religious institution of the Jewish law-givers, adopted from that by the founders of the Christian Church, and perpetuated by the consent of almost all the sects. I felt and preached that the time, thus wrested from the secular concerns of life, ought to be by each one assiduously consecrated to his religious improvement. But I saw and deplored the effect of the superstitious notions, still prevalent in Connecticut, respecting the sacredness of the day itself, and of the strict observance of it that was rigidly enforced. One of the charges alleged by his opponents against my predecessor, Rev. Luther Willson, was that, on a certain Saturday evening, having reached home from a journey, after sundown, and finding that his family were destitute of such wood as could be burned in their fireplaces, he sawed and split up enough to last until Monday! The austere and gloomy aspect given to the day, and to the whole of religion, made Sunday repulsive, especially to the young. A little boy, about six years of age, — Samuel S. Greeley, my nephew, who lived several months in my family after the death of his excellent mother, — said to me one Sunday, "Uncle, I hate Sunday, I do; it is a wooden day." This led me to think much of the better way of employing the time of children on the Sabbath. To this conclusion I came, and have acted upon it, as far as I have been able, ever since; viz., it is incumbent upon all who have the care of children to devote a suitable portion of every Sunday to their thorough religious instruction. When presented properly by a parent or teacher who really loves religion, there is no subject in which even quite young children become so deeply interested, and to which they will for so long a time give their closest attention. Then, children should be taught to consider that their parents, and older persons generally, who value, as they ought, the opportunity which Sunday affords them for religious improvement, will not like to have the quiet of the day unnecessarily disturbed, and therefore they should make as little noise as possible. Children ought not to be wholly forbidden to play on Sunday; for it must be as pleasing to the heavenly, as it is to the earthly, father, to see them enjoying themselves. But they can readily understand that their amusements ought not to be such as will interfere with the comfort of older persons, and prevent them from making the improvement of the hours of Sunday which they wish to do. Therefore it should be enjoined upon children, that their Sunday plays should be as quiet and noiseless as possible.

When I was ordained, my excellent friend, Mrs. Cary, afterwards my step-mother, gave me the elegant silk gown which formerly belonged to her first husband, and which he wore during his short ministry as the colleague of Dr. Freeman, of King's Chapel. My dear Jewish friends, the Misses Hays, also gave me several pairs of very nice bands.* So I commenced my labors as a preacher, attired, as was customary at that time, especially with city preachers, in a flowing black gown, and very white bands. But I had hardly become accustomed to wearing them, before the question arose in my mind, whether dressing up in a particular and somewhat imposing garb, in order to teach Christianity, might not have the effect to separate religion from ordinary, every-day life, and help to make it appear something peculiar to Sunday and the Church. I thought it might, I feared it would, have that effect; and so I threw my bands aside, and gave my gown to a poor woman who needed a comfortable dress.

* In a letter from Slowey Hays, which accompanied this gift, she said, "I have made them, dear Sam, of stiff materials, that they may prick your chin, should you ever say aught unkind of my dear people."

For several years after my settlement, I administered the Lord's Supper in the way that had long been practised in the Church, and was then the universal custom, at the close of the forenoon service, after the benediction, to those only who were called communicants. They were a class of persons admitted to this privilege by vote of those who already belonged to the class, on condition of their making before the whole congregation an acknowledgment of their faith.

The Church of Brooklyn had put aside the Creed, and substituted in its stead a Covenant which set forth only the simple, great doctrines of Christ and his apostles, which all Christians of every denomination acknowledge they taught. This appeared to me an advance in the right direction. It removed, from the approach to the Lord's Table, that impediment which had kept away many believers in God, and in Christ as His beloved Son, who could not assent to the doctrines of the Trinity, or the vicarious punishment of Jesus. But ere long the question arose, by what authority or right a portion (usually a small portion) of a Christian society assumed to themselves the exclusive privilege of one of the ordinances of Christianity. If partaking of the Lord's Supper was a means of spiritual improvement, and not the seal of sanctification, I could not see why any, why all, persons who desired to bring themselves under the influences of that ordinance, should not be freely permitted to do so without the interposition of any conditions, excepting perhaps the avowal of the desire and intention to do so. I could not see why there should be this bar to the

Lord's Table, any more than to the House of God, and the offices of prayer and singing psalms. I could get no evidence that all the persons who were admitted to the Communion were more correct in their belief or more obedient in their lives than many who were excluded. And then, if the outsiders were not so good, but *desired* to become better, it seemed to me our duty was to encourage and urge them onward, instead of putting the slightest hinderance in their way.

The question agitated my mind for some time, and was made the subject of much conference with "the members of the Church," as those who partook of the Lord's Supper were called. Most of them came readily to see and acknowledge that they had been led into an unwarranted assumption of privilege. They therefore consented that, while we should continue "to admit persons to the Church" in the formal manner that had long been customary where persons desired to be so admitted, we should not forbid any others to come to the Lord's Table who wished so to do, without having submitted to the ceremony of admission.

It soon became my practice, at the close of the forenoon service on "Communion Sunday," to announce that the Lord's Supper was then to be administered, and to invite all whose hearts moved them so to do to remain and commune with us. Such, however, was the influence of the long-established custom, that few did so without having been previously "admitted to the Church."

After a while, with the advice and consent of the

church members, I discontinued the preparatory lecture which used always to be delivered on the Friday afternoon before Communion Sunday. This was done for the reason that such an observance tended to separate this ordinance from the other services of public worship, and to hold it up to the people as something more sacred, more to be held in awe, than prayer and the praise of God. So we substituted for the preparatory lecture once a month the weekly meeting for mutual religious improvement, in order that we might help one another to *live*, as well as *speak*, the praise of God, and make life itself a continual prayer.

On my removal to South Scituate in 1836, I induced the Church there to adopt the same plan, I believe with good effect. And when I came to be the minister of the Church in Syracuse, I advised that the administration of the Lord's Supper should constitute the whole service of public worship on the forenoon of the first Sunday of every other month; and that "every person present, who loves the Lord Jesus Christ, and who feels his indebtedness to him for all he has done and suffered for the redemption of mankind, should be invited to commemorate his death and the divine virtue and grace which he manifested in that hour of his utmost trial, by partaking of the Lord's Supper."

This plan was at once adopted, and the ordinance has been so administered ever since I have lived here, now nearly nineteen years. I am unable to ascertain what has been, on the whole, the effect here of my mode of treating and conducting this sacrament. For I have reason to believe that, in this region of our country, the Christian sacraments have never been held in as high esteem as they used to be throughout New England. And then again it is said that the regard for these ordinances is everywhere declining, and in most, if not all, other sects, as well as our own. I regret that more persons have not been, and are not now, more interested in the Lord's Supper as a simple memorial of the faith and the love, — the self-sacrificing love of the Founder of Christianity. It is to me an appropriate and an affecting rite. But many there are, especially those who were formerly of the "Society of Friends," who say they see no significance in eating a piece of bread and drinking a sip of wine. Our congregations are generally about as large on Communion Sundays as on others, although a few persons absent themselves. Those present seem interested; and quite a number have told me they love to be there and to hear my delineations of the character of Jesus Christ, although they have never been moved to partake of the bread and wine.

About ten years ago, Hon. Horace Mann happened to be with us on a Communion Sunday. I observed that he was much affected. As we were walking to my house, he said, "Never before have I seen much significance in the Lord's Supper; never before have I felt moved to partake of it: but to-day I have been affected by your representations of its intention, and your delineations of the character of Christ as revealed in the hour of his death." "Then," I said, "I hope you joined with us in partaking of the bread and wine."

"No," he replied, "I did not. I was withheld by the influence of the old notions and feelings respecting the Lord's Supper, which I imbibed in my childhood from Dr. Emmons, under whose ministry my religious education commenced."

But we must go back again to Brooklyn, where many of my heresies began.

Amongst those of my congregation there who refrained from the Lord's Supper, notwithstanding my cordial invitations to it, was one of the best men in the Society or the town, Mr. Nathan Witter. He was seldom absent from meeting on the Lord's day, always remained to witness the administration of the Supper; but never partook of the bread and wine. I soon inquired the reason of his conduct. He informed me that he deemed it wrong for any one to partake of the Lord's Supper who had not been baptized, and thus regularly admitted into the Church of Christ; and that he had never been baptized according to his understanding of the ordinance of baptism. "True," said he, "I was sprinkled when an infant, at the request of my parents; but I was unconscious of the act. It was not the baptism of a believer; and therefore, I think, not a proper and sufficient introduction into the Church of Christ." I argued with him that the quantity of water used in baptism could not be of any importance if the heart and conscience were right towards God; and that if his parents had fulfilled the promises they made at his baptism, and had brought him up "in the nurture and admonition of the Lord," he was a member of the

Church, as all ought to be, from his birth. But my arguments were of no avail. He was a very staid, conscientious man, somewhat of the stern, puritanical sort, and must needs govern himself by his own convictions. He expressed a strong desire to become a "communicant," but would not, excepting in the way that seemed to him scriptural and proper.

After some consideration of the case, I offered, with the consent of the brethren, to conform to his ideas of what would be right, to baptize him by immersion, and receive him into the Church on his own profession of faith in Christ. He objected that he feared this would be deemed irregular, and that I should bring upon myself the censure of the churches. Dr. Whitney had refused to rebaptize him; and Mr. Willson, under the circumstances in which he was placed, thought it not expedient for him to immerse him. Although I could foresee no evil that could come of my yielding to the conscientious scruples of a good man, I thought it best not to act unadvisedly. Accordingly, I addressed letters to Rev. Dr. Bancroft, of Worcester, and Rev. Dr. Thayer, of Lancaster, Mass., both of whom had assisted in my ordination. I stated the case to them as fully as seemed necessary, and intimated my desire to conform to the wishes of Mr. Witter. Each of those wise and excellent men replied tenderly to my inquiry, expressed sympathy for Mr. Witter, but concluded by advising that, on the whole, it would be better for me not to comply. So doing would be contrary to the long-established usage of the Protestant Churches. It would seem to be an assent to the insufficiency of infant baptism, and might introduce disorder into our churches.

Such advice, for a while, held me in suspense. But the longer I saw that good man submitting without complaint, though sorrowfully, to what he deemed a great privation, the more unwilling was I that he should suffer it. And so, insisting on our right as an independent Church to conduct the services of public worship and to use the ordinances in the way that we thought would conduce most to the edification of our own members, with the consent of the Brooklyn Church I invited the gentleman to be baptized by immersion, and so become a member of our Church in the way he thought right.

He was grateful for our condescension, and, not without hesitation on our account, consented to our proposal. Notice was accordingly given from the pulpit one Sunday that, at three o'clock that afternoon, at a certain place, Nathan Witter would profess his faith in the religion of Jesus Christ, be baptized by immersion, and received into the Church. Of course a large number of people, of the other congregations in the town, as well as our own, went in due season to the appointed place. It was a bright, beautiful afternoon in summer, in a picturesque meadow at a graceful bend of the small river called Blackwell's Brook, where there was a small pebbly beach, over which we could walk, not too suddenly, into the depth of the stream.

After a few introductory remarks and prayer, I read to Mr. Witter the Church Covenant, and, after his audible assent thereto, I took him by the arm, and walked with him into the stream until the water was up to our waists; and then, pronouncing the form of words prescribed by our Lord, I immersed the rest of his body.

The scene was new to myself. I had never witnessed such an administering of baptism by another, and never performed the service in that way but once before. I was almost overcome by my own emotions, and saw that the people were excited above measure. So soon, therefore, as I reached the bank, I admonished them that we ought not to take it for granted that our emotions were purely religious feelings; that the significance of baptism, administered, as they had just seen, by immersion, was no higher than when conferred by sprinkling. That we all were unusually excited, because the performance was a novel one to most of us, and the beautiful surroundings and circumstances of the occasion conspired to give it solemnity; but that we might be solemnized without being sanctified, and might have our religious feelings greatly excited without really giving our hearts to God. And I pressed it upon them not to leave that spot without the assurance that it was not the putting of water upon the body in small quantity or large that was acceptable to God or essential to our salvation, but the denying of all ungodliness and worldly lusts, and living soberly, righteously, and piously in all the relations and intercourse of life.

It being understood, from my procedure in this case, that I held myself in readiness to administer this sacrament in the way that seemed right and scriptural to the recipient, I was several times called upon, while I continued in Brooklyn, to baptize by immersion; and during my too short ministry in South Scituate I admitted a good man and his wife to the Church at the same time, by immersing him in the river and by sprinkling her on the bank.

The Orthodox portion of the original Brooklyn Church, being the smaller, were obliged to leave the old meeting-house in our possession; and, after worshipping awhile in a hall, they built them a small house, capable of holding about two hundred persons. In due time, they invited a candidate, the Rev. Mr. Edson, to settle as their pastor. Knowing that an ordination was an occasion likely to bring together a larger concourse of people than could be accommodated in their small meeting-house, our Society tendered to them the use of our house for that day. The offer was gratefully accepted. People came from all the neighborhood to witness the solemnities, and filled the old meeting-house to its utmost capacity. A prominent, eloquent, and very zealous minister had been invited to preach on the occasion. He came fully prepared, as he felt in duty bound, to denounce the great heresy which had ousted the true Church of Brooklyn from its old home. He arrived but a few hours before the services began, and learnt, to his no little discomfiture, that he was to deliver his philippic against Unitarianism from the pulpit of the Unitarian Church, which had been graciously lent for the occasion. Being a gentleman of quick sensibility to the courteous and right, he was made very uncomfortable by the predicament in which he found himself. He tried, but was not successful in his attempts, to qualify somewhat the severity of his condemnation of us. And I really pitied him so much in his awkward embarrassments, that I forgave his uncharitableness, and felt not the point of his censures.

A bare majority of the communicants under the old *régime* seceded with the Orthodox. In virtue of that majority, they claimed to be the Church of the First Ecclesiastical Society in Brooklyn, Conn., though they could not deny that we were that society. As the church records and communion vessels were left at Dr. Whitney's house, where they had always been kept, we forbore awhile from pressing our claims to them. But so soon as the Orthodox party had organized as the "First Trinitarian Church and Society in Brooklyn," and had settled a minister under that title, at my suggestion a committee of our Church made a written proposal to their Church, that we would appoint our Communion Service on the month alternate to that on which they pleased to have theirs, and would use the sacred vessels in common, always returning them after use to Dr. Whitney for safe-keeping. To this proposal, they replied that they did not know who we were, and would not lend their vessels to be used for any such purpose.

Our prompt rejoinder was, that we were the Church of the First Ecclesiastical Society in Brooklyn, and that we demanded of them certain sacramental vessels belonging to us which were known to be in their possession. That we denied utterly their claim to them; but, as we wished to live in peace and in neighborly kindness, we would consent that they should get the property in their hands belonging to us properly appraised by a competent person, and we would either pay half of the sum so appraised and take the vessels, or they should pay us half the sum and keep them. We added that, if they would not consent to this way of settling the question between us, we should seek redress by the agency of the law. This produced the desired effect. A sum was named, the half of which we thought it not best to pay. So they kept the vessels and paid us the half, with which we were able to purchase a very neat and suitable communion set. Thus all strife between us ended.

I had no religious intercourse with the members of the Orthodox Church, nor ministerial intercourse with their pastor. But I sought to establish and maintain friendly relations with all my neighbors, and was quite successful. They invited me to their houses as a visitor, and they visited me in return.

The prominent physician of the town, Dr. Waldo Hutchins, was a member of the Orthodox Church, and his father and all his relatives in neighboring towns belonged to the same denomination. But he was my medical adviser and personal friend. Four or five years after our acquaintance commenced, he was taken sick and died. When conscious that he was approaching the grave, he sent for me to converse and pray with him. He begged me to visit him often, and sent for me once at midnight. The morning after his decease, I was informed that he was to have a public funeral, and that he had requested his wife and father that I might be called on to preach the sermon, naming his father's minister at Killingly, and two other Orthodox ministers and particular friends, as those whom he wished should officiate in the other services at his house and in the Church. As I expected, and foretold his afflicted family, those gentlemen refused to appear with me in public as a Christian minister. I therefore advised that another should be requested to preach in my stead, and I be allowed to take my place, as I could sincerely, among the mourners. But neither the wife nor the father would consent. The dying request of the dear departed one must be complied with, and they therefore begged me to perform all the services. A large concourse of personal and professional friends attended the funeral, among them several of the Orthodox ministers of the adjoining towns; and, out of regard to the family, some who had refused to take any part with me were obliged to hear my prayers and listen to my sermon. This was a lesson they did not expect would be given them, and they never forgot it.

As a friend of education, and of temperance, the Orthodox men and ministers of Brooklyn and the vicinity united with me in labors for the promotion of those great and good objects. And some joined me in the Peace Society, formed in August, 1826, to co-operate with Dr. Worcester and his followers, who were endeavoring to abolish the custom of war.

Brooklyn was the county town. The court-house and jail were there. Several sessions of the different courts were held there every year; and lawyers and other gentlemen came thither from all parts of the State, with many of whom I became acquainted, and found some of them to be very liberal as well as educated men.

Our meeting-house was the largest building in the place, and therefore county agricultural, masonic, temperance, and other conventions, were often held in it; and I was sometimes called upon to officiate at them. This of course made the only Unitarian minister in Connecticut more widely known to the people.

A year or two after my settlement, I was elected chaplain of the regiment; but I declined the office, because I told the colonel I could not pray that the soldiers might do the very thing they would be mustered to do, but could only pray that they might "beat their swords into ploughshares, and their bayonets into pruning-hooks, and learn war no more."

Not long afterwards, a man was found guilty of the most atrocious murder of his wife, and was condemned to be hanged. I had no doubt of his horrid guilt, and visited him often in his cell, endeavoring to soften his hardened heart and lead him to repentance. The sheriff waited upon me and invited me to officiate at the gallows. I inquired if it was the request of the condemned man that I should do so. He said no, but that he had come in behalf of the State. Then I told him that I could not comply. I would go if the wretched criminal invited me, as the sympathizing friend of a very wicked brother man; but that I could not be, or seem to be in any wise, the agent of the State to do what I did not think the State had any right to do. This led to an earnest discussion of the propriety of the death penalty. I pressed the sheriff with such arguments as I then wielded against the infliction, until he was much moved and expressed a desire to be excused from the awful duty. I afterwards learnt that his heart failed him at the last, and he left it for a stolid deputy to do the deed.

CHAPTER IX.

BROOKLYN, CONN., CONCLUDED.

THE TEMPERANCE MOVEMENT. — BEGINS TO PRACTISE AND TO PREACH TOTAL ABSTINENCE. — HIS "RAISING" WITHOUT SPIRITUOUS LIQUORS. — WILLIAM LADD. — FIRST EDUCATIONAL CONVENTION. — MEETS A. BRONSON ALCOTT. — LECTURES ON EDUCATION. — A POWERLESS HORSE. — CALLED TO PROVIDENCE. — RESOLVES TO STAY IN BROOKLYN.

IN May, 1826, I attended the anniversaries in Boston. Amongst them I attended the annual meeting of the Massachusetts Society for the Suppression of Intemperance, and afterwards a meeting of ministers called together in the vestry of the First Church, the Chauncy Place Church, to consider what was our especial duty as ministers. Several things were said that moved me deeply. At length Dr. Lowell rose, and, having added a few words in further delineation of the frightful ravages of intemperance, said, with his sweet solemnity of manner: "We can at least do one thing: we can ourselves set a good, yes, a perfect, example. Let us abstain wholly from the use of whatever can intoxicate. If such an example should be generally followed, we may be sure the evil we deprecate would be extirpated from the communities in which we live. I know not that this can be done by any other means. This expedient is proposed: let us try it faithfully, at any expense of discomfort, at any sacrifice."

I probably have not reported exactly his words: the above was the meaning of what he said. My determination was formed at the close of his speech.

It had been my habit up to that time, occasionally, at noon on Sunday especially, to take a glass of wine, and to drink a tumbler of cider every day with my dinner; but at that moment these indulgences were renounced. Whether they were salutary or not I cared not to inquire. In the spirit of St. Paul, I said "If wine cause my brother to offend, I will not drink wine while the world standeth, lest I cause my brother to offend."

On my return home, I announced to my good wife my determination that no more wine or cider should be used in my family, and consecrated a hamper of delicious Madeira, that had recently been sent me by my friend Hon. William Sullivan, whose sons were then under my instruction, to the service of the sick alone. She heartily concurred with me in the new measure, and total abstinence was then established as a rule of my household.

That evening, or the next, a party of neighbors came in to welcome my return. At the usual time a plate of cake was handed round, when my sister Abby roguishly said, "If any of you are thirsty, you must go to the well and satisfy yourselves; for my brother has decreed that we shall offer to our friends hereafter nothing better than cold water." This led to an exposition of my new faith, and the terrible statistics of intemperance, which had induced me to adopt the principle of total abstinence. A few evenings afterwards, we returned the call, or rather attended a small party at the house of one of the neighbors alluded to above. Just before we rose to leave, the good lady of the house offered us cake, and pleasantly said, "We are not going to treat you any better than we were treated the other evening at our minister's house: he gave us nothing but cold water; our well is as good as his, and you may have as much cold water as you please. We mean to follow the example of our minister." Thus the doctrine of total abstinence was again made the subject of discussion. But I felt that much more was to be done than merely talk upon the subject at private parties. The statistics published by the Society for the Suppression of Intemperance, and still later by the Total Abstinence Society, were too awful to be readily believed, so I set about investigating the matter for myself. I easily calculated what would be the quota for Brooklyn of all the various evils set forth by the above-named societies as the dreadful consequences of the use of intoxicating drinks throughout our country. It was taken for granted that there was less intemperance in our town than in many others. I therefore did not expect to find our full proportion of the various evils, but supposed I should find enough of them to justify the general statement.

I went personally to every retailer in the town, and ascertained what quantities of the various sorts of intoxicating drinks he sold in the course of a year, and their prices. From the same persons I learnt the number of inebriates in the town. The overseers of the poor enabled me to find out how many persons had been reduced to poverty by their own self-indulgence, or by the intemperance of those on whom they were necessarily dependent. The physicians, the sexton, and the older inhabitants gave me the facts, from which I could estimate how much sickness and how many deaths might be fairly attributed to the use of alcohol. And the records of the court and of the jailer told pretty correctly how many crimes had been perpetrated, during the previous ten years, under the influence of the same demon.

After the most careful examination of all the information thus obtained, I was brought to the conclusion, much to my surprise, that the frightful statements, made in the reports of the temperance societies, of the waste, the miseries, the crimes, the deaths caused by the use of intoxicating drinks, were abundantly sustained by the facts of the case found in our own town.

Thus fortified, I made the evils of intemperance the subject of a sermon, preached to a full congregation. I spread before my hearers the condition of the country in this respect, giving them the statistics published by the societies, that had been formed, if possible, to reform the people. I closed by giving notice that I should resume the subject on the following Sunday. My hearers were much excited; many looked incredulous; some were evidently displeased. As I was coming out of the house, one old man said to me rather roughly, "You'll never make us believe such big stories as you have told us this morning: you had better preach the gospel to us." "My friend," I replied, "wait until you hear what I shall tell you next Sunday."

The next Sunday came. The audience was large, and the people had come eager to hear if any thing more extravagant was to be told them.

I took up the statements I had made the previous Sunday, on the authority of the temperance reports, and then set about to show them by the statistics of our own town, which I had so carefully gathered up and arranged, that if the amount of intoxicating liquors drank by the people throughout the United States was proportionably only as great as the amount used in Brooklyn, and if the evils everywhere produced by that indulgence were everywhere as many and as dreadful as I had found them to be, and no more nor worse, even then the calculations made, and the statistics given, by the friends of temperance must be wholly within the truth.

This exposition evidently made an impression upon the minds of my auditors. A great many adopted the principle of "total abstinence," and the cause of temperance became quite popular. Daniel Frost, a very respectable lawyer of Canterbury, became a convert, and then an earnest advocate, and at length devoted himself almost entirely to the cause.

I lectured frequently on the subject, not only in all parts of Brooklyn, but in all the neighboring towns. We certainly succeeded in diminishing greatly the apparent, if not the real, amount of the evils of intemperance. Numbers of drunkards were reclaimed; several of the retailers abandoned their traffic; and the use of intoxicating beverages was renounced by a great many persons. It seemed as if a general and most beneficent reformation was indeed to be effected. Young persons and old, male and female, signed the pledge of total abstinence. Amongst many very interesting and affecting instances of self-consecration to this work, I remember one with particular pleasure. I went to Norwich, about twenty miles south of Brooklyn, to lecture on the subject. I had a good audience, and was conscious of making no little impression. So soon as I called for signatures to the pledge, a venerable man, more than seventy-five years of age, came forward to give his name. It was General Zechariah Huntington. He was one of Washington's aids during the war of the Revolution, and had ever since sustained a most respectable position in the community where he lived. Before he wrote his signature, he said, "I am now, as you all perceive, an old man. I have been in the habit of drinking alcohol in some of its forms many years, more than fifty. Every day I have taken a dram; but I have seen so much of the horrible effects of intemperance, that I have been upon my guard and have always used rum and wine moderately. I do not believe it has ever done me any harm: it may have done me good. Many persons think that to renounce it, at my time of life, will be injurious, perhaps fatal to me. But I am too much affected, by the fearful ravages of intemperance in the land, to hesitate a moment longer as to my duty. I have often exposed my life upon the field of battle for the redemption of my country from a foreign foe; and I will not refuse any sacrifice that I am called upon to make, to save my country from this far worse, this internal, ay, infernal enemy, even if it be the sacrifice of life." The effect of such an example was more powerful than the most eloquent speech.

Farmers and master-workmen, not a few, refused to furnish spirituous drinks to their hired men; some refused to employ men who persisted in the use of such drinks. And the falsity of the notion, which had been most assiduously disseminated, was thoroughly exposed; the notion that very hard work could not be done without the aid of stimulants. It was shown, too plainly not to be seen, that alcohol conferred no strength: it only excited to undue exertion.

In 1829 I built a house. When the frame was all ready to be put up, I said to my master-workman, "I will furnish the entertainment for the raisers." "I shall be glad to have you do so," was his prompt reply; "but you must have some rum, or spirituous liquor of some kind, for it is always expected on such occasions, and I do not believe the house can be put up without it." "Then it must lie upon the ground," said I; "for I do not mean there shall be a drop of any thing that can intoxicate brought upon the ground." He remonstrated at length, somewhat angrily, but I was inflexible; and he acquiesced on my promise, in case his prediction should be fulfilled, and the frame not be raised, that I would pay him for the work he had done, and whatever damages for the loss of his job might be awarded by an impartial reference.

The day for the raising was appointed. The usual public invitation was given, accompanied by the notice that no spirituous drinks would be furnished or permitted. A large concourse of people assembled; for in our country towns, a raising used to be a great attraction.

The labor commenced at 1 P.M., and before sundown the frames of my house, 42 feet long, 28 feet wide, with an L 24 feet by 18, and of my barn 24 feet by 20, were both standing firm. So soon as the frame of the main part of the house was up, the refreshment I had provided was brought on. It was at once seen to be a generous one, very much more costly than spirituous liquors would have been. A murmur of satisfaction was everywhere audible, and a jolly repast the raisers made of it. They afterwards put their hands and shoulders to the work, with right good-will, and completed the raising of the L and of the barn in the shortest time possible.

Just about the close of the repast, I saw some commotion on one part of the grounds, and heard angry voices. I hurried to the spot, and found it was the expression of indignation at an unprincipled man, who had clandestinely brought a bottle of rum with him, and had invited some others to partake of it with him. His invitation was accepted by no one. Several who were known to be much addicted to the use of rum were too honorable to take it there. They said, "We were invited to a temperance raising: we have been handsomely entertained, and no one shall stay here who attempts to violate the condition on which we were invited." So they broke the man's bottle and drove him away.

As already stated, early in my ministry I commenced preaching the doctrine of peace, and denouncing the custom of war. In the spring of 1825, a most excellent man came to reside in Brooklyn, who was an earnest fellow-laborer and efficient helper in this cause, Mr. George Benson, for many years a merchant in Providence, R.I., a member of the distinguished firm, Brown, Benson, & Ives. He dissolved his connection with them because he could not conscientiously consent to some things which they and most merchants deemed perfectly proper. He was respected by all who knew him, for his steadfast adherence to whatever he believed to be true and right. Although never a member of the Society of Friends, he entertained most of their opinions, cherished their spirit, dressed very much in their style, and generally attended their religious meetings. He was over seventy years of age, very gentle and a perfect gentleman. Able to live comfortably on the interest of his property, for economy's sake, and yet more for the good of his large family, he left the city, and removed to Brooklyn, where he had purchased a large, commodious house, and small farm, near the village. He and his family were a valuable accession to our society, and added much to my personal comfort. His wife, six daughters, and two sons, were all sensible, earnest persons. They conscientiously differed somewhat in their religious opinions, but they were harmonious among themselves, charitable towards others, and all interested in the great work of our Lord, the redemption of mankind from ignorance, sin, and misery. Mr. Benson for several years attended regularly my preaching; but perceiving that my doctrine tended to the humanitarian view of Christ, and having been wrought upon by some of our Orthodox neighbors, he quietly withheld himself from our meetings, and occasionally went to the other church. But this caused no interruption in our frequent intercourse, nor any abatement of its cordiality; for I knew him to be a pure, sincere, practical Christian. Mrs. Benson, one of the most motherly of women; Charlotte, now Mrs. Anthony of Providence; Sarah, a very saint; and Helen, now Mrs. Wm. L. Garrison of Boston, together with George W. and Henry E., were devoted coworkers with me, and constant attendants on my preaching. Frances, the oldest daughter, was very Orthodox, and Mary and Anna were Quakers. I wish I could do better justice to this most estimable family. George W. was a most energetic, fearless, young man in behalf of any thing that he believed to be true and right, and Henry E. was, I think, one of the most faultless persons I ever knew.

Mr. Benson and I soon discovered how much we agreed in our opinions upon the great subjects of war, intemperance, and popular education. He was conversant with most of the best Quaker and other writers upon those subjects, and helped me much to define and settle my opinions. We succeeded in interesting so many persons in our views of war, persons not only of Brooklyn, but of several other towns, that in August, 1826, we called a county meeting of the friends of peace, and succeeded in forming the Windham County Peace Society, which continued its operations so long as I remained in Connecticut. Mr. Benson was the President: I was the Corresponding Secretary. We distributed a great many tracts, and held meetings in most of the towns of the county.

I opened correspondence with many of the prominent friends of peace in this country and in England, with John Bevans, Rev. James Hargreaves of London, and Dr. Thomas Hancock of Liverpool, and with Dr. Noah Worcester of Brighton, Hon. Thomas S. Grimke of Charleston, S.C., William Ladd of Minot, Maine, and Joshua P. Blanchard, of Boston. Through them I obtained the best English as well as American publications on the subject, for my own use and for circulation.

The first pamphlet I ever published was an "Exposition of the Sentiments and Purposes of the Windham County Peace Society," in the fall of 1826.

My correspondence with Mr. Ladd and Mr. Grimke was more frequent than with any others, and was particularly valuable. In the summer of 1827 Mr. Ladd came to visit me. He spent a week or more in my family. He lectured several times in Brooklyn and the neighborhood, and converted many to our faith, and confirmed the brethren. He was a large, coarse-looking man, but refined and delicate in all his feelings. He was well educated and well informed. After leaving college, he led a seafaring life for a number of years, and thus extended considerably his acquaintance with men and countries. Having inherited or acquired a handsome fortune, he retired upon a large farm in Minot, Maine, and there for a while devoted himself to agriculture, the raising of cattle, and to his literary pursuits. The writings of Dr. Worcester arrested his attention, wrought a deep conviction in his heart, and brought him from his retirement to be a public lecturer upon the criminality of the custom of war. His style of writing was piquant and racy. He was forcible in argument, happy in illustration, often witty, and sometimes sarcastic. Although there was no grace in his delivery, he never failed to secure attention, and make a deep impression.

Mr. Ladd was one of the most kind-hearted and genial men I ever knew. His laugh was loud and very contagious, so that it was impossible to be with him without having a merry time. He was, however, a truly, devoutly religious man, and rather Orthodox.

His visit continued, as I have said, through six or seven days, and was most grateful to me and my family. We had a great deal of conversation on several subjects of great interest. I heard all his lectures. He heard me preach, and he took part with me in our morning and evening devotions. How, then, was I surprised at the change which came over him on the morning of his departure! We had taken breakfast together, and had retired to my study to wait several hours for the stage-coach. After a while, his countenance assumed a grave, not to say a dark, look, and in an altered tone he addressed me thus: "Mr. May, I have passed a very pleasant, and, I hope, a profitable, week with you, profitable to ourselves, and to the great Christian reform in which we are both so much engaged. We have conversed, too, upon other important topics; but there is one subject upon which I have not said to you what I ought. I cannot leave you without expressing my utter disapprobation, my dread of your doctrinal opinions, and the false foundation upon which, I fear, you are resting your religious hopes." I soon perceived what was coming. So I threw into my countenance a demure expression, and put myself into the most receptive attitude. He went on, warming as he went, in condemnation of what he considered the dangerous, ay, damnable, errors of Unitarianism, until he had wrought himself into a glow of holy horror.

When he ceased, I looked up and said, "I thank you for what doubtless was intended for my good. I honor you for your fidelity to your convictions. I mean to be equally faithful to my own. And I know not how I can better evince my gratitude for your faithfulness to me, than by being equally faithful to you in return." Then I set before him, as plainly as possible, my view of the Orthodox system of doctrines and "scheme of salvation," showing him how utterly derogatory to God and discouraging to man they seemed to me; and that I did not dread his doctrinal opinions any less than he did mine.

He could hardly wait for me to finish what I had to say, when he replied, "You have served me right. It is just as proper for you to denounce my religious belief as for me to denounce yours. I doubt not you are as sincere in your belief of what seems to me dangerous error, as I am in my belief of what seems to you dangerous error. I consent to what you say about the test of the Christian character. He only ought to be accounted a Christian (whatever be the faith he professes), who manifests the spirit of Jesus, and is laboring to accomplish the work of the Lord, the redemption of mankind from ignorance, sin, and misery. And" he added, with one of his hearty laughs, "I have no doubt that your heart will go to heaven, whatever may become of your head." Thus ended our only talk about theological opinions. Our friendship continued, and, I believe, grew stronger until his death, increased by the not infrequent exchange of letters, and an occasional interview. He devoted the last ten or fifteen years of his life to the dissemination of the pacific principles of the Gospel; and, at his death, bequeathed to the American Peace Society the bulk of his property.

In the spring of 1827, our School Committee had become fully aware of the defects of our common schools in Brooklyn and all that region of the State; and suspecting that they were as numerous and glaring in other parts of Connecticut, they determined to call the attention of the public generally to the subject. Accordingly we issued a circular letter, inviting the people to send delegates to a State Convention in Brooklyn, for the purpose of considering the character and condition of our common schools. I prepared a series of questions, which were printed in the circular, answers to which would elicit the information desired, and would show the people of Connecticut that they had no reason to be satisfied with, much less to be proud of, their system of public instruction.

Copies of the circular were sent into every town in the State, addressed to the School Committees and to individuals, who, it was fairly presumed, would appreciate the importance of such a convention. They were earnestly requested, if they could not come in person to the meeting, to favor us with full and exact replies to all our questions, and with such remarks respecting the schools in their several towns, or the State system of public instruction, as their experience or observation might suggest.

The Convention was held about the middle of May (after planting was over and before the hoeing season had commenced). The attendance was large of delegates from the towns in Windham and the adjoining counties. There were but few from a greater distance, but a number of interesting and valuable letters were received.

In order to unseal the lips of all present, and get from them all they knew about the condition of the schools in their several towns, I commenced the business of the meeting by a full, unsparing exposure of the low state of the schools in Brooklyn, which were reputed to be better than the schools generally in that part of Connecticut. The statements that I made were by no means so creditable as my fellow-townsmen expected. On the whole, the picture that I gave of our schools was quite a sorry one; and many looks of mortification, displeasure, and almost anger, were thrown at me from one and another of my neighbors, who were jealous for the reputation of our town. But their ill feelings were somewhat allayed by what they afterwards heard. My frank exposure of the poor condition of our schools brought out from most of the members of the Convention equally plain statements respecting the schools in their towns; so that, if I had shown our Brooklyn schools to be far inferior to what they ought to be, it was made to appear that the character and condition of the schools in most other towns were still worse.

The result of the Convention was an earnest address to our fellow-citizens of the State of Connecticut, imploring their prompt attention to our system of public instruction; and intimating that the institution of the large fund for the support of the Common Schools, one of the boasts of the State, had, in some respects, operated unfavorably to them. The income from it was so large as to induce the feeling among the people generally that no more need be, or ought to be, appropriated to the cause of popular education. It was indeed large enough to keep the schools going, such as they were, but by no means sufficient to make the improvements in them which were obviously needed, nor sufficient to offer to instructors such compensations as would induce or enable the best qualified persons to devote themselves to this most important service.

I am unable to say what effects were produced in other parts of the State by our appeal. But in Windham County, and throughout the eastern half of Connecticut, the public attention was certainly roused to the subject. We continued to hold, so long as I remained there, annual County School Conventions, which proposed and helped to introduce sundry important improvements. Similar meetings were held in other counties.

Hon. Henry Barnard, who has done so much and labored so many years in the cause of popular education, informed me, ten or twelve years ago, that his diligent researches into the history of our systems of popular education, had failed to discover any *convention of the people* on the subject, prior to the one of which I have above given some account.

Of all the letters received in answer to our circular, the most important was one from Dr. William A. Alcott, subsequently the author of "The House I live in," and other popular books on physical training and moral culture. He was then living in Wolcott, a small town in New Haven County. He was a philosopher and a philanthropist. He had seen so much quackery in his own (the medical) profession, and also in the ministerial, that he had become rather disgusted with both, and was zealous for radical reforms in education, religion, and social life. He wrote, not only to assure us of his lively interest in the object of our convention, and to inform us of the char-

6

acter of the schools generally in his neighborhood; but to give us some account of a remarkable school, kept on a very original plan, in the adjoining town of Cheshire, by his kinsman, Mr. Amos Bronson Alcott. His account excited so much my curiosity to know more of the American Pestalozzi, as he has since been called, that I wrote immediately to Mr. A. B. Alcott, begging him to send me a detailed statement of his principles and methods of teaching and of training children. In due time came to me a full account of the school of Cheshire, which revealed such a depth of insight into the nature of man, such a true sympathy with children, such profound appreciation of the work of education, and withal so philosophically arranged and exquisitely written, that I at once felt assured the man must be a genius, and that I must know him more intimately. So I wrote, inviting him urgently to visit me. I also sent the account of his school to Mr. William Russell, in Boston, then editing the first Journal of Education ever published in our country. Mr. Russell thought as highly of the article as I did, and gave it to the public in his next October number.

Mr. Alcott accepted my invitation. He came and passed a week with me before the close of the summer. I have never, but in one other instance, been so immediately taken possession of by any man I have ever met in life. He seemed to me like a born sage and saint. He was radical in all matters of reform; went to the root of all things, especially the subjects of education, mental and moral culture. If his biography shall ever be written by one who can appreciate him, and especially if his voluminous writings shall be properly published, it will be known how unique he was in wisdom and purity.

My sister Abigail was in my family at the time. I soon saw the indications of a mutual attraction, which afterwards became a strong attachment, that was cemented on the 23d of May, 1830, by their marriage. Louisa May Alcott, the author of "Little Women," is their daughter.

It was, I think, in 1828, that Mr. Josiah Holbrook commenced his enterprise, the institution of the "American Lyceum." The great design of it was to popularize the knowledge of natural history, and of the physical sciences. He came and spent some time with me. He lectured in Brooklyn and in the neighboring towns. We formed a lyceum, and several others were formed in the county. I entered into the work heartily, and delivered quite a number of lectures during several successive winters, in Brooklyn and in other towns. My first lecture was upon the Common Errors in Education, delivered on the 22d of October, 1828. It was published in the "Brooklyn Advertiser;" republished by Mr. Russell in his "Journal of Education;" and, from his types, an edition was printed in pamphlet form, which was, I believe, the second of my book publications.

Here, I may as well record an account of one of my naughty deeds, of which I do not, even now, feel so much ashamed as perhaps I ought to. In the spring of 1830, my wife not being in good health, and having, withal, a young child, I sold an ugly horse that I had owned a few months, and made diligent inquiry for a sound, well-trained, perfectly safe horse, that my timid wife would not be afraid to ride about with, driven by her sister or our hired girl. At length a man, one of my Society, came and offered me his horse. He was not by any means a good-looking animal; but the owner assured me that he had been worn down by hard work, that all his moral qualities were just what I wanted them to be, and that his physical qualities and his appearance would certainly improve under my keeping and with my usage. Said I to him, "I know nothing about a horse. I must rely wholly upon your statements. If I buy him, it will be on your assurance that he is an animal such as I have advertised for." "You may do so," he replied, "and I know that in a few weeks you will be entirely satisfied." So I bought the horse. But, alas! he proved to be a miserable creature, — so weak that he could scarcely drag my chaise up a decent hill; afraid of every thing, and obstinate withal. I was provoked. I had been egregiously cheated, and all my neighbors knew it. So I watched my opportunity to make the man ashamed of himself. It came before long.

Early the ensuing winter, I commenced our lyceum lectures by a course of twelve on natural philosophy. I often had occasion to speak of so much "horse-power." Whenever or several times when the horse-jockey was present, I remarked parenthetically, on using the term "horse-power," "I do not mean my horse, for you all know he has no power." This, of course, always "brought down" the house in expressions that were not complimentary to the man who had cheated me.

In January or February of 1828, I received an invitation from a number of gentlemen in Providence, R.I., inviting me to come to that city and attempt the gathering and institution of a second Unitarian Church, assuring me that another was greatly needed. I accepted the invitation. Accordingly they hired the old Richmond Street meeting-house, which had been recently vacated, the Orthodox Church having taken possession of their new house. I went, and preached four or five Sundays. I then received an urgent "call" to settle as their pastor, with the promise that they would immediately build a new and commodious house. The call was signed by more than eighty gentlemen, many of whom I knew to be men of excellent character, of great earnestness of purpose, and of property enough to support me handsomely without burdening themselves.

The offer was a very tempting one. I had, from the first, found it difficult to live on the small salary paid me by the Church of Brooklyn; and the tardiness with which that had been paid during the past two years had subjected me frequently to great inconvenience. Indeed, I had been obliged to give the committee notice that, unless my salary could be paid more punctually every quarter, I should be obliged to resign my place as their minister, and seek a home elsewhere. My father and family had repeatedly urged me to relinquish my attempt to build up a Unitarian Church in Brooklyn, and expend myself in some wider and more promising field. But my feelings respecting the duty of a minister of the gospel revolted at the thought of withdrawing my plough from a spot that needed to be cultivated, because it was difficult and the remuneration small. Now, however, that a call had come to me so unexpectedly from a place where so much needed to be done, and obviously could be done, in the cause of true Christianity, I was shaken in my determination. I would not consult my father and friends in Boston, because I knew what their decision would be. My wife would not influence me one way or the other; because, she said, it was a question which a minister ought to settle for himself. I could not find to which place she inclined for her own and the children's sake. Repeatedly, in her most unguarded moments, I put questions to her which had only a remote connection with the prominent one in my mind; but she was quick to discern their bearing, and was so adroit in her replies that I could not perceive to which side she really inclined.

But it was known throughout the Society that I had received a call to the new church in Providence, and the members roused themselves with one accord to dissuade me from accepting it. They gave me the strongest assurance that my salary should be promptly paid. They moreover offered to assist me to build a house, in materials, labor, and money to the amount of eight hundred or one thousand dollars. And good Mr. Benson proposed to give me a very desirable building lot, an acre or more, near his house. The anxiety of the people, so emphatically expressed, and their apprehension that the Church would go down if I left them, induced me to decide to remain in Brooklyn.

So in the month of April I went to Providence, and communicated to the new Church there my determination to decline their flattering invitation, and the reasons why I had so decided. Their manifestations of regret were grateful to me, but did not shake the conclusion to which I had come. They then requested me to find the best young man that was to be obtained, for their minister. Thus commissioned, I proceeded immediately to Cambridge; and, after consultation with the professors, I concluded to invite Mr. F. A. Farley (now the Rev. Dr. Farley, of Brooklyn, New York). He went to Providence, and preached several Sundays to the new Church. They were pleased with him, gave him a unanimous call, and he was ordained on the tenth day of the following September. Dr. Channing preached one of his admirable sermons. I delivered the address to the people, which was published in the next January number of the "Unitarian Advocate."

I returned to Brooklyn somewhat sad, not being sure that I had not lost the golden opportunity to improve greatly my own and the condition of my family, and at the same time do even more in the cause of true

Christianity. Nevertheless, I had made my choice, and I resolved to see what would come of it in the good providence of God. I felt that I had now planted myself for life in Connecticut. I set about driving deeper my stakes, and making surer my foundation; and even selected a spot in the burial-ground, where I would have my body deposited when life's labor should be done.

In order to insure the payment of my salary, it was proposed that a fund should be created, the interest of which should partly defray the annual expenses of the Church. This was done. Our friends in Massachusetts contributed something. We funded, in all, enough to yield us about two hundred dollars a year. With this aid it was thought we should get on without much further difficulty. Soon after, the members of the Society began to take measures to help me build my house. This was accomplished honorably on their part, and with the assistance of six hundred dollars loaned me by my father. I have already, in another place, stated that it was done in the course of the year 1829. We took possession of our new home late in the month of November.

CHAPTER X.

FROM THE DIARY.

A Disappointment well borne. — New Year's Meditations. — Fitness for the Ministry. — Sectarianism. — Twenty-five Years Old. — Ordination of a Trinitarian Minister. — Death of his Mother, Sister, and Child. — Anniversary of Marriage. — The Life of Howard. — A Prayer. — Editorial Work. — A Revival. "Coming to Christ."

BESIDES the autobiographical fragment which ended with the last chapter, Mr. May left a diary which was begun in November, 1821, and continued, with varying fulness, through the next twenty years. It was evidently intended to be read by no eyes except his own. The autobiography gives so few dates, that it has been found impracticable to insert passages from the diary at appropriate places, and therefore we must give our extracts from it by themselves. One of the earliest entries relates to his feelings upon learning that he would not receive a call to New York city where he had preached as a "candidate."

November 18, 1821. — Two days since news arrived in town that the parish in New York have given William Ware a call. Many circumstances have made it probable that the choice would fall upon Ware or myself. The reception I met with when there led me to think the probabilities rather in my favor. It is natural that I should have a feeling something like disappointment, and a wish involuntarily arises to know the grounds of the preference which has thus been expressed. Not that I feel at all underrated to be considered second to Ware. I have known him well several years. In the circle of my acquaintances I know but two or three, if any, so free from defects. In such a city as New York there is little doubt of his rapid improvement. There will be a constant demand for his utmost exertion, and like pure metal he will grow brighter with use. I love Ware; and, although it is at the expense of my own disappointment, I do rejoice in his success.

January 1, 1822. — Another year has passed more rapidly and eventfully than any previous one of my life. The great inquiry arises, Has any advancement been made in the high purpose of my being? Am I a better Christian? Am I better qualified to teach by my example and instructions the religion of which I am a minister? Do I understand any better the character and gospel of Christ, and do I possess any more of its spirit? These inquiries lead me to review my studies and the effect of events upon my mind and heart.

. . . .

The circumstances of several parishes to which I have preached rendered it expedient to turn my attention to controverted subjects. It has been my aim to avoid every thing harsh when speaking of the opinions of other sects, and to illustrate my own views as plainly and forcibly as possible. I trust I have not often, if ever, discovered an uncharitable temper. The real feeling of my heart is not so much zeal for the spread of the Unitarian doctrines, as an earnest desire to diffuse throughout the Christian community the idea that religion is something practical, and that, as to the sentiments we may adopt, we have all a right to judge for ourselves.

Brooklyn, Conn., March 18, 1822. — On the 5th inst. my sister Eliza (Mrs. Willis, of Portland) died. She was generous and affectionate, rigidly faithful in the discharge of her duty, and was supported and cheered by a fervent and rational piety. Our whole family are much depressed. My parents have now buried their eighth child. Four only are left. It would have been a comfort to them and delightful to me could I have been established near them; but Providence has ordered otherwise, at least for the present. I pray that I may labor with my might and with good success in this place. But the duty is mine, the event is with God.

Yesterday afternoon I preached from the fourteenth chapter of Romans. I took occasion in this discourse, and not without a very visible effect, to speak to them respecting the unhappy divisions in the town. I asked if they had not been in fault; exhorted them to examine their own conduct, and see if they had not offended against Christian charity; not to seek for palliations for their actions, but to be willing to discover their own errors, and reasons to think and feel more favorably towards their fellow Christians.

September 12, 1822. — To-day completes my twenty-fifth year. I seem now to have entered in good earnest upon the duties of life, and at times I really feel oppressed with care and responsibility. It is six months since I undertook the care of the parish in Brooklyn. Providence has placed me among this people, and I do not see how I can leave them without deserting the post of duty.

April 14, 1824. — This day has witnessed the ordination of Rev. Ambrose Edson as pastor of the First Trinitarian Church and Society in this town. This name denominates those who, several years ago, seceded from the society of which I am now pastor. They are, of course, opposed to us, and it is too true the opposition is bitter. But I cannot bear the thought of considering this man my enemy. It is my wish to make him my friend, and to be a fellow-laborer. What course he means to pursue I know not. I mean to treat him, if possible, with affectionate kindness. If he is an instrument for the promotion of religion in this place, I ought to rejoice; yes, if while he increases I must decrease.

November 5. — This day received the painful tidings of my mother's death. She died October 31. Her children, the sick, and the unfortunate knew her worth in this world, and in the world whither she has gone we shall rise and call her blessed.

November 14, 1828. — This day my sister, Mrs. Louisa Greele, finished her mortal life. She had been sick only about a week.

December 9. — I went to Boston to see and condole with my father and Abby.

December 14. — While sitting in my chamber between the hours of public worship, and preparing myself to preach at the Chapel in the afternoon, my father came into the room and announced to me the heart-rending intelligence that my own little Joseph, my first-born, my only son, was no more. He died on the twelfth, of croup. When I left him he was apparently as well as usual. I hurried home with a brain almost bewildered; reached Brooklyn on Monday at eleven, and found it too true.

December 31, 1828. — This night closes the present year, a most eventful year it has been to me. I wish to review it calmly.

The most prominent event in the past year is the death of my child. The birth of this little being awakened in my bosom a set of affections wholly new. All our recollections of him are delightful. There can be no doubt that infant children are removed to a state of higher felicity. But after all the considerations that may be urged, there are some things inexplicable in the physical sufferings and death of a young child. I do not entertain a doubt that they are all directed by Infinite Wisdom and Love, but the reasonableness of such dispensations is beyond our ken.

The death of my sister Louisa is another event which has thrown its shade over the past year. Her peculiar characteristics had made her a prominent one among us. She was generous, energetic, and affectionate. She was upright, judicious, and engaging. We all loved her, and we were not a little proud of her.

I pray God that these impressive lessons may sink deeply into my heart, and induce me from this time forth to lead a life of greater holiness and devotion to his will and the happiness of my fellow-men.

June 1, 1829. — This day is the anniversary of my marriage. Four years ago I was united in this holy relation, and I can bear a grateful testimony to its influence upon my happiness. My wife's is a mind of singular purity, the utmost tenderness of conscience, and disinterestedness of purpose.

June 16, 1831. — I have just finished reading the "Life of Howard," by James B. Brown. Of no man who has lived since the days of Christ can it be more truly said, "He went about doing good. It was his meat and drink to do his Father's will." God grant that the perusal of this volume may inspire me with greater ardor in the cause of suffering humanity. May

I never be disheartened from attempting a project of benevolence, however many or great may be the discouragements and dangers.

June, 1832.—O God, the Father of my spirit, thou knowest how much I desire to be a follower of thee, as a dear child. Thou knowest how wretchedly I feel, I am, when I have sinned against thee. Thou knowest how heartfelt is my delight when I have obeyed thy will, especially when I have made a successful struggle against the enemies of my virtue. And O Thou from whom my help cometh, to thee is known how strong my temptations often are. To thee I look up in fervent prayer. Assist me to keep a more vigilant watch against the first approach of sin. May I be more continually on my guard, watching unto prayer. Let no sin have dominion over me. Give me wisdom to discern clearly the heinousness of the offences I am sometimes tempted to commit, and aid me to flee from the first approach of evil.

December 31, 1832.—Since last April I have been the editor of a paper, "The Christian Monitor and Common People's Adviser." Its object is to promote the free discussion of all subjects connected with happiness and holiness. The success of it has been as great as I could expect.

January 4, 1833.—Since the first of the month there has been in this village a protracted meeting held by the Orthodox Society. I have attended four times. I have not discouraged my people from going, but quite otherwise. I have rather wished them to go. Surely, if there is any good to be obtained, I fervently pray that my people may share in it. I feel too deeply the momentous interests they have in eternity, to assume to myself all the responsibility of instructing them. I dare not say to them, "I am the only safe guide. I alone am a teacher of the truth." My wish is that they should hear what other ministers of the Gospel may think, and carefully compare all they hear from others or from myself with the declarations of Scripture.

None of the gentlemen that I heard gave any explanation of their meaning when they exhorted their hearers to "come to Christ." When I exhort my people to come to Christ, I mean by it that they should take him for their instructor, guide, example. I assure them that, if they will obey the precepts and copy the example of our Lord, they will be saved, and not otherwise. On this point I mean to question some of them before the public.

Such is the management at these meetings that a person must have great strength of nerve, or a most phlegmatic temperament, to retain his self-command if he submits himself to the whole series of operations. There is something like manœuvre in this, which I cannot approve.

God knows my heart, that I fervently, unfeignedly desire the good of this whole people. I am not so anxious to have my Society increased as I am to have true religion increase among us. If I am wrong, I pray that none may be misled by me. Sometimes the sense of responsibility weighs so heavily upon me that I long to be released. But imperative duty seems to demand of me to persevere. I pray God to direct me, to guide me, to support me. Make me useful to him in the cause of truth and righteousness, and not suffer me to live a moment to do harm.

CHAPTER XI.

ANTISLAVERY.

Impression received from Daniel Webster's Oration at Plymouth in 1820. — Rev. John Rankin, of Kentucky. — Benjamin Lundy. — Hears William Lloyd Garrison. — Becomes one of his Disciples. — Sermon in Rev. Dr. Young's Pulpit. — Great Sensation. — Entreats Mr. Garrison to be less severe. — Mr. Garrison's Noble Reply. — Prudence Crandall's School. — Her Persecutions. — Mr. May becomes her Champion. — Publishes "The Unionist." — Miss Crandall's School abandoned. — Mrs. L. M. Child's Dedication. — Attends Convention called to form a National Antislavery Society. — Letter from John G. Whittier concerning the Convention and Mr. May. — Mr. May reproves Rev. Dr. Channing. — Pro-slavery Feeling in Boston. — Mr. May General Agent and Corresponding Secretary of the Massachusetts Antislavery Society. — His Manner as an Antislavery Lecturer. — Letter from Rev. J. H. Heywood. — Mr. May is mobbed. — Defends the Abolitionists before a Joint Committee of the Massachusetts Legislature. — Harriet Martineau's Tribute.

IT was at the very height of the Missouri Controversy and of the interest it had awakened in the question whether slavery was to become permanent in the United States, that Mr. May entered upon the labors of his profession.

Just at the close of 1820, very soon after he had received the approbation of the Boston Association of

Ministers as a candidate for the Christian ministry, he preached at Springfield, Mass., for his particular friend, Rev. W. B. O. Peabody. In his "brief account of his ministry," which he gave in a discourse at Syracuse, when seventy years of age, he said:—

"It is not an insignificant fact in my history, that, though in the trepidation of the moment, my voice must have been very little 'like a trumpet,' I read in the morning service the fifty-eighth chapter of Isaiah. I know not what prompted me to do so, unless it may have been the impressive words on slavery uttered a few days before at Plymouth by Daniel Webster, whom I then revered more than any of our statesmen."

In that oration Mr. Webster said of the slave trade: "I invoke the ministers of our religion, that they proclaim its denunciation of these crimes, and add its solemn sanctions to the authority of human laws. If the pulpit be silent whenever or wherever there may be a sinner bloody with this guilt within the hearing of its voice, the pulpit is false to its trust."

A few years later, about 1825, Mr. May became deeply interested in a book on Slavery by the Rev. John Rankin, of the Presbyterian Church in Kentucky, addressed to a brother in Virginia who had then recently become a slave-holder. It denounced slavery as "a never-failing fountain of the grossest immoralities, and one of the deepest sources of human misery;" insisting that "the safety of our government and the happiness of its subjects depended upon the extermination of this evil."

In the month of June, 1828, Benjamin Lundy, whose paper, "The Genius of Universal Emancipation," was for a long time nearly the only voice that warned the people of the United States of their guilt and peril, visited Brooklyn, Conn. Mr. May was deeply impressed by Mr. Lundy's exhibition of the wrongs of slavery and the suffering of its victims, although he had serious doubts of the wisdom and justice of the proposed plan of removing the blacks to some of the unoccupied territory of Texas or Mexico. It was not until two years later, however, that Mr. May listened to one whose words on this subject satisfied both his mind and heart, and led him to enlist "for the war" in the army of freedom.

"It so happened, in the good Providence 'which shapes our ends,' that I was on a visit in Boston in October, 1830. An advertisement appeared in the newspapers, that during the following week W. Lloyd Garrison would deliver to the public three lectures, in which he would exhibit the sinfulness of slave-holding; expose the duplicity of the Colonization Society, revealing its true character; and, in opposition to it, would announce and maintain the doctrine, that immediate, nnconditional emancipation is the right of every slave and the duty of every master. The advertisement announced that his lectures would be delivered on the Common, unless some church or commodious hall should be proffered to him gratuitously. If I remember correctly, it was said that Mr. Garrison had applied for several of the Boston churches, and been refused, because it was known that he had become an opponent of the Colonization Society. A day or two after the first, I saw a second advertisement, informing the public that the free use of Julien Hall, occupied by Rev. Abner Kneeland's church, having been generously tendered to Mr.

Garrison, he would deliver his lectures there instead of on the Common. I had not then seen this resolute young man. I had been much impressed by some of his writings, knew of his connection with Mr. Lundy, and had heard of his imprisonment [in Baltimore, at the suit of a slave-trader from Massachusetts, whom he had exposed]. Of course I was eager to see and hear him, and went to Julien Hall in due season on the appointed evening. My brother-in-law, A. Bronson Alcott, and my cousin, Samuel E. Sewall, accompanied me. Truer men could not easily have been found.

"The hall was pretty well filled. Among some persons whom I did, and many whom I did not, know, I saw there Rev. Dr. Beecher, Rev. Mr. (now Dr.) Gannett, Deacon Moses Grant, and John Tappan, Esq.

"Presently the young man arose, modestly, but with an air of calm determination, and delivered such a lecture as he only, I believe, at that time, could have written; for he only had had his eyes so anointed that he could see that outrages perpetrated upon Africans were wrongs done to our common humanity; he only, I believe, had had his ears so completely unstopped of 'prejudice against color' that the cries of enslaved black men and black women sounded to him as if they came from brothers and sisters.

"He began with expressing deep regret and shame for the zeal he had lately manifested in the Colonization cause. It was, he confessed, a zeal without knowledge. He had been deceived by the misrepresentations so diligently given throughout the free States by Southern agents, of the design and tendency of the Colonization scheme. During his few months' residence in Maryland he had been completely undeceived. He had there found out that the design of those who originated, and the especial intentions of those in the Southern States who engaged in the plan, were to remove from the country, as a disturbing element in slave-holding communities, all the free colored people, so that the bondmen might the more easily be held in subjection. He exhibited, in graphic sketches and glowing colors, the suffering of the enslaved, and denounced the plan of Colonization as devised and adapted to perpetuate the system and intensify the wrongs of American slavery, and therefore utterly undeserving of the patronage of lovers of liberty and friends of humanity.

"Never before was I so affected by the speech of man. When he had ceased speaking I said to those around me: 'That is a providential man; he is a prophet; he will shake our nation to its centre, but he will shake slavery out of it. We ought to know him, we ought to help him. Come, let us go and give him our hands.' Mr. Sewall and Mr. Alcott went up with me, and we introduced each other. I said to him, 'Mr. Garrison, I am not sure that I can indorse all you have said this evening. Much of it requires careful consideration. But I am prepared to embrace *you*. I am sure you are called to a great work, and I mean to help you.' Mr. Sewall cordially assured him of his readiness also to co-operate with him. Mr. Alcott invited him to his home. He went, and we sat with him until twelve that night, listening to his discourse, in which he showed plainly that *immediate, unconditional emancipation, without expatriation, was the right of every slave, and could not be withheld by his master an hour without sin.* That night my soul was baptized in his spirit, and ever since I have been a disciple and fellow-laborer of William Lloyd Garrison.

"The next morning, immediately after breakfast, I went to his boarding-house and stayed until two P.M. I learned that he was poor, dependent upon his daily labor for his daily bread, and intending to return to the printing business. But, before he could devote himself to his own support, he felt that he must deliver his message, must communicate to persons of prominent influence what he had learned of the sad condition of the enslaved, and of the institutions and spirit of the slave-holders; trusting that all true and good men would discharge the obligation pressing upon them to espouse the cause of the poor, the oppressed, the downtrodden. He read to me letters he had addressed to Dr. Channing, Dr. Beecher, Dr. Edwards, the Hon. Jeremiah Mason, and Hon. Daniel Webster, holding up to their view the tremendous iniquity of the land, and begging them, ere it should be too late, to interpose their great power in the Church and State to save our country from the terrible calamities which the sin of slavery was bringing upon us. Those letters were eloquent, solemn, impressive. I wonder they did not produce a greater effect. It was because none to whom he appealed, in public or private, would espouse the cause, that Mr. Garrison found himself left and impelled to become the leader of the great antislavery reform.

"The hearing of Mr. Garrison's lectures was a great epoch in my own life. The impression which they made upon my soul has never been effaced; indeed, they moulded it anew. They gave a new direction to my thoughts, a new purpose to my ministry.

"I was engaged to preach on the following Sunday for Brother Young, in Summer Street Church. Of course I could not again speak to a congregation as a Christian minister, and be silent respecting the *great iniquity* of our nation. The only sermon I had brought from my home in Connecticut that could be made to bear on the subject was one on Prejudice, a sermon about to be published as one of the Tracts of the American Unitarian Association. So I touched it up as well as I could, interlining here and there words and sentences which pointed in the new direction to which my thoughts and feelings so strongly tended, and writing at its close what used to be called an *improvement*. Thus: 'The subject of my discourse bears most pertinently upon a matter of the greatest national as well as personal importance. There are more than two millions of our fellow-beings, children of the Heavenly Father, who are held in our country in the most abject slavery, regarded and treated like domesticated animals, their rights as men trampled under foot, their conjugal, parental, fraternal relations and affections utterly set at naught. It is our *prejudice* against the color of these poor people that makes us consent to the tremendous wrongs they are suffering. If they were white, ay, if only two thousand or two hundred *white* men, women, and children in the Southern States were treated as these millions of colored ones are, we of the North should make such a stir of indignation, we should so agitate the country with our appeals and remonstrances, that the oppressors would be compelled to set their bondmen free. But will our *prejudice* be accepted by the Almighty, the impartial Judge of all, as a valid excuse for our indifference to the wrongs and outrages inflicted upon these millions of our countrymen? Oh, no! oh, no! He will say, "Inasmuch as ye did not what ye could for the relief of these, the least of the brethren, ye did it not to me." Tell me not that we are forbidden by the Constitution of our country to interfere in behalf of the enslaved. No compact our fathers may have made for us, no agreement we could ourselves make, would annul our obligations to suffering fellow-men. Yes, yes,' I said, with an emphasis that seemed to startle everybody in the house, 'if need be, the very foundations of our Republic must be broken up; and if this stone of stumbling, this rock of offence, cannot be removed from under it, the proud superstructure must fall. It cannot stand, it ought not to stand, it will not stand, on the necks of millions of men. For God is just, and his justice will not sleep for ever.' I then offered such a prayer as my kindled spirit moved me to, and gave out the hymn commencing,

'Awake, my soul, stretch every nerve,
And press with vigor on.'

"When I rose to pronounce the benediction, I said: 'Every one present must be conscious that the closing remarks of my sermon have caused an unusual emotion throughout the church. I am glad. Would to God that a deeper emotion could be sent throughout our land, until all the people thereof shall be roused from their wicked insensibility to the most tremendous sin of which any nation was ever guilty, and be impelled to do that righteousness which alone can avert the just displeasure of God. I have been prompted to speak thus by the words I have heard during the past week from a young man hitherto unknown, but who is, I believe, called of God to do a greater work for the good of our country than has been done by any one since the Revolution. I mean William Lloyd Garrison. He is going to repeat his lectures the coming week. I advise, I exhort, I entreat—would that I could compel!—you to go and hear him.'

"The excited audience gathered in clusters, evidently talking about what had happened. I found the porch full of persons conversing in very earnest tones. Presently a lady of fine person, her countenance suffused with emotion, tears coursing down her cheeks, pressed through the crowd, seized my hand, and said audibly, with deep feeling: 'Mr. May, I thank you. What a shame it is that I, who have been a constant attendant from my childhood in this or some other Christian church, am obliged to confess that to-day, for the first time, I have heard from the pulpit a plea for the oppressed, the enslaved millions in our land!' All within hearing of her voice were evidently moved in sympathy with her, or were awed by her emotion. For myself I could only acknowledge in a word my gratitude for her generous testimony.

"The next day I perceived, on his return from his place of business in State Street, that my revered father was much disturbed by the reports he had heard of my preaching. Some of the 'gentlemen of property and standing' who had been my auditors said it was fanatical, others that it was incendiary, others that it was treasonable; and begged him to 'arrest me in my mad career.' The only one, as he soon afterwards informed me, who had spoken in any other than terms of censure, was the great and good Dr. Bowditch, who said, 'Depend upon it, the young man is more than half right.' My father tried to dissuade me from engaging in the attempt to overthrow the system of slavery which Mr. Garrison proposed. He had come, with most others, to regard it as an unavoidable evil, one that the fathers of our Republic had not ventured to suppress, but had rather given to its protection something like a guaranty. He thought, with most others at that day, that slavery must be left to be gradually removed by the progress of civilization, the growth of higher ideas of human nature, and the manifest superiority and better economy of free labor. He admonished me that, in assailing the institution of American slavery, I should only be 'kicking against the pricks,' that I should lose my standing in the ministry and my usefulness in the church. I need not add that he failed to convince me that 'the foolishness of preaching' would not yet be 'mighty to the pulling down of the stronghold of Satan.' In less than ten years he was reconciled to my course.

"A few days afterwards I gave my sermon on Prejudice to my most excellent friend, Rev. Henry Ware, Jr., for the American Unitarian Association. He accepted the discourse as originally written, but insisted that the interlineations and the additions respecting slavery should be omitted. He would not have done this, nor should I have consented to it, a few years later. But we were all in bondage then. Unconsciously to ourselves, the hand of the slave-holding power lay *heavily* upon the mind and heart of the people in our Northern as well as Southern States.

"What a pity that my words in that sermon respecting slavery were not published in the tract! They might have helped a little to commit our Unitarian denomination much earlier to the cause of impartial liberty in earnest protest against the great oppression, the unparalleled iniquity of our land. Of whom should opposition to slavery of every kind have been expected so soon as from Unitarian Christians?"
—*Recollections*, pp. 17–24.

Though he was now fully committed to all the principles of the movement against slavery, and fully in sympathy with Mr. Garrison, he still questioned with himself whether the latter would not better help his cause by a more restrained and moderate advocacy of it. And he frankly told him his doubts.

"Mr. Garrison will perhaps remember that, a few months after he commenced the 'Liberator,' when almost everybody was finding fault with him or wishing that he would be more temperate, I was one of the friends that came to remonstrate and entreat. He and his faithful partner, Isaac Knapp, were at work in the little upper chamber, No. 6 Merchants' Hall, where they lived, as well as they could, with their printing-press and types, all within an enclosure sixteen or eighteen feet square. I requested him to walk out with me that we might confer on an important matter. He at once laid aside his pen, and we descended to the street. I informed him how much troubled I had become for fear he was damaging the cause he had so much at heart by the undue severity of his style. He listened to me patiently. I told him what many of the wise and prudent, who professed an interest in his object, said about his manner of pursuing it. He replied somewhat in the way he has so often done since: 'Do *the slaves* think my language too severe or misapplied? Do that husband and wife, that mother and daughter, who have just been separated for life, by sale on the auction-block, think my denunciation of the man who inflicts that wrong too severe?' 'But,' said I, 'some of the epithets you use, though not perhaps too severe, are not precisely applicable to the sin you denounce, and so may seem abusive.' 'Ah!' he rejoined, 'until the term "slave-holder" sends as deep a feeling of horror to the hearts of those who hear it applied to any one as the terms "robber," "pirate," "murderer" do, we must use and multiply epithets when condemning the sin of him who is guilty of the "*sum of all villanies.*"' 'Oh,' cried I, 'my friend, do try to moderate your indignation, and keep more cool! why, you are all on fire!' He stopped, laid his hand upon my shoulder with a kind but emphatic pressure that I have felt ever since, and said slowly, with deep emotion, 'Brother May, I have need to be all on fire, for I have mountains of ice about me to melt.' From that hour to this I have never said a word to Mr. Garrison in complaint of his style. I am more than half satisfied now that he was right then, and we who objected were mistaken." — *Recollections*, p. 36.

In Windham County, Conn., Mr. May stood quite alone, being the only minister of his denomination in the whole State, and finding little sympathy with his antislavery convictions beyond his own parish, where the people welcomed Mr. Garrison to their pulpit, and, with a few exceptions, heartily co-operated with their pastor. He suddenly found himself called to confront the entire political, social, and religious sentiment of his county, besides entering upon a contest with the officers of the law.

In 1833, Miss Prudence Crandall, a well-educated lady, who had an excellent boarding and day school for girls in Canterbury, in a house which she owned, after some hesitation received a bright young colored woman of fine character as a pupil. When the parents of some of the white scholars threatened to remove their children if the "nigger girl" was permitted to remain, and Miss Crandall saw that, without doing what she believed to be mean and wrong, she could no longer expect to have a full school from that neighborhood, she gave notice in Canterbury, and advertised in the "Liberator," that her school would be opened "for young ladies and little misses of color." This excited the fiercest wrath of the community.

Hearing of her noble stand, Mr. May wrote Miss Crandall a letter of encouragement; and, although warned that he should be in personal danger if he appeared in Canterbury as her friend, he soon went there at her request. He found that she had been grossly insulted, and threatened, and that a town-meeting was to be held to adopt such measures as "would effectually avert the nuisance, or speedily abate it."

To this meeting a multitude came, many from the neighboring towns. Strong resolutions were offered and abusive speeches were made by men of prominence; and when Miss Crandall, by a note to the chairman, asked that Messrs. May and Arnold Buffum might be heard in her defence, fists were doubled in their faces, and they were not permitted to speak.

The school opened with fifteen or twenty colored girls from different parts of the country. But no storekeeper or dealer in provisions in the town would furnish needful supplies. Miss Crandall and her pupils were insulted in the street, "the doors and door-steps of her house were besmeared, and her well was filled with filth." The old vagrant law was revived, and its enforcement attempted "upon Eliza Ann Hammond, of Providence, a fine girl of seventeen years," notwithstanding a bond in the sum of $10,000 had been given to the town treasurer of Canterbury by several gentlemen of

Brooklyn, to save the town from all charges on account of any of Miss Crandall's pupils. This law required that *whipping on the naked body, not exceeding ten stripes*, should be inflicted on any person refusing to leave the town after ten days' warning. Miss Hammond dared to stay, but her persecutors did not venture to proceed to the extremity of the whipping.

But on the 24th of May, 1833, the legislature of Connecticut enacted a law known as "The Black Law." It provided, under heavy penalties, that no school should be established in any town of the State, for the education of colored persons of other towns, "without the consent in writing, first obtained, of a majority of the civil authority, and the selectmen of the town." Miss Crandall was arrested and lodged in the county jail at Brooklyn. Messrs. May and George W. Benson gave the required bonds the next day, and she returned to her school.

Reports of a calumnious character against Miss Crandall, her pupils, and her friends, were circulated and printed; and all corrections, with all defences of the school, were refused insertion in the county papers. To Mr. May's surprise and delight, he received a letter from Arthur Tappan, of New York, pledging money to secure the best legal counsel for Miss Crandall. Mr. Tappan soon visited Mr. May, and suggested the starting of a newspaper as a needed auxiliary. In "The Unionist," which was continued about two years, Mr. May was assisted by the since distinguished brothers, Charles C. and William H. Burleigh.

At Miss Crandall's first trial the jury did not agree. A new indictment was hastily drawn, and a verdict was given against her. The case was then carried up to the highest tribunal of the State; but upon the vital question the Court gave no decision at all, merely quashing the indictment on account of its defects!

Miss Crandall's house was set on fire, but by timely exertion saved from destruction. At about midnight of the 9th of September, the house was assaulted by a band of persons with heavy clubs and iron bars, who broke in and destroyed windows, rendering a portion of the house quite untenantable, and alarming the pupils exceedingly. They now became afraid to remain another night. In his "Recollections of the Antislavery Conflict," Mr. May says: —

"After due consideration, therefore, it was determined that the school should be abandoned. The pupils were called together, and I was requested to announce to them our decision. Never before had I felt so deeply sensible of the cruelty of the persecution which had been carried on for eighteen months, in that New England village, against a family of defenceless females. Twenty harmless, well-behaved girls, whose only offence against the peace of the community was that they had come together there to obtain useful knowledge and moral culture, were to be told that they must go away, because the house in which they dwelt would not be protected by the guardians of the town." "The words almost blistered my lips. My bosom glowed with indignation. I felt ashamed of Canterbury, ashamed of Connecticut, ashamed of my country, ashamed of my color. Thus ended the generous, disinterested, philanthropic, Christian enterprise of Prudence Crandall."

While Mr. May had so much local odium and persecution to bear, there were true-hearted ones, both near at hand and far away, who gave him cordial assurance of their admiring sympathy in his noble course. In July, 1833, Mrs. L. Maria Child published "An Appeal in favor of that Class of Americans called Africans," a work never superseded, and which may yet be consulted with profit. She dedicated it in these terms: "To the Rev. S. J. May, of Brooklyn, Conn., this volume is most respectfully inscribed as a mark of gratitude for his earnest and disinterested efforts in an unpopular but most righteous cause." When he received his copy of this work and read the dedication, which was a complete surprise to him, Mr. May was deeply moved, and said to his cousin Samuel, "Now, indeed, I *must* go forward. I can never draw back."

In December, 1833, Mr. May attended the convention in Philadelphia which had been called to form a National Antislavery Society. A letter from John G. Whittier gives an interesting account of the important part which was assigned to them at that memorable gathering, as well as other illustrations of Mr. May's fidelity in those days that tried men's souls.

"Amesbury, 3d, 11th mo., 1871.

"I am very glad to know that the biography of my old and dear friend, Samuel J. May, is in such good hands. I have known him well for nearly forty years. I first met him at the convention in Philadelphia which formed the American Antislavery Society in 1833; and, like everybody else, loved him at first sight. I remember he was on the sub-committee with Garrison and myself, to whom was assigned the task of drawing up the Declaration of Sentiments, a draft of which Garrison read to us by candle-light in the early December morning. I was with him in the season of the Boston mobs, and went with him to visit Garrison in the Leverett Street jail. I was associated with him and Dr. Follen and Professor Ware in preparing the Address of the New England Antislavery Convention. His labors in the cause were abundant, and prosecuted under circumstances which would have appalled a less brave and hopeful spirit. In my native town, Haverhill, he was assailed by a ferocious mob; and narrowly escaped personal indignity and injury by his cool firmness and self-possession, passing through the enraged crowd after the lecture, with no other escort than my sister and her friend, daughter of the late Judge Minot, of Haverhill, now Mrs. Pitman, of Somerville. Through all the trials and vicissitudes of the antislavery struggle he bore himself with a serene and cheerful courage, and a hope which never failed in the darkest hours.

"He was a favorite with all classes and parties in the antislavery reform. Orthodoxy forgot his liberalism, New Organization forgave his adherence to the Old. Nobody doubted his sincerity. I had reason to know that his bitterest political enemies loved and honored him in their hearts, even while denouncing him with their lips. His last visit to me was but little more than a year before his death. We spent a happy day together, talking over the old times, and calling up the dear old friends who acted with us."

Prejudice against the Abolitionists at this time was exceedingly strong and bitter; and, to some extent, it was shared by the most intelligent and worthy men. The story of Mr. May's noble reproof of Dr. Channing, and the latter's equally noble confession that it was deserved, was first published in the "Memoir of Chan-

7*

ning;" but it cannot be spared from the Life of Mr. May.

"Late in the year 1834, being on a visit in Boston, I spent several hours with Dr. Channing in earnest conversation upon Abolitionism and the Abolitionists. My habitual reverence for him was such that I had always been apt to defer perhaps too readily to his opinions, or not to make a very stout defence of my own when they differed from his. But at the time to which I refer I had become so thoroughly convinced of the truth of the essential doctrines of the American Antislavery Society, and so earnestly engaged in the dissemination of them, that our conversation assumed, more than it had ever done, the character of a debate. He acknowledged the inestimable importance of the object we had in view. The evils of slavery, he assented, could not be overstated. He allowed that removal to Africa ought not to be made a condition of the liberation of the enslaved. But he hesitated still to accept the doctrine of immediate emancipation. His principal objections, however, were alleged against the severity of our denunciations, the harshness of our epithets, the vehemence, heat, and excitement caused by the harangues at our meetings, and still more by Mr. Garrison's 'Liberator.' The Doctor dwelt upon these objections, which, if they were as well founded as he assumed them to be, lay against what was only incidental, not an essential part of our movement. He dwelt upon them until I became impatient; and, forgetting for the moment my wonted deference, I broke out with not a little warmth of expression and manner.

"'Dr. Channing,' I said, 'I am tired of these complaints. The cause of suffering humanity, the cause of our oppressed, crushed, colored countrymen, has called as loudly upon others as upon us Abolitionists. It was just as incumbent upon others as upon us to espouse it. *We* are not to blame that wiser and better men did not espouse it long ago. The cry of millions, suffering the most cruel bondage in our land, had been heard for half a century, and disregarded. "The wise and prudent" saw the terrible wrong, but thought it not wise and prudent to lift a finger for its correction. The priests and Levites beheld their robbed and wounded countrymen, and passed by on the other side. The children of Abraham held their peace, and at last "the very stones have cried out" in abhorrence of this tremendous iniquity. You must not wonder if many of those who have been left to take up this great cause do not plead it in all that seemliness of phrase which the scholars and practised rhetoricians of our country might use. You must not expect them to speak and act with all the calmness and discretion that clergymen and statesmen might exhibit. But the scholars, the statesmen, the clergy did nothing, did not seem about to do any thing; and for my part I thank God that at last any persons, be they who they may, have earnestly engaged in this cause; for no *movement* can be in vain. We Abolitionists are what we are, babes, sucklings, obscure men, silly women, publicans, sinners; and we must manage this matter just as might be expected of such persons as we are. It is unbecoming in abler men who stand by and do nothing to complain of us because we do no better.

"'Dr. Channing,' I continued with increased earnestness, 'it is not *our fault* that those who might have conducted this great reform more prudently have left it to us to manage as we may. It is not *our fault* that those who might have pleaded for the enslaved so much more wisely and eloquently, both with the pen and the living voice, have been silent. We are not to blame, sir, that you, who, more perhaps than any other man, might have so raised the voice of remonstrance that it should have been heard throughout the length and breadth of the land, have not so spoken. And now that inferior men have been impelled to speak and act against what you acknowledge to be an awful system of iniquity, it is not becoming in you to complain of us because we do it in an inferior style. Why, sir, have you not taken this matter in hand yourself? Why have you not spoken to the nation long ago, as you, better than any other one, could have spoken?'

"At this point I bethought me to whom I was administering this rebuke, the man who stood among the highest of the great and good in our land, the man whose reputation for wisdom and sanctity had become world-wide, the man, too, who had ever treated me with the kindness of a father, and whom from my childhood I had been accustomed to revere more than any one living. I was almost overwhelmed with a sense of my temerity. His countenance showed that he was much moved. I could not suppose he would receive all I had said very graciously. I awaited his reply in painful expectation. The minutes seemed very long that elapsed before the silence was broken. Then, in a very subdued manner and in the kindliest tones of his voice, he said: 'Brother May, I acknowledge the justice of your reproof. I have been silent too long.' Never shall I forget his words, look, whole appearance. I then and there saw the beauty, the magnanimity, the humility, of a truly great Christian soul. He was exalted in my esteem more even than before.

"The next spring," Mr. May adds, "when I removed to Boston and became the General Agent of the Antislavery Society, Dr. Channing was the first of the ministers there to call upon me and express sympathy with me in the great work to which I had come to devote myself. And during the whole fourteen months that I continued in that office he treated me with uniform kindness, and often made anxious inquiries about the phases of our attempted reform of the nation." — *Recollections*, p. 172.

It will be very difficult for most readers at this day to comprehend the extent and force of the hostility to the Abolitionists in 1835. Something of it may be imagined from the fact that, in the city of Boston, deemed the home of liberal thought, the "cradle of liberty," and the seat of education and every benevolent object, not a single church could be obtained for a meeting or lecture on slavery; not a minister, excepting Dr. Channing and the pastor of Pine Street Church (Rev. A. A. Phelps?), would even read a notice of such a meeting; and no public hall of any size and commodiousness could be hired for such use. Faneuil Hall even, which surely should have re-echoed all appeals for liberty and justice, was refused, though asked for in a respectful petition signed by one hundred and twenty-five gentlemen of irreproachable character. But the same hall was readily granted for a meeting of citizens to denounce the Abolitionists, and assure the slaveholders that Boston would give them no trouble. As the combat thickened, Mr. May felt bound to devote more time and strength to the cause of the slave.

"The demand for antislavery lectures came from all parts of New England, and from many parts of the Middle and Western States. A great work was to be done. The fields were whitening to the harvest, but the laborers were few. I therefore accepted the renewed invitation of the Massachusetts Antislavery Society to become its General Agent and Corresponding Secretary, and removed to Boston early in the spring of 1835. Many of my nearest relatives and dearest friends received me kindly, indeed, but with sadness. They feared I should lose my standing in the ministry, and become an outcast from the churches. For a while it seemed as if their apprehensions were not groundless. None of the Boston ministers, excepting Dr. Channing, welcomed me. Dr.

Follen, Dr. Ware, Jr., and Dr. Palfrey were then resident in Cambridge; Mr. Pierpont was in Europe. James Freeman Clarke had not left Louisville, and Theodore Parker was a student in the Divinity School. I was, indeed, soon made to feel that I was not in good repute. Dr. Ware, Senior, who had charge of the Hollis Street pulpit in the absence of the pastor, invited me to supply it, if I found I could do so consistently with my new duties. I engaged for two Sundays. But, at the close of the first, one of the chief officers of the church waited upon me, by direction of the principal members, and requested me not to enter their pulpit again, assuring me, if I should do so, that a dozen or more of the prominent men with their families would leave the house. Of course I yielded; and I was not invited into any other pulpit in the city, excepting Dr. Channing's, during the fifteen months that I resided there." — *Recollections.*

We cannot give a better description of Mr. May's manner as an antislavery lecturer, or a finer example of the impression that he often made, than will be found in this letter from one who caught his spirit, and has emulated his fidelity: —

LOUISVILLE, KY., May 16, 1872.

DEAR BROTHER MUMFORD, — A deeply interesting reminiscence of Mr. May has often touched and thrilled me. In its visitings, it has seemed more like the presence of an angel form hovering near, than of any well-defined, earthly being; for I cannot give to the scene which it brings before me exact date or certain local habitation, and yet the scene itself is distinctly visible, and its impression as fresh and deep as if made yesterday.

It was in the town hall of Worcester, I think, and when I was thirteen or fourteen years of age, that I saw and heard our revered and beloved friend for the first time, and received the ineffaceable impression. He was speaking upon the subject of slavery, and I was not then prepared to listen to him with entirely unprejudiced mind. When a child, I had gone with my parents to New Jersey, and had lived there five years. At that time slavery was dying out in that State under gradual emancipation. Its last remnants only were to be met with; but I saw enough of the relations which existed between old family servants and their former masters to teach me that the service, repulsive as it was to my inborn, New England love of universal freedom, was not mere chattelism unrelieved by thoughtful kindness, and that slaveholders personally had often risen above the influences of the slave system. You will readily understand, therefore, why the reformers, whom our friend represented, should have appeared to me somewhat unwise ultraists, extremists who were not altogether just.

Mr. May spoke then as he always spoke. You know he never compromised, but always said just what he thought truth and duty required. His analysis of slavery was keen, and his denunciation of it scathing, withering. Some of his statements seemed too unqualified and severe, but all present listened intently. We could not do otherwise, so earnest and rapt was he.

After he had spoken for a considerable time, a Southern gentleman, who chanced to be present, asked permission to express his dissent from the views advanced. "By all means," said Mr. May, with the fairness and courtesy always characteristic of him, and urged the stranger to speak at length and with perfect freedom. When he had finished, Mr. May replied; and it was his manner and his looks, as well as his words, while making the rejoinder, that moved my heart to its depths and filled me with admiration, almost with awe. So strong and frank was he, yet so mild and calm, so unfaltering and so loving in spirit, so complete his self-control, and so evident his heart-felt desire to do justice to all, that I could not but feel that we were in the presence of one whose allegiance to truth was entire, and who would always, prophet-like, speak what he thought God bade him speak.

Years passed before I saw him again, but his kindly, truth-illumined face never vanished from my mind; and I have always been grateful for the influence then exerted and for the illustration which the consecrated man then gave of that highest, most Christ-like attainment and grace, — the power of speaking the truth in love.

Truly, your brother,

JOHN H. HEYWOOD.

He was mobbed five times; his meetings at Rutland and Montpelier, Vt., and at Haverhill, Mass., being "dispersed with violence." Demands came from several of the Southern legislatures "to suppress all Abolition societies, and make it penal to print, publish, or distribute newspapers and tracts having a tendency to excite the slaves to insurrection and revolt." In his Annual Address to the Legislature of Massachusetts, in January, 1836, Governor Everett not only severely censured the Abolitionists, but intimated his opinion that they were guilty of offences punishable at common law. This portion of the Governor's address was referred to a joint committee of two from the Senate, and three from the House of Representatives. By order of the managers of the Massachusetts Antislavery Society, Mr. May, as their general agent, addressed a letter to this committee, asking permission to appear before them, and show reasons why there should be no legislative action of the kind called for by the Southern legislatures. The request was granted, and the 4th of March fixed for the hearing. Mr. May opened the case, set forth the principles of the Abolitionists, the grounds and methods of their action, and the objects they desired to attain. He showed that their warfare on slavery was by moral means, appealing always to the honor and conscience of the people, and to the beneficial effects which must follow from a great act of justice. He laid before the committee copies of the constitutions of the antislavery societies, their rules of membership, and also their publications generally. He was ably supported by Dr. Follen, Ellis Gray Loring, S. E. Sewall, Esq., William Goodell, and others. They did not speak in vain.

Harriet Martineau was in our country during some of the earlier struggles of the antislavery cause, and she has left on record, in her "Society in America," vol. iii. page 280, her estimate of Mr. May: —

"I believe Mr. May had the honor of being the first Unitarian pastor who sided with the right. Whether he has sacrificed to his intrepidity one Christian grace; whether he has lost one charm of his piety, gentleness, and charity amidst the trials of insult which he has had to undergo, I dare appeal to his worst enemy. Instead of this, his devotion to a most difficult duty has called forth in him a force of character, a strength of reason, of which his best friends were before unaware. It filled me with shame for the weakness of men, in their noblest offices, to hear the insolent comparison with which some of his priestly brethren spoke of a man whom they have not light and courage enough to follow through the thickets and deserts of duty, and upon whom they therefore bestow their scornful pity from out of their shady bowers of complacency."

CHAPTER XII.

SOUTH SCITUATE, 1836-1842.

The Cold Water Army. — A Peace Society. — The Misses Grimké. — A Manly Letter. — Theodore Parker's Sermon. — Interest in Education. — Sympathy with Children. — Miss Caroline Tilden. — Rev. W. P. Tilden. — Accepts the Charge of the Lexington Normal School.

MR. MAY was installed pastor of the Church in South Scituate on the 26th of October, 1836, and his six years' ministry there was a very happy and useful one. It is still fondly remembered by many grateful hearts which were first moved to give themselves to God and humanity by the influence of his life and spirit. His presence and labors occasioned a great revival of practical Christianity, which was not limited to his own parish, but spread throughout Plymouth County in churches of all denominations. Conventions in behalf of many philanthropic causes were called, and largely attended by deeply interested persons.

At that time drunkenness was more common than it is now; and Mr. May, while doing his utmost to impress his adult hearers with a sense of the enormity of the evil, and the extent of their peril, devoted himself mainly to saving the young from this vice. He enlisted a Cold Water Army composed of children from all parts of the town, procuring music, and preparing banners with appropriate devices designed by himself, and mottoes inscribed in his own handwriting. Many of these are still carefully preserved. Although not remarkable as works of art, they are very creditable specimens of his taste and skill, and must have produced a fine effect when he marshalled his five hundred young followers under these flags, and all recited in concert, —

> "So here we pledge perpetual hate
> To all that can intoxicate."

Often they marched through the streets with Mr. May at their head; but sometimes they held picnics in the groves and fields, a field near his own house being called The Field of Waterloo.

All the rum-shops in town were closed with one exception, and finally this obstinate seller capitulated. Mr. May resolved to have a public execution of the last enemy. He got hold of the remaining liquors in the man's shop, procured an old horse and cart to carry the barrels to the scene of action, and summoned his little army. They came in full ranks to the appointed grove. He made an address, led them in singing, and then took an axe and beat in the head of every barrel. As the contents flowed forth upon the earth, the children are said to have cheered as boys and girls have seldom cheered. His precepts and example made such an impression upon some of their minds that, when they afterwards became members of the church, they would never partake of wine even at the Lord's Supper.

He organized a Peace Society in the Sunday school, and gave six copies of "A Kiss for a Blow" to the library, so that every child might be sure to read it. Most of the children received his Gospel of Universal Freedom with prompt enthusiasm, and became stanch adherents of the antislavery cause. One of them wrote, long afterwards: "When I first read of our immortal Lincoln signing that glorious Proclamation of Emancipation, next to my rejoicing for the poor slave was the thought, 'Oh, how happy Mr. May is now! I am so glad he has lived to see this day.'"

Early in 1837 Sarah and Angelina Grimké, of South Carolina, came to Massachusetts, invited by the State Antislavery Society to address meetings of their own sex. At first Mr. May's sense of propriety was somewhat disturbed, but he soon saw that it was "a miserable prejudice that would forbid woman to speak in behalf of the suffering just as her heart may prompt, and as God has given her power." He invited the Misses Grimké to his house, and made arrangements for their meetings in Scituate, Hingham, and Cohasset.

He was so active in the antislavery cause and in other great reforms, while at South Scituate, that some persons thought that he was not so useful in the ministry as he might have been if he had restricted himself to what was then called "the Gospel." But his course was always without concealment, and without compromise. We are not fully acquainted with the circumstances alluded to in this letter which we have found among his papers, but the letter itself has a very manly ring:—

SOUTH SCITUATE, June 25, 1839.

REV. C. BRIGGS,
Cor. Sec'y of the American Unitarian Association.

DEAR SIR, — Yours of yesterday came to me this afternoon. I am ready and willing to go to East Greenwich and labor to bring those who will hear me to the knowledge of Christian truth as it is understood by Unitarians. But if I go under the auspices of the American Unitarian Association, I must go feeling that I have the confidence of its Executive Committee. Unless they can trust me, they ought not to send me.

And what do they mean by "Unitarian cause exclusively"? I believe that the Unitarian cause includes every thing that Christianity includes. Do they restrict it to something less? Or do they suspect me of wishing to spend my strength for any thing that Christianity excludes? If they wish me purposely to omit, in my preaching, any of the doctrines or precepts of Christ, I cannot act as their agent. If they apprehend that I shall propound some false doctrines, or inculcate false principles, they ought not to send me forth. Are they unwilling I should show the people, if I can, that Unitarian principles are fundamental to all individual improvement, and to all social reform? And that Unitarian Christians, if consistent, will be heartily disposed to every good work? If they are thus unwilling, I cannot consent to go for them.

But I am reluctant to believe they meant what their note implies. On further consideration, I hope they will strike out the condition they have prescribed, and let me go to Greenwich as a man, and a Unitarian Christian especially, ought to go.

I shall be happy, unless prevented by something now unforeseen, to preach at East Greenwich the second and third Sundays in August next.

Yours truly, SAMUEL J. MAY.

We give the following anecdote as it has been related by Mr. Parker Pillsbury: —

"When Theodore Parker preached his memorable sermon at the ordination of Mr. Shackford, at South Boston, Mr. May was the settled minister of South Scituate, Mass. The sermon was printed, and, with a copy of it in my valise, I called, in my regular round of antislavery lecturing, on Mr. May. He and Mrs. May had other company, but insisted on my remaining during the afternoon, and till lecture time. In course of conversation, the new heresy and its author came up, and I asked if any one present had seen the sermon. None had, and so I produced it. Mr. May proposed that I should read it. He and others declining, I did so. I had read it, and had marked some passages as of peculiar significance, and so endeavored to give them what emphasis I could in this second, but wholly unexpected, reading, and to an audience so worthy. The company heard me in silence to the last word.

"After a pause, Mr. May said: 'Oh, is not that a beautiful sermon?' To which all assented in general terms; but some present took exception to some passages. Mr. May, however, defended the discourse in the main, praised the ability and extolled the heroism of its author, at the same time murmuring the fear that, as a recognized Unitarian minister, he had sealed his doom.

"Mr. May's conduct towards Mr. Parker ever after, while he preached in Boston, and while he lived, proved how sincere, manly, and brotherly was his regard for him and his work."

Mr. May was unwearied in his interest in education. Through his instrumentality several bright young women were persuaded to go to the Normal School, and be partially sustained there. Their own fathers could hardly have taken greater interest and pride in their subsequent success. To one of them, Mrs. Helen J. Parmenter, now of Arlington, Mass., we are indebted for the following letter relating to school days at Scituate, addressed to Rev. W. P. Tilden:—

"We used to enjoy having him come into school. He was always delighted with us if we did well, and had such pleasant things to say to us. He was particularly desirous that we should be good readers and spellers; and to this day I hardly ever write the word *separate* without thinking of him, he used to ask us so often whether there should be an *a* or an *e* after the *p*.

"He used to bring his father in to see us when he came to Scituate, and in so many ways made us children in that little, old, poor school-house feel that we were of some account. When I got to be one of the largest girls, he used to bring into the school letters for us to copy. He had so many letters to write that, when he wanted duplicates of any, we often used to help him. Very careful we were, I can assure you, that there should be no words spelled wrong, and that the writing should be our very best.

"One thing that endeared him very much to the children was his sympathy with them in their enjoyments, and the interest he showed in promoting their pleasure in every possible way. As an instance of this, he had a nice swing put up under a large tree near his house, between the school-house and his home.

"But how interminable would be the list of kind and helpful deeds with which his long life was filled, more than filled, running over! I wonder if you have the same feeling that I have when you come across persons that never saw or knew him, a feeling of commiseration, as if a great blessing had been withheld, as if their lives must necessarily be by so much the poorer?

"I suppose they told you in Scituate all about his last visit, when they had a picnic and such a grand reception for him. Emily read a poem of welcome. Mr. May tried to reply, but could not, for tears."

Miss Caroline Tilden, of South Scituate, afterwards became Mr. May's assistant in the Normal School at Lexington. He said, in 1867: —

"I discovered her genius while she was the modest mistress of a village school, and induced her to go to the Normal School at Bridgewater. She prepared herself to be the inspiring genius of many who were seeking to acquire the art of teaching."

In his life at Scituate nothing interested Mr. May more, or gave him greater satisfaction, than his success in confirming the purpose of Rev. W. P. Tilden to become a Christian minister. He always looked back to the instruction and encouragement given to this dear son in the faith with especial pride and delight. What this intimate and tender relation was to Mr. Tilden, we may learn from his tribute to the memory of his spiritual father, in the "Religious Magazine."

"Perhaps I cannot better hint of the blessing he was to *many* than by first telling a little of what he was to *one*. I first became acquainted with him in South Scituate about thirty-five years ago, when he came, fresh from his faithful service as General Agent of the Antislavery Society, to become the minister of my native parish. I was at this period using what time I could spare from daily toil in study, hoping, if possible, some day to enter the Christian ministry. But I soon found that the path from the ship-yard to the pulpit was not carpeted with flowers. 'The pursuit of knowledge under difficulties,' so fascinating in books, I found a somewhat different thing in real work-day life; and I confess that at times the sky grew very dark. The light of hope, at first so bright, receded from a star of the first magnitude to a far-off glimmer in the upper deep, and sometimes threatened to go out in darkness. Just at this time came Mr. May. He took my hand; the sky cleared. He clasped it in that broad, warm, loving palm: the star came back, full-orbed and glorious. Oh, what a clasp that right hand had! He never gave his finger-tips. He gave the whole palm, and it carried with it a whole flood of sympathy and strength. He seemed to have an extra set of nerves made for the special purpose of transmitting sympathy and cheer straight from his heart to ours. For three blessed years I was in almost daily intercourse with him. I heard him preach on Sundays, and, what was better, saw him practise through the week what he preached. I read with him, studied with him, talked with him, laughed with him, prayed with him, worked with him; went to temperance, antislavery, and peace meetings with him; superintended his Sabbath-school: till at last he entrapped me to preach for him, and then sent me out with his blessing to preach to others. How brightly the light of those golden days shines through the azure distance of thirty years!"

On the 12th of September, 1842, Mr. May made the following entry in his diary:—

"This day I have left South Scituate and removed to Lexington, to take charge of the Lexington Normal School, instituted three years ago for the preparation of female teachers for our common schools. I have been induced to take this step by the urgent solicitation of Hon. Horace Mann, Secretary of the Board of Education, and of Rev. Cyrus Pierce, the former teacher of this school, who, by the multiplicity of his cares and the severity of his labors, has been overborne and obliged to retire. He and Mr. Mann have not indeed persuaded me that I am competent to the place, but they have induced me to attempt to do the duties that are incumbent upon the Principal of the school. I pray God for wisdom to direct me, and for strength to sustain."

CHAPTER XIII.

PRINCIPAL OF THE STATE NORMAL SCHOOL AT LEXINGTON.

Letter to Horace Mann about the Advantages of Normal School Education. — The Spirit in which he goes to his New Duties. — His Qualifications for the Work. — Becomes Discouraged. — Cheering Letters from Messrs. Pierce and Mann. — Defence of his attending an Antislavery Meeting and taking some of his Pupils. — Resigns in Favor of Mr. Pierce. — The Secret of Mr. May's Success as a Teacher. — "Love the Unlovely."

MR. MANN found a warmer living interest in common school education in Plymouth County than almost anywhere else, and traced it, in a large degree, to the active interest of Mr. May, in speaking of whom it is not just to forget the zeal and activity of Rev. Charles Brooks, in another part of the county.

On Feb. 13, 1842, Mr. Mann received the following letter: —

Hon. Horace Mann.

Dear Sir, — I heard, a few days ago, that application is to be made to our legislature, during the present session, for a grant of means to sustain our Normal Schools, at least for another term of three years. Let it be done, and earnestly done. I cannot think it will be unsuccessful. It ought not to fail. There is no project which the legislators of a free people should be more careful to encourage than one for the better education of the whole people. . . .

I have *heard* of good done by the Normal Schools at Lexington and Barre, but I have *seen* the good effects of our own school at Bridgewater, although it has been in operation only seventeen months.

He then gives several instances of striking success in the teaching of young persons who, before they went to the Normal School, had been rather poor teachers.

One kept, in this town, the Union or High School. Many thought she had undertaken more than she could perform. . . . I confess I trembled for her. But the success of her labors was complete; it was beautiful. For the first two or three weeks, appearances were squally. She had not the physical ability, if she had had the disposition, to force her pupils to observe her directions and attend diligently to their studies. At the close of the first month, however, the clouds had dispersed, and the sunshine of peace and love had settled upon her school. She had succeeded in perfectly establishing her authority, by inspiring her pupils with respect and affection for herself, and so generally with a desire to learn, that the public sentiment of the school was favorable to study and good order. . . . The discipline of the school was unusually strict; not the least whispering was allowed. . . . I never was in a school so still. . . . A strict account was kept of the deportment of the pupils, and the number of violations of the rules of the school was incredibly small. More progress had been made, when I visited the school, at its close, than I have ever known to be made in any common school during the same length of time; and the recitations of the pupils were altogether more satisfactory. . . . Perhaps some may surmise that this young lady has naturally an aptness to teach. I think it probable that she has. But her talent was developed at the Normal School; for she had tried school-keeping before she went to Bridgewater, and had not been very successful, for the want of something which she acquired under Mr. Tillinghast's instructions. . . .

I am, very respectfully, yours,

SAMUEL J. MAY.

When Mr. Cyrus Pierce, the first Principal of the State Normal School, broke down from over-exertion, Mr. Mann urged Mr. May to take his place. It was in vain that Mr. May declared his incompetency to the duties of teaching, and entire content with his place and office in the pulpit. Mr. Mann insisted; and Mr. May consented to go, on condition that Miss Caroline Tilden, "who did know how to teach," should accompany him. In a letter to Mr. Mann, of July 29, in answer, he says: —

"Nothing prevents my saying, at once, that I will accept the appointment, if the Board see fit to make it, but the consciousness of my inability to perform well all the duties of the station. I do not know of any other place of usefulness into which I should so rejoice to be put, if I were competent to fill it as it ought to be filled."

These misgivings were compelled to give way to the urgency of Mr. Mann and Mr. Pierce.

On August 17th he writes: —

"DEAR SIR, — It has leaked out that I am to be Mr. Pierce's successor. The girls suspected as much from my visit of two days last week; . . . and Mr. Pierce, taking it for granted that your nomination would fix the choice of the Board, allowed himself to encourage their suspicion, so that yesterday it went forth on the wings of common report. So far as my feelings are concerned, this need give you no pain.

Much as I long to give myself to the cause of education, which alone can effect that reform, or those reforms, in the personal and social state of man which it is my heart's desire and prayer to witness, the load of responsibility, care, and labor that Mr. Pierce has laid down is so weighty that I shall feel relieved if I may be excused from taking it up.

"Of course you will inform me, so soon as the decision of the Board is known to yourself. I have a surgical operation to go through, in separating myself from my people at South Scituate, which cannot be despatched in a day."

On the 5th of November, he writes to Mr. Mann: —

"My dear Sir, — I have passed the Rubicon, and burnt up my boats. I went last Saturday to Scituate, took a final leave of my Society, demolished my home, removed my furniture, and came back to Lexington, resolved to give up myself, *body* and *soul*, to the cause of education. You can have little idea of the struggle it has cost me. But, now it is over, I feel relieved, calm, resolved, cheerful. I dread nothing save the question, between myself and the Board, respecting the admission of a colored girl. That, however, may never arise. I think it never will arise. If it should, I hope I shall be directed into the right course."

Mr. May and Miss Tilden went together to the school at Lexington, where Mr. May supplied his deficiencies in experience and practice by qualities higher than mere skill in teaching, though that is a very high, and was then a very rare, quality; and Miss Tilden, who had been instructed by Mr. Tillinghast, introduced a style of teaching which was unsurpassed, and, perhaps, unsurpassable.

It is a precious fact that Mr. May, by the purity, elevation, and disinterestedness of his Christian character, without large experience or skill in teaching, should have been able to raise the tone of a school, the excellence of which, from the integrity, devotedness, and skill of its first teacher, Mr. Pierce, had secured the blessings of Normal School instruction to the schools of Massachusetts.

On the 29th of next September, however, he writes to Mr. Mann:—

> "DEAR SIR,—I have made up my mind to resign my place as Principal, . . . and wish you to consider this a tender of my resignation."

After enumerating various difficulties, especially the severity of the labors and cares, and their effects upon his nerves, so that he cannot sleep, and upon his lungs, so that he can hardly speak, he adds:—

> "But, more than all, I find myself incompetent to the duties of the place. The Institution, I fear, will decline in my hands. I know what it should be; but I have so little facility in managing the details of the plan, that dissatisfaction has been the reward of my labors, almost every night.
>
> "Were it not for this, if I could see the Normal School flourishing, or foresee that it would flourish, under my administration, I should 'count it all joy' to spend and be spent in its behalf. It seems to me that I would willingly die, if by such a sacrifice I could make the school what it should be.
>
> "I will remain at Lexington, if you wish, several weeks, that you may have time to find a successor."

After suggesting the names of several persons as likely to fill the place successfully, he concludes:—

"In resigning this most interesting charge, I cannot withhold heart-felt expressions of gratitude to you, sir, for the favor you have intended, and for the great kindness you have uniformly shown me."

To this doleful letter Mr. Mann made a cheerful and most witty answer, and really laughed him out of his downheartedness. He received a letter from Rev. C. Pierce, Sept. 27, 1843, in which he comes to Mr. Mann's aid:—

"DEAR MAY,—Yours of the 23d instant, which came to hand yesterday, though a very good and interesting letter on the whole, has, in one part, so troubled me that I cannot longer defer answering it. The amount of it is this: In very smooth and pleasant, yet in very plain terms, you charge upon me the enormity of 'enticing and flattering you away into the Normal School;' and, in language of grave reproof, put the interrogatory, 'How could you, after thirty years' experience, think I was fit for it?'

"Now, *dear child*, hear my defence, as strange as it may seem to you. I thought *then*, and I think *now*, there was no person into whose hands I could so safely commit the school as into yours. My reasons are these: 1. God has blessed you, as I think, with the right temper and disposition for a schoolmaster (a very important qualification); 2. You have a deep interest in children and school education; and, 3. The *drift* of your reading, habit of thinking, and general knowledge have been such as to adapt you to the office of teacher. If I did not make allowance enough on the score of difficulty from the want of *experience*, . . . yet still, in one calculation, I was not in error; namely, that your diligence and aptness to learn would fast make up for any want of experience. Time, if I do not misjudge, is rapidly showing that I was right in my conjecture. Resign! resign!! You have begun auspiciously. *Perge quo cœpisti.* The school has risen and enlarged in your hands. What would you have? . . . Dismiss all thoughts of resignation, and hold on the even tenor of your way, steady as the needle to the pole."

In the course of the next winter, however, Mr. Mann wrote to him, finding fault with his having gone to an antislavery meeting at Waltham, taking some of his pupils, and making a speech there. To this he immediately answered: —

LEXINGTON, Feb. 8, 1843.

HON. HORACE MANN.

MY DEAR SIR, — I am sorry to have caused you so much anxiety, and hasten to relieve you as far as I may.

As to the lecture, from the delivery of which you apprehend so much evil, I made up my mind, several days ago, that I could not take time enough to prepare such a one as I should be willing to deliver in the proposed course, without neglecting my immediate, paramount duties here ; and therefore determined to withdraw my name from the list of lecturers. Accordingly, I wrote to my antislavery friends to this effect.

It is my wish still to be known of all men as an Abolitionist. Nothing seems to me so impious, foolhardy, fanatical, as the attempt to perpetuate slavery in our country, although I see so many of "the wise and prudent" enlisted on that behalf. It is my intention to do what I may, without neglecting or slighting my duties to the Normal School, to aid the antislavery cause. I declared this intention to you, most explicitly, in our first conversation at Bridgewater. I told you that, whenever I could, without a dereliction of duty, I should attend antislavery meetings ; that I should retain my office in the Massachusetts and American antislavery societies, — and contribute to their funds all the more, because I should not be able to serve them otherwise, as I have been wont to do. I assured you, if I took charge of this Institution, that the care of it should be my first object of attention, and that to its interests I would devote the best powers of my mind. And I predicted that I should have but little time or thought to spare to other subjects, however important. I have thus far done as I promised; and if I continue here I shall be as devoted as I have been.

My going to Waltham, and carrying with me a number of my pupils, was no departure from the course I prescribed to myself at first, nor did it involve any neglect of duty. My speech there took up no more of my time than was occupied in the utterance of it. It was not a written nor a premeditated address, but wholly extempore. The meeting was held on a Saturday evening. I could therefore go without leaving any thing undone. Many of my pupils are Abolitionists. They were so when they came here, or were made so by Father Pierce. They expressed a desire to attend the meeting, to which they, with the rest of the people, were invited by placards sent over from Waltham and scattered through our village. It was very fine sleighing, which made them more desirous to go. The getting ready took but a short time. We went, and enjoyed the meeting highly, excepting an injudicious speech. If the young lady to whom you referred in a former letter really was prevented from joining our school by the reason you have assigned, she must be, I think, in mind and heart very inferior to many who are now in it.

Nor was my consenting to be one of the lecturers of the proposed course any breach of my important trust. I consented, supposing my turn would come in my next vacation, and that I should be left to take a subject upon which I have a carefully prepared address. But when I saw the advertisement of the course, I found that another (Wendell Phillips) had taken my subject, and that another subject had been assigned to me, upon which I felt little inclined to write, and unable to do so well, without a careful revision of my former opinions, and much study of recent documents. This determined me to withdraw from the course.

I have gone thus at length into an account of myself, because I wish to satisfy you, if I may, that I have not been unmindful of my charge, and that I shall not be.

And now, my friend, allow me to say to you, that I think your fear of the effect of my Abolitionism upon the prosperity of the Normal School is undue. This heresy is rapidly becoming orthodoxy in our Commonwealth. It is embraced by a much larger portion than you are aware of, of that class of the people which furnishes the most of our school-teachers. I have myself been surprised to find so large a part of my pupils zealous in the antislavery cause. But if you and the other supporters of the school are to be made unhappy, and filled with alarm, whenever I do or say any thing that shows how deeply I am interested in the redemption of our country from the curse of slavery, it will certainly be better for me quietly to withdraw, on the plea of my incompetency, and leave the Institution in better hands.

Yours very truly, SAMUEL J. MAY.

I am happy to inform you that the Normal School is full, and that there are thirty pupils in the Model School, which is doing finely.

The school continued to flourish and to increase rapidly in numbers. When he took it there were thirty-one pupils: in June, 1844, he wrote to Mr. Mann that there were sixty-six, of whom thirty-one belonged to the Freshman class.

In July, he tells Mr. Mann that he hears that Mr. Pierce has almost entirely recovered his health, and, "if he can be induced to return," he says, "I cannot persuade myself that I ought to remain here. He has much vigor of mind and body left, and it is a pity that his experience, wisdom, and skill should not be given to the Normal enterprise. I presume the Board would rejoice to have him again in their service; and I hope, before the close of this term, to send you my resignation in his favor."

Very soon after, he sends to Mr. Mann the following letter: —

LEXINGTON, July 17, 1844.

HON. HORACE MANN.

DEAR SIR, — I hasten to forward you the enclosed from Mr. Pierce.

Knowing, as I do, how highly you and other members of the Board esteem Mr. Pierce as a teacher, I doubt not you will all rejoice to see him again in the place where he did you and the Commonwealth such good service.

If he will accept, as he seems disposed to do, the arrangements I have made, he will keep even a better school than he did before. If he will retain Miss Tilden and Miss Lincoln as his assistants, and keep up the musical and the drawing departments, — with his vigilant oversight and vigorous and exact executive talents, he will make this Institution much more efficient than it was before in his hands, and incomparably more so than it would ever be in mine. I am too indulgent, and cannot help being. I am not, therefore, sufficiently thorough and exact in all my requirements. Mr. Pierce is as kind a man as lives; and yet he never swerves from the line he has marked, nor allows others to swerve. He is the man for this place, and I am confident that I am doing the cause of education a better service in resigning this school into his hands than I could do by retaining it.

In a few days I will send, through your hands, to the Board of Education my formal resignation. I despatch this to you, that you may have all the time you can have between now and the opening of the next term to make what arrangements you may wish to make with my successor.

During the vacation, if possible, but certainly before your annual report is presented, I mean to furnish you with evidences of the usefulness of this Institution.

With great esteem, yours,

SAMUEL J. MAY.

Mr. May's success in the school was complete, giving entire satisfaction to all but himself. In the following extracts from a letter to Mr. Mann, of Oct. 20, 1844, after he had left the school, he gives the secret of his success: —

"MY DEAR SIR, — I thank you heartily for giving me notice of the Essex County Teachers' Convention. I went to it, and rejoice that I did so. It was a large gathering; and there were several choice spirits there besides D. P. Page, who is first-rate. . . .

"I ventured to address the meeting upon the subject of the management of schools; and the reception given to my remarks (I say it *sub rosa*), while it gratified me much, surprised me not a little. I first dwelt for a few minutes upon the importance of attention to little things, applying to schools the old adage, 'Take care of the pence, and the pounds will take care of themselves.'

"And then I urged, at some length, that teachers should go into their schools in the spirit of Christ, meaning to seek and to save them that are lost; being especially mindful of the neglected, ill-looking, ill-dressed, ill-tempered, not wishing them away, but rejoicing to have an opportunity to do for them in school what is not done for them at home. Let this class of children be at once made to feel that they are really cared for; that they are not shunned, but sought after; not despised, but valued; not doubted, but trusted; not despaired of, but hoped for: let them be treated thus, and a prolific source of trouble in schools would be dried up. Love the unlovely, and they will put their unloveliness away.

Several arose in quick succession, and declared this to be the most important suggestion they had yet received. Father G. said (*mirabile dictu!*) that this was entirely new to him; that he had never before heard this method proposed; that he felt deeply that there was a great truth in it; and that he would go home and try to act in accordance with it. So said several others; and 'love the unlovely' was heard from various quarters as we were going out of the house, along the road, and after we had reached the hotel. I was really a little disconcerted to find that it was a new discovery to so many, that 'evil might be overcome with good' in schools no less than elsewhere."

On the 20th of August, 1844, Mr. May writes to Mr. Mann: —

"Father Pierce spent Saturday night and Sunday with me. It did my heart good to see how much he has revived since his reappointment. Now that all the teachers of the Normal School are of my selection, I am confident it will flourish as it never could have done under the Principal you persuaded to take it two years ago. So confident am I, that I will almost promise, if I am disappointed, to assist you to get the last incumbent back and never stir a finger to remove him again.

"I settled my account with the treasurer yesterday, allowing my connection with the school to cease with the close of this month; so that Father Pierce's salary may commence with the first of September. . . .

"A few weeks hence I hope to be more at liberty, and then I will devote some time to lecturing in the cause of education. Respectfully, your obliged friend,

"Samuel J. May."

CHAPTER XIV.

MINISTRY AT SYRACUSE.

GAVE HIS VIEWS OF REFORMS WHILE PREACHING AS A CANDIDATE. — STAYS IN LEXINGTON TO SETTLE A DIFFICULTY ABOUT A CHURCH FUND. — HIS PREACHING. — HIS PASTORAL LIFE. — OUTSIDE MINISTRIES. — THE CANAL BOYS. — POPULAR LECTURES. — ASYLUMS. — THE ONONDAGA INDIANS. — THE RIGHTS OF WOMAN. — SERMON BEFORE THE GRADUATING CLASS AT CAMBRIDGE DIVINITY SCHOOL. — PUBLIC DISCUSSION OF THE DOCTRINE OF THE TRINITY. — THEODORE PARKER. — LUTHER LEE. — MARKET-HALL DISCUSSIONS. — RESIGNS HIS PASTORATE. — MISSIONARY OF THE AMERICAN UNITARIAN ASSOCIATION.

IN 1843, while on a journey to Niagara Falls, Mr. May occupied the pulpit of Rev. J. P. B. Storer at Syracuse, for several Sundays. When Mr. Storer's sudden death deprived this young church of their pastor, they sent for Mr. May; and, after hearing him again, gave him a unanimous invitation to become their minister. The call was accepted the more readily because, during the week between the two Sundays when he was preaching practically as a candidate, he had delivered addresses on the reforms in which he was deeply interested. He said, "I intended they should clearly understand whom they were calling, if they called me."

He began to discharge the duties of his new post in April, 1845. In one of the notes appended to his "Brief Account of his Ministry," he says: —

"I should have come to reside in Syracuse several months sooner than I did, but for a serious, vexatious difficulty in which the churches of Lexington had been involved for twenty years or more, respecting a large fund for the support of the ministry of the town. The fund was created by subscriptions and donations at an early day, when there was only one Church there. But in process of time differences of theological belief had arisen amongst the people, and churches of several denominations had been gathered. Each of these claimed a share of the fund. It became the subject of repeated litigation. The decisions of the courts and of the legislature, to whom at length the matter was carried, were that the income of the fund legally belonged to the old, original Church. But the claimants were not satisfied, and discord and strife continued. When I became the temporary minister of the Old Society, I looked into the matter and became satisfied that, if the law gave the fund wholly to that Church, Christian equity did not; and that there would never be peace and good-fellowship among the people of the different churches until the income of the fund should be equitably divided. I was confident that what ought to be done could be done. I was allowed to devise the plan of settlement, and remained there long enough to see it accomplished."

Mr. May was nearly forty-eight years old when he began his work at Syracuse, and his pastorate extended through more than twenty-two years, ending at the close of his seventieth year. In all this time he was very diligent in the work of the ministry.

One striking proof of his love of his calling may be seen in his power to inspire young men with a desire to engage in the work of the ministry. We know of more than half a score who became clergymen under his leadership. Messrs. Frederic T. Gray, Samuel May William P. Tilden, Thomas J. Mumford, and several others, pursued at least a part of their professional studies as his pupils.

Looking back upon his life, he expressed his regret that he had left undone some things "immediately promotive of the improvement and prosperity of a church;" but although a great deal of his time and much of his strength were given to the causes of peace, temperance, freedom, and popular education, his professional duties were remarkably well performed. Scores of his sermons, suggested by the events of the times, were published in the daily journals; but the greater part of his preaching always related to the religious life and the formation of Christian character. He was fond of announcing courses of sermons which enabled him to treat subjects somewhat methodically, and also gave an enforced direction to his own studies. The nature, history, and claims of the Bible, were most grandly presented. He made Scriptural characters the subjects of many of his most interesting and popular discourses. But the life and spirit of Jesus were his favorite topics. Of course there was a practical purpose in all his preaching, and he excelled particularly in the application of Christianity to domestic, social, and business life. His delineations of true fathers and mothers, wives and husbands, brothers and sisters, sons and daughters, will never be forgotten by those who listened to them. His views of the use and abuse of property, the conditions of real respectability, and the tests of a noble manhood, were very impressive. He thought that lawyers, doctors, merchants, and journalists ought to be solemnly ordained at the beginning of their professional careers, and his sketch of a Charge at the installation of an editor was especially memorable. Rev. C. D. B. Mills, one of his most intelligent and appreciative parishioners, says of Mr. May's work in the pulpit:—

"As a preacher Mr. May was always perspicuous, intelligent, and impressive. His evident sincerity, earnest love of truth, and devotion to his kind invested all that he said with interest and attractiveness. He was not always equal with himself. If his sermons ever seemed dry and uninteresting, it was when he handled, which he sometimes did (though quite rarely), doctrines belonging more purely to the domain of mere speculative theology. I think he never felt at home there, and he grew more to disuse such subjects in the pulpit. Rarely what would be called eloquent, he rose not unfrequently to heights of true inspiration and commanding power. This was almost uniformly when treating of themes of great practical duty. The heart seems to have overshadowed the head, making all else beside it to have appeared comparatively trivial and cheap; but he was certainly a man, on the intellectual side, of greatly superior endowment. Some of his sermons were models in thought and expression; and I have heard from him discourses that in point of quality, in all ways, I think I have never known surpassed. Those that seemed such to me were not, I believe, generally in his view among his best. I hope certainly that some of them may, at no distant day, see the light. He felt the call to direct practical work for his kind so imperative, that he left all to follow it, finding comparatively little time for studies as such, albeit his was a mind of fine general cultivation; but had he been able to give himself with more of fulness in this direction, I doubt not he would have wrought results in the sphere of pure intellectual inquiry of no common-place or ordinary character.

"His benediction was always emphatically a blessing, such a beam of the eye, and such clear fervor of the spirit going out with the invocation of benefit: it was well worth a good journey to see and hear this alone of a Sunday, say nothing of any sermon."

In the pastoral office Mr. May was unsurpassed, seldom, if ever, equalled. His great, warm heart was always ready to respond to any call for sympathy. In times of trial and distress, his people found him the best of comforters. It was easier to bear pain in his helpful presence, and to believe in the Divine tenderness and forgiving love, while witnessing such a wealth of human affection and forbearance. Hundreds outside of his own congregation sought for him in seasons of distress and bereavement. He was often called to neighboring, and even distant, towns on sacred errands of consolation. A family of Episcopalians were present at the funeral of a child which was conducted by Mr. May. Losing one of their own little boys soon afterwards, and yearning for such faith and hope as they felt that only Mr. May could impart, they sent for him. A few months later he went to Europe, and the grateful father sent him a hundred dollars to purchase memorials of his travels, in remembrance of his kindness in the time of darkness.

We were at Syracuse once when an old gentleman from Trenton, who had come to attend an Autumnal Convention, was drowned in the canal, and at the same time a train on the New York Central Railroad ran off the track a few miles from Syracuse. Several persons were severely injured, while a lady from Toronto, Canada, was instantly killed. In addition to his labors in behalf of the convention, who were the guests of his people, Mr. May devoted much time to efforts to find the drowned man, who, before his fate was ascertained, was supposed to have wandered off into the country; and he would also go to the hotel where the sufferers from the railroad accident were lying, and carry from room to room the blessing of his tender words and loving acts. He found that he could not do all that he was desired to do, because the bereaved families at both Trenton and Toronto asked for his presence at the burials; and he had to choose between the funeral occasions.

While Mr. May was an acceptable preacher and a beloved pastor, his own parish did not absorb all his interest and energy; for he was active in every good work.

The first year that he lived in Syracuse he had occasion to pass and repass the bridges every day, and he was shocked by the loathsome condition of the thousands of boys employed upon the Erie Canal, their terrible profanity and disgusting obscenity. In December, 1845, Mr. May was invited to a clerical party at the house of Rev. Dr. Adams, pastor of the First Presbyterian Church. He told the ministers what he had heard of the wrongs and exposure of the canal boys, and what he had seen of their degradation; and a Memorial was at once prepared and sent to the legislature, asking for the passage of such an Act as would secure to the canal boys protection of their persons, and compensation for their services; homes and suitable instruction in the winters for that large portion of them who were parentless; and a Reformatory for those who should become delinquents. Public meetings were held, correspondence was opened with men of influence along the lines of the canals of the State, and the cause was earnestly advocated in the Senate and Assembly of New York. The legislation upon the subject was not satisfactory to Mr. May, but it became more difficult for the public to wholly forget the claims of an unfortunate class upon their sympathy and help.

He was chiefly instrumental in instituting courses of popular lectures in the town, and became known as an enlightened and devoted friend of education, delivering many lectures on public instruction and assisting at Teachers' Institutes and Educational Conventions. To Cornell University he gave his large collection of books and pamphlets relating to slavery and the antislavery contest in this country. He was known far and wide as an earnest friend of temperance. He was deeply interested in the Asylum for the Feeble-Minded, the hospital, city library, and reading-room.

It was hard for him to regard the Indians as a hopeless race. He helped those in his neighborhood to raise the means to build a school-house; procured a good teacher; obtained from the Superintendent of Public Instruction an annual appropriation for her support, and for that of her successors, for twenty years. He visited the school frequently, and obtained money from Boston to aid in the support of the Mission established by the Methodist Conference. He was repeatedly called upon to settle the difficulties of their teacher and missionary, and the Indians themselves often resorted to him for all sorts of advice and help. Sometimes groups of them would sit stolidly in his study for hour after hour Whenever he visited the Reservation their faces lighted up with joy and welcome. The whole tribe knew him. A friend who accompanied him the last time he visited these Indians says: "An Indian boy overtook us, and ran nearly half a mile beside the carriage to talk with Mr. May."

In 1846 he preached and published his first sermon on "The Rights of Woman." It was republished in this country and in England, having a larger circulation than any other writing that he ever gave to the press. He never wavered in his convictions, and declared, near the close of his life:—

"I am fully persuaded that never will our governments be wisely and happily administered until we have mothers as well as fathers of the State."

In 1847, the graduating class of the Cambridge Divinity School invited Mr. May to preach before them. On the 11th of July, he delivered a sermon on "Jesus the Best Teacher of his Religion." At the close he said:—

"Young gentlemen, by whose invitation I am here on this interesting occasion: you are about to go forth as ministers of Christianity, at a day when courage, as well as piety and learning, will be needed by you. May you have all the gifts and graces of true followers of Christ. If you go to your work in the simplicity, the truthfulness, the faith, the love of Jesus, you will not preach in vain. Go, I trust you will, not to be masters of ceremonies, but to be earnest, hard workers in the service of God and mankind. Care not so much whither you go, as in what spirit you go. There may be a choice in places, but there is no choice for you in purposes. Wherever you go, you should go with the determination to do the work of the Lord, to redeem men from ignorance, sin, and misery. This is the end for which Christ lived and died. This is the end to which you should live, and *die*, if fidelity to your duty demands the sacrifice."

In 1854, Mr. May had a discussion of the doctrine of the Trinity with Rev. Luther Lee, a distinguished Wesleyan minister. It began on Feb. 28, 1854, and ended on March 23. Eleven evenings were devoted to it, and the City Hall was filled with "an immense audience, hundreds being unable to get in." The speeches were carefully reported, and afterwards published together. There was much excitement, but the controversialists preserved their self-control, and there was no breaking off of their friendly relations.

Mr. Lee tried to identify Mr. May's opinions with those of Theodore Parker, which were the objects of especial dread on the part of most of the religious people of Syracuse. Mr. Parker and Mr. May were very intimate friends, and loved each other dearly. Early in their acquaintance, Mr. May had warned Mr. Parker most faithfully against his tendency to indulge in harsh and bitter personalities; but this candor was received as kindly as it was given. Mr. May sold large numbers of Mr. Parker's books, and procured many invitations for him to lecture in Central New York. Mr. Parker often preached in Mr. May's church. This fact Mr. Lee sought to turn to controversial account, but Mr. May replied: —

"Mr. Lee has endeavored to associate me in your minds with Theodore Parker. Of this I do not complain, though it has nothing to do with our argument. But why should Mr. Lee, and my Orthodox neighbors generally, take it for granted that my theological opinions are coincident with Mr. Parker's, because I have invited him to preach in my pulpit and have myself preached in his? I have had the same friendly intercourse with Swedenborgian, Methodist, Baptist, and Presbyterian (or Orthodox Congregationalist) ministers. They have preached in my pulpit, and I in theirs; yet I never heard the intimation that Mr. May had become, or was becoming, 'evangelical,' when any of these last-named exchanges took place.

"The ground of my great regard for Mr. Parker personally, and of my ministerial intercourse with him and with some preachers of the different Orthodox sects, has not been an agreement in our system of theological belief so much as a mutual recognition of our right to differ in our interpretation of the Bible; and, still more, a similar appreciation of the great practical purposes of the gospel, and of the demands of our Lord that are upon us all to co-operate with him, and with one another, in the redemption of the world from ignorance, sin, and misery. I respect Theodore Parker because he is a man of great intellect and of wonderful acquisitions. I love him because he consecrates so much of his knowledge, his genius, and his eloquence to the cause of suffering, outraged humanity. I honor him because he is no respecter of persons, doth not regard the rich more than the poor. As Jesus, our pattern in all things, did, so does he assail, frequently and fearlessly, 'the high and lifted up' in Church and State, because the giant sin of our time and nation is entrenched behind their example and influence. He is hated, sir, in Boston, as our Lord was in Jerusalem, not because of his heterodoxy in theology, I believe, so much as because of his exposure of the vices of the Scribes and Pharisees, the rulers of the people.

"I have been shocked at some of Mr. Parker's opinions, and sometimes offended at his way of stating truths; but when I see the tremendous blows he strikes at the foundation vices of society, I respect and love him, his opinions on some points notwithstanding. And his opinions, let me add, are less shocking, less derogatory to God, less discouraging to man, than the doctrines which are given us in the Presbyterian Confession of Faith, and the Thirty-Nine Articles and Creeds of the Episcopal Church; doctrines which, if they should be intelligently read to the people, and enforced individually upon their reception, as the condition of continued membership, would empty those churches apace."

At the close of the discussion Mr. May said:—

"When I first heard of you, Brother Lee, it was as a man who had generously espoused the cause of the wretched slaves in our country. I honored you for your fidelity to the right. Since you came to this city, I have heard of your kindnesses to the outcasts, the fugitives from our American despotism; how you have sheltered them under your roof, fed them at your table, and helped them on their way. My soul has been drawn towards you as a good son of God.

"I cared not much to know what your theological opinions might be, to enable me to form an estimate of your Christian character. And now that I have found, in the course of this discussion, what your opinions are; although they appear to me very unscriptural, very irrational, very inconsistent with themselves and self-contradictory, still I will not withdraw my confidence from you as a man and a Christian so long as I see that you abound in love and good works. And here, Brother Lee, after all our disputing, is my right hand of fellowship, if you are willing to receive it."

Mr. Lee said: —

"I take your hand, and fellowship you as a man and a philanthropist; but I have no fellowship with your theology."

Mr. May replied: —

"Nor I with yours! I suppose your theology is just as unlike to mine as mine is to yours."

Then (turning to the audience) he said: —

"I thank you, fellow-citizens, for your long-continued and patient hearing of what we have had to say. I have only to beg you to read what we have said, and consider it well, that you may understand; compare our doctrines and arguments with each other as impartially as you may be able, and both with the teachings of the Bible, and judge for yourselves which of the two is nearer the right."

For several years free meetings, for the consideration of religious and philanthropic subjects, known as "The Market Hall Discussions," were held on Sunday afternoons in Syracuse, and very largely attended by members of all the Protestant denominations as well as the independents and "unbelievers" of the vicinity. All questions were open questions; and, sooner or later, about every thing was debated with the utmost freedom. Mr. May was the only clergyman who attended regularly, and he bore himself so nobly that the extremest free-thinkers were ready to admit that there was one minister who had no priestcraft in him. His presence secured the order and dignity of these remarkable gatherings. Of course, absurd things were sometimes uttered; but nobody, even in the heat of debate, became so forgetful of the claims of courtesy as to indulge in wrangling. It was a school of politeness and of reciprocal regard for honest convictions, as well as an assembly for free discussion.

Agreeably to his long cherished purpose, he tendered his resignation as pastor of the Church of the Messiah upon the completion of his seventieth year, and delivered "A Brief Account of his Ministry" on the 15th of September, 1867. His people were hardly reconciled to their loss, some of them going so far as to say: "We would rather have Mr. May sit in the pulpit, and only smile upon us, than to hear the most eloquent sermons from any other preacher." But they soon found that they had love enough to satisfy two ministers, and Mr. Calthrop's coming was an occasion of pleasure to themselves and to their old pastor.

After he was released from the care of the parish, Mr. May became a missionary of the American Unitarian Association throughout Central New York, and many listened with respect to what they considered serious theological error because of their faith in the practical Christianity of its well-known representative.

CHAPTER XV.

1859, EUROPE.

The Missionary to India. — Treatment of Sailors. — London Dirt and Fogs. — The Houses of Parliament. — Scenes at Rome. — Wayside Chapels and Monasteries. — Vienna. — Heathenish Sculptures. — Royal Stables. — Jews' Quarter at Prague. — Out-door Work of Women on the Banks of the Elbe. — Bridal Procession at Dresden. — Cigar Makers. — Crown Jewels. — Grave of Goddard near Zurich. — Descent of Rhigi. — Publication of Coleridge's "Hymn before Sunrise in Vale of Chamouni." — Mr. May sitting in John Calvin's Chair. — English Friends. — Letter to Theodore Parker. — Third Class Car in Scotland. — Fellow Travellers in Europe. — Miss Hoar's Letter. — Hears of John Brown at Harper's Ferry.

IN the summer of 1858, Mr. May became so worn out with his labors and cares that his friends saw the need of his having a completer rest than could be obtained in America; and it was soon proposed that he should go to Europe. He sailed in December, on the steamer "Arabia," and arrived in London, Jan. 12, 1859.

After a few days he went to Paris, stopping but a short time; and then directly to Naples, by steamer from Marseilles by the coast route, touching at Genoa, Leghorn, and Civita Vecchia. He spent a month in and about Naples, and went to Rome by *vettura* over the Pontine Marshes, arriving in Rome on the last day but one of the Carnival. On the last day he rode in the line of carriages through the Corso, in domino, throwing *confetti*, and enjoying the fun highly. After a considerable stay in Rome, he went to Florence, Venice, Vienna, Prague, Dresden, Leipsic, Nuremberg, Augsburg, and Munich. From Munich he went into Switzerland by the Lake of Constance. He visited all the principal places of resort in Switzerland in the course of three weeks, and went to Baden-Baden, stopping at Strasbourg. He enjoyed Heidelberg, and descended the Rhine to Cologne. From there he went to Amsterdam, Rotterdam, the Hague, and Antwerp, and afterwards to Brussels and Paris. From the latter city he went to England, and remained until the last of October, when he sailed for Boston in the steamer "America."

We have gleaned from his numerous letters such passages as seem to us most interesting and characteristic.

"OCEAN STEAMER, ARABIA,
January 7, 1859.

"A gentleman now sitting opposite to me, the Rev. Mr. Baume, of the Methodist Church, late of Chicago, is bound to Calcutta, with his young wife and beautiful infant boy, there to devote himself to the work of a missionary of the gospel in the city and neighborhood of Lucknow. My heart has been much drawn out towards this soldier of the Cross, and I have been most happy to give him a letter to a friend of mine in that country, which will be of service to him."

"January 8.

"I have had much conversation with four intelligent American captains, respecting the deterioration of the character and the degraded condition of sailors. The slaves of our country hardly make louder demands upon our sympathy, or call more earnestly for deliverance, than do the sailors. I have read to these gentlemen the article in the last 'Atlantic Monthly,' entitled 'The Men of the Sea.' They unitedly pronounced it true, wise, excellent."

"PARIS, January 20.

"Of course, I passed though many streets of London, saw many of the great public edifices, and several lofty columns and statues of distinguished men; but, at first, I could take notice of nothing so much as of the dirtiness of every thing: houses, stores, churches, palaces, statues, all looked begrimed, smutched. Oh! if the dense black smoke of the coal which everybody burns in London would but deposit itself in even, regular layers, one might suppose that the English people were particularly fond of black marble and ebony. But, as it is, the buildings, columns, and statues in London do not look black so much as very, very dirty. Even the statue of their justly admired Queen, in the Royal Exchange, looks as badly as the person of a coal-heaver. I accused several English ladies and gentlemen, whom I chanced to meet, with a great want of loyalty, that they did not keep a maid or man there to wash the face of her Majesty. But, notwithstanding the first impression of London was so disagreeable, I soon found much to admire. Fortunately for me, the weather during my stay in the great city was unusually pleasant for the season. I saw the sun more or less, less rather than more, every day excepting one. But he always looked more like the Queen of Night than the King of Day.

"It was so cold and damp in Westminster Abbey, that I took but a hasty glance at the wonderful structure, and a few of the countless monuments that line its walls. The Houses of Parliament I surveyed more deliberately. My friend, Mr. George Thompson, formerly a member of the House of Commons, accompanied me, and made my visit much more interesting than it would otherwise have been. He pointed out the seats of the distinguished members, and explained to me the etiquette of the two bodies. But nothing in London interested me quite so much as the immense Library in the British Museum."

"ROME, April 26, 1859.

"We have been here at the very time of the year when most is to be seen of the rites and ceremonies of the Roman Catholic Church; and we have improved our opportunities. I have witnessed the most pompous and gorgeous parades. No description could give you an accurate idea of them. On Ash Wednesday I succeeded in getting into the Sistine Chapel; and there, after standing nearly two hours, I saw eighteen or twenty cardinals, splendidly dressed, come in through a file of soldiers, each one of them followed by two attendants bearing his long purple silk train, while he knelt for a minute in the attitude of prayer, and then accompanied him to his seat and adjusted his robes for him, and sat down at his feet. When all the cardinals had thus paraded into their places, his Holiness, the Pope, came in with a large escort of military men and ecclesiastics of various orders. He had six attendants to hold his train, and take off and put on his mitre, and adjust his robes when he knelt in prayer, and when he rose up, and when he sat down. So soon as he got settled on his throne, the officiating priests read some portions, and the choir chanted other portions, of the service for the day. When that was over, the cardinals arose, each one in his order; and having been divested by their servants of one splendid robe, and clothed again with another, they walked to the feet of the Pope, and, humbly kneeling there, his Holiness put upon their heads a sprinkling of ashes, made upon it the sign of a cross, and gave them his blessing. Then they arose, kissed reverently his hand, and went back to their seats. When all the cardinals had gone through this ceremony, countless bishops, monsignori, and other ecclesiastics, and then the ministers and other diplomatic servants of foreign courts (who were Roman Catholics), and after them numerous generals and other military men went up, in like manner, and kneeled to the Pope and received the ashes upon their heads, with the sign of the cross, and the benediction of his Holiness, and then bowed themselves still lower and kissed his foot. This I actually saw more than a hundred men do.

"The following Friday we were summoned, by the trumpet of common report, to be at St. Peter's by twelve o'clock, to witness the Pope at his prayers. We were there, of course. And we found there a large company of soldiers, keeping an open passage-way from the front door of the church to one of the chapels on the right side, where it seemed his Holiness had appointed to pray. At the appointed hour the huge doors of St. Peter's were thrown open, and in came a military guard, and after them a retinue of ecclesiastics, and then the Pope, followed by a long train of cardinals and bishops. Arrived at the cushion placed for his accommodation at the door of the chapel, one of his six special attendants took off his mitre, another received it in charge. Three or four others adjusted his robes, and his Holiness knelt. At the same moment cardinals, bishops, the military guard, and all true Catholics in the church, fell upon their knees, and there was silence for ten minutes. It was an imposing spectacle. But I could not see in it any thing better than an *imposing spectacle*.

"At the expiration of ten minutes the Pope arose from his knees. The attendant who had taken charge of his mitre handed it back to the one by whom it was given to him, and he replaced it upon the head of his Holiness. The other attendants then took up his train, and the Pope, preceded and followed as before, walked reverently to the bronze statue of St. Peter (once a statue of the heathen god, Jupiter), and impressed a kiss upon the great toe of its right foot, which, by the bye, had just been most assiduously wiped by one of the attendants. He then went on to a cushion in front of the High Altar; and his mitre having been taken off as before, and his robes adjusted by those appointed for that pious office, he and all his retinue knelt again; and again there was a silence for the space of ten or fifteen minutes. At the conclusion of this ceremony he arose, his mitre was put upon his head, his train was taken up by the officials of his person, and he went back to his palace as he had come from it. Comment is unnecessary. Let me only say, the scene reminded me of those in our Saviour's day who loved to pray at the corner of the street and market-places, to be seen of men.

"The following Friday I witnessed a ceremony of a different sort. It was enacted in one of the churches in the centre of the city. His Holiness came thither in great pomp, in a splendid coach drawn by six black horses, with a postilion, dressed in red satin, on one of the leaders, and the others driven by a coachman in similar costume, and three footmen, likewise dressed, riding behind. The Pope's carriage was followed by ten or twelve cardinals, whose equipage and liveried servants were almost as splendid; and they by other high officials in Church and State, and generals of the French and Italian armies; the whole escorted by the Pope's Guard of Nobles, and a large body of cavalry, elegantly mounted. Arrived at the church, his Holiness was taken in a gorgeous chair upon a platform covered with the richest velvet, upon the shoulders of twelve men, elegantly dressed, under a silken canopy borne by eight other gentlemen, and on either side one bearing on a long handle an immense fan of white feathers. Thus supported, and followed by his cardinals and bishops on foot, the Pope was carried up and down the aisles of the church, and then placed upon a throne, near the High Altar. Here he attended Mass. After that, fifteen or twenty girls, eighteen or twenty years of age, dressed alike in virgin white, were conducted to his feet. There, upon their knees, they received his benediction, and each a present of money, called a dowry, or marriage portion. The Pope was then taken upon the shoulders of men, in the same manner as before, carried up and down the church again; and so being conducted to his carriage, he returned to his palace, with the same escort and retinue with which he had come to the church. Of course, all that I have attempted to describe was a splendid pageant; but I could not see any thing Christian in it.

"The parade on Palm Sunday in St. Peter's Church was much more showy; but I have no time now to describe it.

"On Holy Thursday, the day before Good Friday, were played what I must be allowed to call the Farce of Humility and the Farce of Hospitality: the former in the Chapel of St. Peter's, on the right of the High Altar; and the latter in the hall over the vestibule of the church. All possible accommodations in the way of seats had been prepared, so as to enable as many as possible to see what great humility the Pope and cardinals could practise.

"Arranged upon a high bench, so as to be very conspicuous, were thirteen men, selected for the purpose, on what principle I know not. They were all dressed alike, in long white woollen gowns, and whiter capes and whiter kid boots. They all looked more like women than men. In due time, the Pope, in a simple dress, accompanied by some of his cardinals and bishops, without parade, came in through the side aisle. A short service was read; after which a white apron was tied around his Holiness, and he proceeded to wash the feet of the men who were there, I suppose, representing the Apostles. But it was only a shallow ceremony. The feet of the men were already very clean, so they did not need washing. Nevertheless, I will tell you how it was done. A priest had gone before, and taken off the shoe, or rather boot, on the right foot of each of the *quasi* Apostles, and slipped it down to the heel, so that it would be readily shuffled off; then came a cardinal or bishop, with a pile of small napkins; next the Pope, dressed more simply than I had ever seen him, and with his white apron on; just behind and below him, another bishop or priest holding a golden basin; and next, a priest with a large golden pitcher. This last poured a little water upon the foot that was extended to be washed, while the one with the basin held it to catch the drops. Immediately the Pope clapped a napkin, received from his attendant, upon the slightly wet foot, wiped it quickly, impressed a kiss upon it, gave to its owner a bouquet and a golden medal or coin, and then passed to the next, and so on until all had received the ablution, and, I should have added, each kissed the hand that had wiped the foot.

"This farce I saw with my own eyes, until seven of the thirteen had been so washed. And then I joined most of those around me, who hastened from that, to get places where they might also see the other farce, *the feeding of the poor.* But I missed my way, or was less nimble than others, so that I did not get within sight of the table. It was spread, as I have stated, in the hall, over the vestibule of St. Peter's. It was laden with the good things for the palate, both solid and liquid. And, as I was told by many who saw the farce, the same men whose feet had been washed were conducted thither, seated at the table, and *served* by the Pope and cardinals. But, as I did not see it, I will not attempt a description.

. . . .

"Indeed, after all I have seen at St. Peter's, and of the condition of Rome, I have come to feel that St. Peter's is nothing more than *a splendid theatre*, and the Pope, cardinals, bishops, and priests are only the *dramatis personæ;* and that *religious plays* are acted by them for the amusement of many, and, perhaps, the edification of some of the people."

"INCISA, May 1, 1859.

"All along these roads one is often reminded that he is in a Roman Catholic country, by the little chapels, and pictures and images and crosses, that recur at least once in every mile. But the frequency of these things lessens the effect they are intended to produce. The people seemed to pay them no more respect than they pay the guide-boards or mile-stones.

"Then, frequently upon the highest hills, steep, barren, solitary, almost inaccessible, are to be seen the monasteries in which the several orders of monks have secluded themselves, there to lead lives utterly useless to their fellow-men, and therefore unacceptable to God, who has commanded us to evince our love of him, whom we cannot directly benefit, by doing what we may to promote the happiness and highest welfare of our brethren of the human family."

"PRAGUE, May 26, 1859.

"When I was a little boy, I used to listen with great admiration to my sister's playing of "The Battle of Prague," then a very famous and favorite piece of music; and here I am at the place which was the scene of the terrible conflict described in that music. When I was old enough to study the elements of astronomy, I learnt the name of Tycho Brahe, and committed to memory some account of his contributions to that noble science; and here I am in sight of the observatory where he studied the heavens. When I opened the volumes of ecclesiastical history, I was soon brought to know something of John Huss, the great Protestant Reformer; and here I am close by the convent where he first came to the discovery of other and higher truths than the Church was pleased to communicate to the people, and which he converted into a school of freer and better theological doctrine. I shall soon go out to explore the city, and visit the spots so sacred. But before I go, let me tell you a little about Vienna.

. . . .

"We went to one of the public gardens of Vienna, in the centre of which there is a building like the Temple of Theseus at Athens, erected to hold an immense piece of statuary by Canova, "Theseus killing a Centaur." I have no doubt it is an admirable piece of work; but it is a disgusting subject, as are too many of the sculptures that I saw in the cities of Italy, representations of deeds of violence or revenge. It may be well enough to save such sculptures that may be found among ancient ruins; but for modern Christian artists to spend their time upon the barbarous fables of heathen mythology seems to me a sad misuse of their talents.

"We went to see the Royal stables. They are three stories high, built around a rectangular court, four hundred feet long and one hundred and fifty wide, and look very much like a palace. The lower story, on three sides, is devoted to horses; on the fourth side to a riding-school. There were stalls for six hundred horses. More than five hundred of these were occupied. The tenants of the others, we were told, had been taken to the war. Never before had I seen so many beautiful horses. They were of every choice variety that is known, and they looked as much cared for as if they were members of the Emperor's household. Some young friends of mine, that I could name, would have been especially delighted, and might have been led to wish that they had been born sons of an emperor. No such wish was awakened in my bosom. I came away saying with more emphasis than ever: 'What a pity, what a wrong, that so much wealth and power should be allowed to accumulate, and to be retained by inheritance in the hands of one person. No one man was ever, or will ever be, wise and good enough to use so much wealth and power judiciously, beneficially to others or happily for himself.'"

"DRESDEN, May 28, 1859.

"At Prague we crossed the river in a ferry-boat, several hundred feet below the bridge, and landed in the Jews' quarter of the city. Descendants of Abraham have lived on that spot, it is said, longer than in any other part of Europe.

"We went first to their old burial-ground. It was literally full of grave-stones and monuments, many of them several hundred years old. One is said to date from A.D. 606. We were conducted through the very narrow, winding path, to the graves of Rabbi Abignor Karo and Rabbi Lowi, said to have been very learned and pious men: one, the intimate friend of Tycho Brahe; the other, the founder of two hospitals. So Miss E. H. and I each put a stone upon their monuments, that being with the Jews an expression of respect for the dead, and came away.

. . . .

"Our sail down the Elbe was very agreeable. The country through which we passed, Saxon Switzerland, was all that its name led us to expect. Sometimes the mountains overhung the river; at other times they were sufficiently far from it to give a margin of highly cultivated land. In the fields there were more women than men at work; and even at the coal-yards, along the river, we saw them, in great numbers, doing their share of lifting and shovelling. I cannot be reconciled to this use of women. It is too severe for their physical constitutions, and must tend, it seems to me, to depress their spiritual nature, and to deaden their moral and domestic sensibilities."

"DRESDEN, June 2, 1859.

"We found the city given up to preparations for the reception of Prince George, a son of the Elector of Saxony, with his bride, Maria Anna of Portugal. I perched myself upon the seventh round of a ladder that was placed against the front of our hotel, and from my elevated but uncomfortable seat saw the whole. The procession must have been a mile in length, and was partly military, partly civic. Companies of infantry and cavalry preceded and followed the carriages containing the bridal party. And then came, with bands of music at proper intervals, companies of all the different tradesmen and mechanics, of which the most conspicuous (I am sorry to say it) were cigar-makers, some of whom were in a long, covered wagon, busily engaged in making the noisome, noxious things, much to the amusement of all beholders, excepting the few who, like myself, utterly disapprove of the use of tobacco. But I shall not be able to stay long enough in Europe to persuade the people, certainly not the Germans, to abandon the use of this nasty weed.

"One forenoon we spent two hours in what is called the Green Vault. It is the depository of the jewels and precious keepsakes of the Court of Saxony. They occupy eight rooms, and are said to constitute the most valuable collection of the kind in Europe. I cannot describe them. Every article, useful and ornamental, to be worn upon the persons of men or women, to be set upon the tables or the toilettes of kings and queens, or to gratify their love of the beautiful or curious, was there displayed, in bronze, in ivory, silver, gold, crystals, emeralds, jaspers, pearls, onyxes, diamonds, and every other precious and half precious stone. I came away without the slightest wish to be myself the possessor of so much useless treasure, but only wishing that it could be exhumed from that tomb, and converted to some beneficent purpose.

"HORGEN, June 15, 1859.

"Ever since the year 1820, the name of Zurich has sent a thrill through my heart. In that year, a particular friend of my youth lost his life in this lake. He was a young man of an excellent spirit, full of hope and high aspiration; but he was afflicted with an infirmity of sight, that obliged him, at the age of nineteen, to relinquish his plan of study, and devote himself to the pursuit of health. He came to Europe, hoping that he should by travel enrich his mind at the same time that he was invigorating his body. He came to Zurich, and was sailing upon this beautiful lake, when a squall suddenly struck and overset the boat. He was unable to swim, and was drowned.

"The first thing I did after my arrival at Zurich, day before yesterday, was to go to the cemetery, and search for the grave of my friend; but without success. Yesterday morning, I found an intelligent *valet-de-place*. He took me to the Rath Haus, or City Hall, where, in one of the offices, we found a gentleman who well remembered the sad event. From him I learnt that the disaster happened about five miles above, near the village of Kusnacht, and that my friend's body was deposited there.

"Yesterday afternoon, we took a carriage and rode out to the place. There, on the wall of the village church, we found a black marble monument, upon which was the following inscription in gilt letters, still bright, though it is thirty-nine years since they were made: —

"'Here rests F. W. Goddard, from Boston, in America, a youth of nineteen years, who, far from his home, in a storm on Lake Zurich, struggling with the waves, found his death. He died at Goldbach, near Kusnacht, on the 22d of August, 1820.'

"There was a sad pleasure in standing upon the spot where the person of my early friend disappeared from this world, and seeing that the good people of the place had done all they could do to evince their pity for the young stranger, and their sympathy for his distant relatives. They buried him in a conspicuous place, next to the one in which, two or three years afterwards, they deposited the remains of their beloved and excellent pastor, if the epitaph upon his monument tells truly the regard in which he was held.

The poet Wordsworth was in Zurich at the time of the catastrophe. He had learned somewhat of the character of my young friend, as well as the circumstances of his untimely death; and you may find, in the collection of Wordsworth's Poems, some appropriate and touching 'Lines upon a young American, Mr. F. W. Goddard, who was drowned in the Lake of Zurich.'"

"HOTEL BYRON, LAKE OF GENEVA,
June 24, 1859.

"At nine o'clock we left the Mountain House (Rhigi), and commenced our descent on the opposite side. As I had before determined, I would not venture upon a horse's back down the many very steep places that I was told were on the way. I had not strength enough to walk to the bottom so soon as our party wished to get there. Nothing else could do, therefore, but take a '*chaise à porteur*,'—a stout arm-chair with a foot-board, swung between two long poles, and carried by two men. It proved to be an easy, and, on the whole, an agreeable mode of conveyance over such a road. One has to reconcile himself to the apparent misuse of his fellow-men, in thus subjecting them to the work of horses. But I found men there eager for the job. They could earn more money in that way, in three hours, than they could in two days at farming; and, as one of them said to one of my lady companions, who expressed her unwillingness to impose on them such hard work, 'Oh! God gives us the strength to do it, and gives you the money to pay for it.' So I made myself easy, and more easy by occasionally getting out of my chair and walking a half mile."

"CHAMOUNI, June 28.

"In December, 1820, I went to Springfield, Mass., to visit my friend, Rev. W. B. O. Peabody, and preach my first sermon from his pulpit. He was a true poet himself, and an ardent lover of the good poetry of others. During my stay with him, he repeated to me many choice pieces. One in particular is now brought most effectually to my remembrance. It was Coleridge's 'Hymn to Mont Blanc, written at Chamouni, an hour before sunrise.' I was so much delighted with it that I copied it, and committed it to memory. It had not then been published in our country. Mr. Peabody had recently received it, in manuscript, from a friend in England. It was too good to be kept for the gratification of the few.

So I sent a copy of it to Rev. H. Ware, Jr., the editor of the 'Christian Disciple,' Boston, and it was published in that excellent periodical in the course of the year 1821."

"GENEVA, June 29, 1859.

"This forenoon I went to the large old cathedral church where John Calvin preached for more than twenty years. It was despoiled of every vestige of the Roman Catholic worship, for which it was built. But it is ill adapted to the Protestant service, which it is intended the people should hear and understand. The voice of the preacher reverberated so from the lofty arches of the Gothic building, nave, aisles, transept, and apse, that I could not perceive the articulation of half the words the reverend gentleman uttered. His manner was earnest, impressive, eloquent, but his words I could not hear; and, I am ashamed to say (such is my ignorance of the French language, in which he spoke) I should not have understood half if I had heard all.

"At the conclusion of the service, I went to the foot of the pulpit stairs, and waited until the minister descended. I found he understood no more of my language than I did of his. But I communicated to him my wish to know if that was indeed the church and the pulpit in which John Calvin used to preach. He assured me they were the same; "and there," said he, "is the chair in which he sat." So I ascended the pulpit stairs, and sat down awhile in the very chair of the great Reformer.

"As I was coming out of the church, an agreeable-looking young gentleman accosted me in correct but imperfectly pronounced English. I soon learned that he was a Norwegian, taking Switzerland on his way to one of the universities in Germany, whither he is going to study theology. We were not long in getting acquainted sufficiently to walk together to the house in which Calvin dwelt nearly all the while that he lived in Geneva. It is now occupied by the Sisters of Charity.

"On my return to our hotel, I met, upon the bridge that connects the old part of the city with the new, a blind old man, with a bundle of papers, which he was loudly crying for sale. I bought one, and found it, as I expected, an extra filled with items of news from the seat of the war, and from other parts of Italy; items that will reach you, no doubt, before this letter can. Truly, the last battle has been a fearful one; almost without a parallel in the history of modern warfare."

During the three months which he spent in Great Britain, Mr. May lectured upon slavery, by request, to large audiences in several of the chief cities of the kingdom, and had meetings for conversation with the prominent Abolitionists, especially in London, Glasgow, and Dublin. He enjoyed meeting Miss Carpenter, Miss Estlin, Miss Cobbe, Richard D. Webb, Lord Morpeth, Mr. Martineau, and many other persons in whom he had long been interested. We have heard that Miss Cobbe said that if any one could reconvert her to Christianity it would be a person of Mr. May's spirit, and his attractive way of presenting the claims of Jesus; and that she acknowledged his success in satisfying her, for the first time, of the justice and importance of the movement in behalf of the rights of women. He must have written many letters from Great Britain, but only two have come into our possession. The first is addressed to Theodore Parker.

LONDON, Aug. 5, 1859.

MY DEAR FRIEND, — I reached this city yesterday afternoon, and to-day have learnt your place of residence.

You left Paris a few days before I arrived there, and were

probably going up the Rhine about the same time that I was coming down; thus showing that you have brought your contrary, perverse spirit all across the Atlantic with you. Oh, my dear friend, when will you learn that you ought to go just the same way that others do; and that it is much easier to swim with the current than against it? Well, well, if my example has had no effect, it will be useless for me to spend words upon you.

But I did not "take my pen in hand" to reproach you for wrongheadedness, but to make an earnest inquiry about your health. Do tell me exactly how you are, if you feel a consciousness of returning soundness. I would give much to set eyes on you, and judge for myself; though your testimony, even then, would be of more value than my own judgment. I saw Charles Sumner in Rome. He looked well, but was much more disconcerted by coming up two or three flights of stairs than a strong man would have been. However, I pressed my inquiries about his health, and received very satisfactory replies. He told me of the changes that had taken place in his physical condition, and assured me he felt confident that the effects of the injury he received were well-nigh obliterated. I pray that it may be so.

You have heard, no doubt, that his Alma Mater has at length put forth her tender hand, and applied her LL.D lotion to his wounds. This, of course, will complete the cure, and efface even the scar.

And now, dear Parker, do let me know just how you are; what remedies you are trying, and with what effect. I hope you will not allow yourself to attempt much, bodily or mentally. I hope you are in a quiet place, a sweet retirement. Rapid journeyings and daily sight-seeing I find are not very beneficial to a jaded, nervous system. I have erred somewhat in that direction, and mean to be much more moderate.

My tour has been most interesting and instructive to me. Would I had taken one like it thirty years ago! But what I have learnt may be of some use to others as well as myself even now, before I quit the body; and afterwards — surely, the knowledge we acquire in this life will not be all lost.

Give my best regards to your wife and Miss Stevenson, and be assured of the love of,

Yours truly, SAMUEL J. MAY.

August 8.

William and Ellen Crafts speak of you with the warmest affection, and desire me to send their love to you and Mrs. Parker. I took tea with them last evening. They are living (with their three beautiful little boys) very neatly and prettily. I am ashamed to add, they have no wish to go back to our country.

August 9.

I have just read with delight your beautiful letter of June 25, in the "Liberator" of July 22, which George Thompson put into my hand last night. But is it possible the date given in the "Liberator" is correct, the 25th of June? I left Hotel Byron on the morning of that day, and was in the village of Montreux for an hour, the afternoon before. Mrs. Edward and Miss Elizabeth Hoar (of Concord) and I went over from Hotel Byron to Montreux to see Mr. and Mrs. Hawthorne, who, we were told, were there. We then visited together the Castle and Dungeon of Chillon. Can it be that I was so near you then, and did not know it? I will not believe it on the authority of a newspaper.

GLASGOW, Aug. 23.

The train did not come up until fifteen minutes after I reached the station. So I took out my fac-simile of the Cotter's Saturday Night; and in full view of the beautiful hills and valleys of the Ayrshire, upon which the eye of Burns had so often dwelt with delight, I read this most exquisite poem with a deeper enjoyment of its beauties than ever before.

In order that I might see more of the Scotch people, and at the same time save two dollars, I took a seat in a third-class car. It was filled with well-behaved persons of various social positions. Two young country squires rode with us fifteen or twenty miles, having their dogs, and their bags, full of grouse, under their seats. Not far off sat a well-dressed, pretty lassie, of seventeen, with a large frame, containing, I suppose, a picture she had just finished at some boarding-school. But, alas ! right before me sat two Highlanders, in full costume, each with a bagpipe, upon which they played most of the time with stentorian lungs, making music about as agreeable as that of a large locust in a hot summer's day, accompanied by a stout boy blowing a squash-vine trumpet.

. . . .

I have been exceedingly fortunate in the companions that I have had. [In his tour through Europe.] They have been persons of my own land and other nations, but from every one I have received kindnesses that have made me their debtor for ever. I wish particularly to report that I have uniformly found the English people with whom I have travelled courteous, obliging, and sociable. In several instances they have made the first advance, have proffered me some favor, and have taken pains to oblige me.

The impression which Mr. May himself made upon his fellow-travellers may be learned from a letter written, in response to our inquiries, by a lady whose society abroad gave him very great pleasure: —

CONCORD, MASS., Dec. 17, 1871.

I do not know that I can tell you any thing about him which will add to your store of illustrations of those beautiful traits which made him so beloved and honored. His histories of a life so full and so beneficent were endlessly entertaining to us all, as we passed over long distances together in railway or post carriage. They came without egotism, quite impersonally, as illustrations from experience of some general remark or opinion of others or his own. And through all shone the same single-hearted righteousness, love of God and man, wisdom and courage born of love, which "goeth and passeth through all things by reason of her pureness." He made friends with children and mothers as we travelled, in Italy, in Germany, and France, where they had no word of language in common. But they felt and loved the tenderness and good-will which could not refrain from blessing the little children.

The variety and extent of his activity and his sympathy impressed us all very much. His stories of his father and mother, their adopted children, his father's death-bed, when he said: "'And now you must let the old man go.' And I put my arms round his neck, and said, 'Father, you shall!'" It was all a part of the same poem. Every thing seemed touched with the same sweetness; and withal he had great spirit and vivacity, and sense of humor and fun, when it was due, and little flashes of dramatic power in relating exciting or amusing conversations. And in all these four months, when we were together almost from morning to night, in the chances and fatigues of travelling, I never saw a shadow of selfishness on his face; and we shaped our plans of travel with the first consideration that "we should not lose Mr. May."

And we *cannot* lose Mr. May. The remembrance of him, the presence of such a life, is a joy for ever, though great is the sorrow that we can see his face here no more. "Where'er he be, God grant us there to meet." I feel almost as if I were sending my love to him by you, in writing this very imperfect acknowledgment of the honor done me in speaking of me as one of Mr. May's friends.

With much regard, yours truly,

ELIZABETH HOAR.

On arriving at Halifax, Nov. 3, 1859, Mr. May heard of Captain John Brown's attack upon Harper's Ferry, and wrote in his Diary: —

"I have read the accounts of the attempt of Captain Brown to get up an insurrection at Harper's Ferry. This, I apprehend, is but the beginning of sorrows; the pattering of the rain before a hurricane."

When Mr. May reached Syracuse, a public reception was given to him. An address of welcome was delivered, and speeches were made by the gratified pastor and Rev. Joseph Angier, who had taken good care of his flock during his absence.

CHAPTER XVI.

ANTISLAVERY.

THE UNDERGROUND RAILROAD. — VISITS CANADA IN BEHALF OF THE FUGITIVE SLAVES. — THE JERRY RESCUE. — TEST OF HIS NON-RESISTANCE PRINCIPLES. — CORRESPONDENCE ABOUT HOLDING AN ANTISLAVERY CONVENTION. — THREATENED WITH VIOLENCE. — HIS FIRMNESS. — HE IS MOBBED, AND BURNED IN EFFIGY.

AFTER his removal to Syracuse, Mr. May continued to be very active and prominent in promoting the antislavery reform. He soon became known far and wide as a fearless and uncompromising Abolitionist. He lectured in many places; and antislavery conventions were often held in Syracuse, which, on account of its central position, is, like Worcester, Mass., sometimes called "The City of Conventions." Whenever the friends of freedom assembled in his vicinity, Mr. May's hospitality was limited only by the size of his house and the length of his table.

As early as 1834, while living at Brooklyn, Conn., he had fugitive slaves consigned to his care, and he forwarded them to the next station on "The Underground Railroad." At Syracuse, a great deal of human freight passed through his hands upon the invisible route. Hundreds of men, women, and children, fleeing from bondage, and bound for Canada, came to him for

10

protection and help, and they never came in vain. In his "Recollections of the Antislavery Conflict" he gives an account of the appearance and adventures of some of these victims of American despotism. The mysterious trains used to arrive at Mr. May's house about eleven o'clock at night, and he was sometimes kept busy until two o'clock in the morning conducting the passengers to places where they could stay in safety until the road to Canada should be reported free from all obstructions. Sometimes, in defiance of the Fugitive Slave Law, he would announce from his pulpit the presence of fugitives in the city, and take a collection in their behalf. He visited Canada, and made an extended tour among the colored settlements, to satisfy himself as to their prospects there.

In October, 1850, many of the best citizens of Syracuse publicly declared that the Fugitive Slave Law should not be enforced in that place, and a vigilance committee was appointed. A large number of persons made an agreement to stand by each other in resisting the law. A rendezvous was fixed upon; and it was agreed that any member of the association who might hear of a person in danger should toll the bell of an adjoining meeting-house in a particular manner, and that, on hearing that signal, all the rest should hasten to the spot.

The determination of many of the best citizens of Onondaga County was well known throughout the country; and in June, 1851, Mr. Webster, as a representative of the government, made a speech in Syracuse which seemed designed to intimidate the opponents of the infamous law. He called them traitors, and declared that the law should be enforced in that place, in the midst of the next antislavery convention, if there should then be any occasion to enforce it.

On the first day of October, 1851, just as Mr. May was about to rise from dinner, he heard the signal bell, and hurried to the appointed place, a mile from his house. On the way, he learned that Jerry McHenry had been arrested as a fugitive slave, and taken to the office of the commissioner. Proceeding to the court-room, Mr. May found the prisoner manacled, and not allowed to state his own case, nor to refute the testimony of his adversary. Not being very closely guarded, Jerry soon slipped out of the room, and ran for his liberty. He got off nearly half a mile before he was retaken, and then surrendered only after a furious fight in which he was seriously injured. He was thrown into a wagon, two policemen sat upon him, and so they rode, through the central streets of the city, back to the commissioner's office.

The people were very much excited, and told Mr. May that, if he would speak the word, they would have Jerry out. But he advised them to wait until it should become dark. The chief of police asked Mr. May to talk with Jerry, who needed to be soothed. In the course of this interview, Mr. May managed to make Jerry understand that he had friends who did not mean that he should be taken back to slavery. Mr. May then went to the office of the late Dr. Hiram Hoyt, where he found twenty or thirty picked men, including Gerrit Smith, who happened to be in town attending a Liberty Party Convention. The plan of a rescue was discussed, and all the arrangements for it were made with skill and despatch. Strict injunctions were given not to injure the policemen intentionally, and Mr. May said, "If any one is to be hurt in this fray, I hope it may be one of our own party."

About eight o'clock in the evening, the police office was in the possession of the opponents of the law, and the officers were overpowered. Jerry was taken to a place of refuge, where his shackles were cut off, and, after several days' concealment, he was sent to Canada, in spite of the utmost vigilance on the part of the administration.

Then began a series of persecutions. Eighteen persons were indicted, and taken to Auburn. They went accompanied by nearly a hundred of their fellow-citizens, including ladies. At Auburn, Hon. W. H. Seward put his name first upon the bond required from their sureties, and invited "the rescuers of Jerry" and their friends to accept the hospitality of his house. A mass convention of citizens of Onondaga County met, and justified the rescue. Some of the public journals denounced Mr. May as the most responsible person in this act of "treason." Mr. May, Gerrit Smith, and Charles A. Wheaton published an acknowledgment that they had assisted all they could in the rescue of Jerry; that they were ready for trial; that they would give the Court no trouble as to the fact, and should rest their defence upon the unconstitutionality and extreme wickedness of the Fugitive Slave Law. As it was not found expedient to punish the chief persons concerned in the rescue, and it was not creditable to the government to continue its prosecutions of obscure offenders while distinguished ones, who avowed their responsibility, were unmolested; and it was impossible to empanel a jury which would not contain persons who had formed an opinion against the law, the "Jerry Rescue Causes" were finally abandoned. For several years afterwards, the anniversary of the rescue of Jerry was duly celebrated at Syracuse with great enthusiasm.[1]

Just after the election of President Lincoln, the fierce threats of disunion made by the slaveholders caused the leading politicians of the free States to become very desirous that no imprudent utterances concerning slavery should be made at the North, at least until the new

[1] When Mr. May was accused of inconsistency because, although an avowed friend of peace, he counselled determined opposition to the Fugitive Slave Law, he replied: "I only insisted that all good men and true ought to withstand the execution of that infamous law, in the way and by the means that they each one of them conscientiously believed to be right. I declared I had no confidence in the use of deadly weapons; that I would not carry even my cane to the rescue of one who should be seized under the law. I would hold a man who was attempting to execute it, if I could; overpower him, if I had strength so to do; but not intentionally harm a hair of his head. Nevertheless, I did solemnly enjoin it upon those who believed it right, in the sight of God, for them to fight for their own liberty, or for the liberty of a white brother; I did enjoin it upon them, if it should seem necessary, to fight for the rescue of any black man from the horrors of a return into slavery."

administration should be in full possession of the power to which it would soon be entitled. The Abolitionists, however, were equally desirous that the Northern people should not be intimidated by threats, nor misled by apprehensions of material losses. Therefore they proposed to continue the holding of their conventions, and to urge the people not to recede an inch on account of Southern menaces. But their meetings were violently assailed in Boston and other cities. The Mayor of Syracuse earnestly requested Mr. May to prevent the holding of a meeting in that city, lest it should provoke a riot, although he acknowledged their right to assemble, and promised to protect them. Twenty of the most influential gentlemen of Syracuse, nearly half of whom were his parishioners, addressed a letter to Mr. May, informing him that they were credibly informed that an organized and forcible effort to prevent the holding of the Abolition Convention would be made. These gentlemen declared that it would be their duty, as good citizens, to protect the Convention; but they urged Mr. May to exert his influence to prevent its assembling, because, in the excited condition of the public mind, it could only be productive of evil.

Probably this was one of the severest tests to which Mr. May's loyalty to his own convictions was ever subjected. He had the most affectionate regard for some of these gentlemen, and the greatest confidence in their wisdom and fidelity in ordinary matters; but he also felt that liberty of speech was in peril, and he felt bound to answer them with the same respectful firmness that he had shown in his reply to the Mayor: —

SYRACUSE, January 28, 1861.
1.45 P.M.

GENTLEMEN, — Your communication requesting me to exert my influence to prevent the assembling of the Anti-Slavery Convention, called to meet on the 29th and 30th, came to hand at a quarter to twelve.

The Committee of Arrangements have not yet come to the city; and I have no authority to postpone the Convention on their behalf. They may not arrive until this evening or to-morrow morning. Meanwhile, there is not time for me to see enough of the friends of the antislavery cause, residing in Syracuse, to sustain me in assuming the responsibility of preventing the meeting for the reasons you assign. In common with my associates, I am very sincere in believing that the principles we inculcate, and the measures we advise, are the only ones that can extirpate from our country that evil which now overshadows us, and threatens our ruin as a nation. We have much to say to the people, much that we deem it most important that they should hear and ponder, lest they bow themselves to another compromise with the slaveholding oligarchy, which for the last twenty-five years has ruled our Republic, and which nothing would satisfy but the entire subjugation of our liberties to their "peculiar institution."

We perceive that the "strong" men of the Republican party are trembling, and concession and compromise are coming to be their only hope. We deprecate their fears, their want of confidence in moral principle and God. We do not consider the reunion of our divided States of so much consequence as we do a steadfast adherence to the true and the right. We, therefore, feel deeply urged to cry aloud, and warn the people of the snare into which politicians and statesmen would lead them. We should at least *offer* to speak, whether the people will hear or whether they will forbear.

If, gentlemen, you had assured me that our proposed

meeting will be violently assaulted; that those who may assemble peacefully to listen to us will not be allowed to hear us; that they will be dispersed with insult, if not with personal injury; and that you, gentlemen of influence as you are, shall stand aloof and let the violent have their way: then I should have felt it to be incumbent on me to advertise the friends of liberty and humanity that it would not be worth their while to convene, as it would be only to be dispersed.

But, gentlemen, as you generously "affirm" in the letter before me "that your duties as citizens would require you to aid in extending protection to our Convention, in case it shall be convened, in the exercise of all the rights which all deliberative bodies may claim;" and as the Mayor of our city has assured me that "he shall fearlessly use every means at his command to secure order, and to prevent any interference with our proceedings," I feel that I should not be justified in assuming the responsibility of postponing the Convention. For, gentlemen, if you will do what you acknowledge to be your duty, and if the Mayor will fulfil his generous promise, I am confident the rioters will be overawed, the liberty of speech will be vindicated, and the city rescued from a deep disgrace.

Yours, gentlemen, in great haste, but

Very respectfully,

SAMUEL J. MAY.

P. S. POLICE OFFICE, 4½ P.M. — Since the above was written, the Committee of Arrangements have arrived; and without knowing what I have written above, they, each of them, after hearing your communication and the Mayor's letter, determined that it was our duty to go on with the Convention; to present ourselves at the time and place appointed, and offer to the people the advice we have to give in this emergency of our country. S. J. M.

Before the hour appointed for the meeting of the Convention, rioters took possession of the hall which Mr. May had hired for the occasion; fists were thrust into his face, and rough men swore that they would knock him down and put him out of the hall if he said another word. As the Convention was not protected either by the officers of the law or by good citizens, some of its members retired to a private house, and adopted a series of resolutions. Soon afterwards the victorious mob celebrated their triumph by an evening procession led by a band of music. Their transparent banners bore these inscriptions: "Freedom of Speech, but not Treason;" "The Rights of the South must be protected;" "Abolitionism no longer in Syracuse;" "The Jerry Rescuers played out." An effigy bearing Mr. May's name was prominent in the procession. After it had been carried through some of the principal streets, it was burned in Hanover Square, the centre of the business part of the city.

It was not long before the firing upon Fort Sumter put an end to such shameful proceedings in the free States.

CHAPTER XVII.

SANITARY COMMISSION, AND SOLDIERS' AND FREEDMEN'S RELIEF.

ACTIVE IN SENDING SUPPLIES TO THE ARMY. — VISITS THE CAMP, AND MINISTERS TO THE WOUNDED AFTER THE BATTLE OF YORKTOWN, VA. — HIS INDIGNATION ON ACCOUNT OF SWINDLING PENSION AGENTS. — "NOTHING BUT SLAVERY SO BAD AS WAR." — TEACHERS FOR THE FREEDMEN.

THE years of the war brought Mr. May deep anxiety and redoubled activities. His soul was deeply stirred by the awful thought of a nation plunging into the bloodshed and waste of war, and his heart was touched with a constant sympathy for the various classes of sufferers. As a long-time advocate of peace, he was brought to face a problem difficult to solve, when the action of the South forced upon the nation a choice between war and the dismemberment of the Republic. That he solved it to his own perfect satisfaction we can hardly assert. He confesses at one time that "the conduct of the rebels and the impending fate of our country has shaken my confidence in the *extreme* principles of the non-resistants." But he never lost his faith or relinquished his advocacy of peace principles as an ideal, nor ceased to be acutely sensitive to the wickedness and horror which follow in the train of warfare. Neither did he gain much confidence that, as a measure of self-protection, it was really much to be relied on. The preparations for it filled him with sadness; although he said often, to those who thought war right, that they were called on not to shrink from upholding their principles in the terrible crisis our country had arrived at. Attending a war-meeting in the early days of the struggle, he records: "I cannot find it in my heart to urge men to enlist." His great concern was the spirit and views of those influential in its direction; and it is true that these often seemed to him so imperfect, influenced so much by a temporizing disposition, and long so wanting in just apprehension of the true cause of the war and a just interest in directing it to the issue of universal emancipation and enfranchisement, that he was doubtful of its result, and depressed with painful anticipations, not only of military defeat, but still more of political infidelity and its consequences.

But his abhorrence of war, and doubt of the spirit and aims with which ours seemed for a time to be conducted, did not impair the readiness with which he devoted himself to mitigating its evils. We can go little into details of his philanthropic activity; but it is perhaps true that he became at once the centre of the efforts made in his own vicinity on behalf of the soldiers, and afterwards of the freedmen. Before the formation of the Sanitary Commission, he aided and superintended the collection of clothing and other necessaries for the soldiers, packing and despatching boxes with his own hands; and when the Commission was established, earnestly promoted its success, co-operating constantly with its leaders and officers. To ascertain the condition and wants of the soldiers of Onondaga County, he made, at the request of the citizens of Syracuse, one or two journeys to the scene of operations of the Potomac army, carrying supplies and ministering to the moral and spiritual wants of the well and the invalid. On one occasion he arrived at White House when a great number of wounded were coming in from the recent battle at Yorktown. He stopped at once, and devoted several days to them, assisting to dress their wounds, comforting them by cheerful sympathy, and taking messages to be forwarded to their friends. "The most touching thing," he says, "was the patience and fortitude I everywhere witnessed. I did not hear a murmur or complaint all that terrible time."[1] At home he gave much time to the welfare of the soldiers' families, obtaining help for them, and securing to them the pensions which became their due. He co-operated in an attempt to form an association for the protection of this unfortunate and exposed class; but this was apparently merged in the Sanitary Commission. For the wretches who availed themselves of the inexperience of the victims of the war to defraud them, he kept a constant look-out. A friend, who rode with him for an afternoon on errands of this sort, describes finding one poor woman who had already made

[1] On arriving home, he makes this record in his Diary: "Never so glad to enter my own door, but I would go off again to-morrow if I could contribute to the comfort of the poor soldiers."

partial arrangements for obtaining her pension through a notorious swindler. She had not, however, surrendered her papers; and Mr. May enjoined it on her not to do so. "But he will demand them," she replied, anxiously. "Tell him when he comes that Samuel J. May told you *not* to give them to him!" was his reply.

All the incidents of the war he followed with keen interest, earnest in his hopes for the success of the Union cause, while often disappointed and grieved by the conduct of the administration, which he, nevertheless, deemed it his duty to sustain by his vote. In July, 1862, he makes this minute in his Diary: "I have thought and felt so much about our army near Richmond that my mind and heart are weary." Again, a little later, visiting a camp near home, to examine the condition of the soldiers, he says: "Nothing but slavery seems to me so bad as war." By such conflicting sentiments was his heart oppressed.

During all these years his ordinary activities continued unabated. Ministrations to his parish, and to hundreds of other persons demanding every kind of aid or sympathy, filled his days to overflowing.

For the freedmen his anxieties and labors were peculiar, for he knew well the apathy of Northern sentiment towards their race; and, in the preoccupied condition of the public mind, found it hard to secure to their claims the interest and attention due them. He occupied himself unceasingly in measures for their relief and education; forming an auxiliary association, appealing for aid through the press, delivering lectures and sermons, securing, advising, and corresponding with their teachers, and giving unstintedly of his time and money to their cause. He was often pained by the difficulty he found in securing interest and assistance for them. Even the charitably disposed were often weary and exhausted in means by the demands of the white sufferers. "I find," he writes on one occasion, in his Diary, "that the burden of this effort is to come upon myself." For three or four years his Diaries are sown with minutes of his exertions. Often he despatched boxes of goods to the soldiers in Virginia, and similar ones to the freedmen of South Carolina or on the Mississippi, on the same day; or, having spent the forenoon with teachers on their way to freedmen schools, he occupied the afternoon visiting soldiers' families and the camp, and in helping the ladies working for soldiers' relief.

Of all this, however, we can only speak in these general terms. His brief records are the outline, not now to be filled up, of constant, unwearied, but, it would appear, most exhausting activity.

CHAPTER XVIII.

CHARACTERISTICS.

"My Most Moving Speech." — "The Lord's Chore Boy." — A Hard Man to hate. — Considerate Courtesy. — Conquered with Kindness. — Moral Power. — Memories of his Childhood. — "The Prophet of the Everlasting Covenant." — A Terror to Evil Doers. — "I did Mean You." — Unexpected Gratitude. — The Letter of Introduction. — Candor at Funerals. — The Right and the Expedient. — May and June. — Too Many Friends. — Mr. May and Dr. Lyman Beecher. — A Strange Request. — Giving and taking Frankness. — Applauded in Church. — The Power of Kindness. — Political Preaching. — How to turn away Wrath. — The Family Pledge. — Love of Children. — Geniality. — The Ideal and the Actual. — Ashamed to Die. — "The Lord knows I do." — A Merited Reproof. — A Death-bed Repentance. — Sleeping with a Madman. — Keeping a Promise to a Lunatic. — Mr. May's Roman Catholic Cane.

WHAT HE CALLED "MY MOST MOVING SPEECH."

MR. MAY made an address to an assembly of Onondaga Indians, including several chiefs. In the plainest terms he told them that, if they expected or desired to prosper, they must overcome their contempt for hard work, and devote themselves to regular and constant industry. As soon as he ended and "paused for a reply," an old chief arose, with an expressive grunt of disgust, and stalked off in silent dignity.

He was followed by all the other hearers, until the offending speaker was left entirely alone.

"THE LORD'S CHORE BOY."

Mr. A. B. Alcott was once at Syracuse when Mr. May was engaged from morning until night in errands of mercy, — visiting the sick, burying the dead, helping fugitive slaves and canal boys, and prisoners who wished to reform. When he reached home at evening, and was drawing off the boots from his weary feet, Mr. Alcott said: "I have found a new name for you. You are the Lord's chore boy. You do the Lord's chores."

A HARD MAN TO HATE.

An active politician, who frequently denounced Mr. May in the bitterest terms, and expected to be regarded by him as an enemy, was so overcome by Mr. May's kindness that he said in his despair of effecting a quarrel: "I have got to give up trying to hate that man. You know I have a sick child, but I went to a meeting to abuse the Abolitionists. Soon after I heard Mr. May's voice calling my name in the street. Turning round, I found his face full of neighborly tenderness; and all he said was, 'I do hope your little boy is better.'"

CONSIDERATE COURTESY.

Mr. May once had a parishioner who was so offended with him on account of his preaching in behalf of reforms, that he would not listen to his pastor, but would be sure to attend church if he knew that another minister would officiate. As soon as Mr. May learned how this man felt towards him, he never failed to send word when he was about to exchange, so that Mr. —— might have as many church privileges as he would accept.

CONQUERED WITH KINDNESS.

Mr. May once preached very earnestly in his church upon some doctrinal topic; and, as soon as he pronounced the benediction, an excited man began to lift up his voice in the most righteous indignation against the soul-destroying heresies to which he had listened, and to reflect quite severely upon the preacher. Some of the people were provoked; but Mr. May begged them to give their respectful attention, and urged the protestant to come forward to the pulpit where he could be seen and heard better, assuring him that he should have a fair chance. He started full of zeal, but when he went up the steps, and took the outstretched hand and looked into the beaming face of his opponent, he was completely disconcerted; and, after a few tame words, ended by thanking Mr. May for his manifestation of brotherly love.

MORAL POWER.

Once seeing a crowd collected around two men who were fighting in the middle of the street, he broke the ring, separated the men, who were overawed by his presence, told the dispersing assembly that he was ashamed of their meanness in encouraging their brothers to make brutes of themselves, and received the congratulations of an Orthodox minister on a curbstone, who said, "I had been aching to interfere, but did not know just where to take hold."

MEMORIES OF HIS CHILDHOOD.

"He told me he could remember when a boy being in his father's office, and Chief Justice Parsons came in, and asked his father to call in several gentlemen, naming them; and when they were present, he asked them to sit down and give him the benefit of their experience and common sense in making up judgments in cases reserved in court for consideration. Then he took from his green bag papers. A. B. had come into such and such relations with C. D., and there had been such and such transactions, and such and such events in consequence. What was justice between them? Several cases were thus submitted, without names; and the great jurist took the thought and conscience of his business friends, to prepare himself for his great work upon the bench.

"Once, he said, when the family assembled for breakfast, his father came in from his usual morning walk, and said, 'I have seen something wonderfully interesting this morning. As I passed the Old Granary burial-ground, I saw that the tomb was open, in which I knew were the remains of James Otis; and, with the help of the sexton, I opened the lid of Otis's coffin, and behold the coffin was full of the fibrous roots of the elm, especially thick and matted about the skull; and going out I looked up at the noble, verdant elm, and there in transfigured glory was all that was material of James Otis.' G. W. Hosmer."

THE PROPHET OF THE EVERLASTING COVENANT.

"In the winter of 1816–17, Mr. May taught school in Concord, Mass. It was his senior year in college. One cold Sunday morning we all were assembled in church. The first hymn had been read and sung, and Dr. Ripley had prayed. As the prayer closed, the front door was opened, and a large man, with dignified, benignant bearing, entered the church, and went to the pew in which Mr. May was standing to receive him. It was Colonel Joseph May, who had come from Boston to Concord to worship with his son. He might then have been fifty-five years old; his black hair was silvered a little, and he wore that morning a drab kersey overcoat, which gracefully set off his manly figure. That drab overcoat is the subject of my story.

"Twenty years ago, the ministers along the line of the New York Central Railway knew an eccentric man, who believed that he was sent of the Lord, and he styled himself the Prophet of the Everlasting Covenant. Certainly he took no purse nor shoes; but he had, alas! he had script, a book in manuscript, which he wanted the ministers to read and commend to a publisher. The Prophet haunted Brother May at Syracuse, in whose great heart he found room. One cold day he came, shivering in his scanty attire, and asked Brother May to lend him an overcoat for the day. There was no overcoat in the house for him, it was said; but Mr. May laid his hand upon this dear old relic, the drab coat of his father. He would not say, 'Corban,' it is sacred to a dead man's memory, when a living man, suffering with cold, stood before him; and so he lent the coat. The next morning the Prophet came again. The weather was intensely cold, and the coat was so comfortable; and the Prophet asked for it as a gift. 'But,' said Mr. May, 'it was my father's: how can I part with it?' 'Ah!' said the Prophet, 'it is precious to you; but only think of this coat of your father cherishing and keeping alive the Prophet of the Everlasting Covenant!' And the Prophet got the coat. G. W. Hosmer."

A TERROR TO EVIL-DOERS.

"Belonging to my Society, in Brooklyn, was a very worthy colored family. They were required to sit in the negro pew, which was as far back from the rest of the congregation as it could be placed. Being blessed with a numerous family, as the children grew up they were uncomfortably crowded in that pew. Our church occupied the old meeting-house, which was somewhat larger than we needed, so that the congregation were easily accommodated on the lower floor. Only the choir sat in the gallery, except on extraordinary occasions. I therefore invited my colored parishioners to occupy one of the large, front pews in the side gallery. They hesitated some time, lest their doing so should give offence. But I insisted that none would have any right to be offended, and at length persuaded them to do as I requested. One man was, or pretended to be, much offended. He said, with great warmth, 'How came that nigger family to come into that front pew?' 'Because,' I replied, 'it was unoccupied: they were uncomfortably crowded in the pew assigned them, and I requested them to remove.' 'Well,' said he, 'there are many in the Society besides myself who will not consent to their sitting there.' 'Why?' I asked. 'They are always well dressed, well behaved, and good-looking withal.' 'But,' said he, 'they are niggers, and niggers should be kept to their place.' I argued the matter with him till I saw he could not be moved, and he repeated the declaration that they should be driven back. I then said, with great earnestness, 'Mr. A. B., if you do any thing or say any thing to hurt the feelings of that worthy family, and induce them to return to the pew which you know is not large enough for them, so sure as your name is A. B. and my name is S. J. M., the first time you afterwards appear in the congregation I will state the facts of the case exactly as they are, and administer to you as severe a reproof as I may be able to frame in words.' This had the desired effect. My colored friends retained their new seat." — *Recollections*, p. 270.

"I DID MEAN YOU."

On one occasion, Mr. May preached in his searching and faithful manner upon the subject of selling rum;

and the sermon created a good deal of excitement in the parish. A few days afterward there met him in the street the prominent retail dealer of the village, much disturbed in manner, and apparently greatly grieved, as if innocent, and as if injured by the discourse Mr. May had given. In his hurried way, he went on to speak about the sermon, and to tell about the general or universal interest it had awakened, the talk it was giving rise to, and the strong terms of censure the people were using about the rum-seller in correspondence with the language heard from the pulpit. "And," said the unhappy man, in deprecation of the severity with which the trade had been handled, "they say you mean me!" "Well," said Mr. May, to the great amazement of his hearer, "I did mean you!"

UNEXPECTED GRATITUDE.

After Mr. May went to Syracuse he was stopped in the street in New York city one day by an apparent stranger, who begged him to call at a certain place of business, and receive his thanks for old kindnesses. When Mr. May called at this prosperous establishment, the master of it said: "When I was a boy, and had nobody to help me, you interested yourself in my behalf, and got me a good place in a store. Thanks to that start, I have made my own way in the world.' He took Mr. May to his house, introduced him to his family, and at their parting pressed a roll of money into his hand.

THE LETTER OF INTRODUCTION.

A young man whom Mr. May knew and loved, a bright, agreeable, capable fellow, but somewhat inclined to associate with dissipated companions, asked his minister for a letter of introduction to the father of a young woman in whom he had become deeply interested. Mr. May immediately granted the request, and prepared a note in which he spoke in the highest terms of his young friend, and added that, if he manfully overcame his temptation to indulge in doubtful associations, he would be a most desirable companion and friend. He gave the letter to the young man, unsealed, saying, "You can read it, if you please." We do not know that it was ever delivered; but we have heard that the parties were happily married, and that Mr. May did not lose the fondest regard of the young man with whom he had dealt so directly.

CANDOR AT FUNERALS.

Mr. May was sometimes sent for to attend funerals when persons had died under discreditable circumstances, including cases of delirium tremens. It was known that he was merciful, and a believer in the final reformation of all mankind. It was his general rule, however, to refuse to officiate upon such occasions unless he should be left entirely free to speak of the awful warning suggested by the sad close of an evil life. His manner was tender, but indescribably solemn; and the impressions made by such services were wide-spread and lasting.

THE RIGHT AND THE EXPEDIENT.

Colonel Higginson remembers Mr. May's telling him about a passage-at-arms with Horace Mann. Mr. Mann said, "I hate your doctrine that we should think only of the right, and not at all of the expedient." "And I hate your doctrine," retorted Mr. May, "that we should think of the expedient, and not only of the right."

MAY AND JUNE.

While Mr. May was once riding late in the afternoon, his horse lost a shoe, several miles from a convenient stopping place. Passing by a blacksmith's shop, he stopped, and asked the smith whether he would set the shoe. As he was just shutting up his shop, he declined doing it. Mr. May urged him, saying, among other things, "I was in hopes that the consideration of our relationship might induce you to oblige me." "How relationship? How am I related to you?" "Why, I see by your sign that your name is June. My name is May. Are not May and June nearly related?" The man laughed, saying, "Doubtless they are; so I suppose I ought to do your job for you." Whereupon he put on his apron, and set himself to the work. While he was engaged in it, Mr. May entertained him, in his usual way, with anecdotes and conversation, and so pleased him that he not only would receive no pay, but said he should be glad to shoe the horse "all 'round."

TOO MANY FRIENDS.

In 1857, Mr. May wrote to Horace Mann:—

"I am vexed, without any abatement of my vexation, whenever I think of my failure to see you during my visit to Massachusetts friends. But when I go to spend a few days in Boston I am like the boy who got his hand into a narrow-necked jar of filberts, and filled his hand so full of nuts that he could not get it out of the bottle. I undertake to do so much that I do nothing, or nothing well."

MR. MAY AND DR. LYMAN BEECHER.

We are indebted to James Freeman Clarke for the following anecdote:—

"Mr. May sent a note to his friend, Rev. Thomas K. Beecher, of Elmira, N.Y., telling him that he knew that the Beechers were afraid of nothing, but that he now was about to give his courage a pretty severe trial. 'I invite you to exchange with me, who am a Non-Resistant, Woman's Rights, Anti-Capital Punishment, Garrisonian Abolitionist.' To which Mr. Beecher replied: 'Pooh-pooh! that is nothing. Come and exchange!' Mr. May went and preached. Dr. Lyman Beecher, whose noble intellect was then giving way to age and infirmity, was staying with his son, and went to hear Mr. May preach. When he came home he said: 'Mr. May, if I understood your discourse correctly, and I think I did, for I paid strict attention, I liked it well. I understood you to say that you expected to be saved by the merits of Jesus Christ!' 'Oh, no! Dr. Beecher,' said Mr. May, 'I do not believe that any other person's merits will ever help me to salvation. I must be saved by my own character, if I am saved at all.' At this Dr. Beecher was displeased, and answered, 'Then I did not like your sermon at all.' After a while he added, 'Do you think it right, or gentlemanly, or Christian, to go into another man's pulpit, and try to destroy the work he has been doing?' 'No, Dr. Beecher,' said Mr. May, 'I do not, and I never do any such thing.' 'You did it this morning,' said the old man, and walked away. But when evening came, Dr. Beecher forgot his anger, and talked a long time with Mr. May on those subjects wherein they agreed, as temperance, education, and the like. And at the close of the conversation, subdued, as all others were, by the fascination of the honesty, sweetness, truthfulness, and kindness of this remarkable man, Dr. Beecher said, on taking his bed-light to retire, 'Well, Mr. May, I shan't see you to-morrow morning. I'll bid you good-by now. I *do* like you, after all.' "

A STRANGE REQUEST.

Mr. May was so brotherly towards all his fellow-men that the humblest persons felt perfectly sure of his sympathy, and approached him with such faith and freedom as are seldom inspired.

He befriended a poor woman and her daughter. The latter was an invalid, and, while her mother was away at her work, she enjoyed the companionship of a fine cat. One day Mr. May was told that these persons had called upon him. He found them in the parlor. The mother had a basket which contained something that was nicely covered with a white towel. Mr. May's first thought was that they had brought him some gift; but he soon noticed that they were very sad. When he asked what troubled them, they burst into tears, and told him that boys in their neighborhood had set dogs on the cat, and it had been worried to death. Mr. May expressed his regret. Then the mother said that the cat's body was in the basket, and they had brought it there to see if it could be buried in Mr. May's premises. They did not own their house-lot, and they feared that if the cat should be buried there it would be dug up by the dogs.

"We should not think of asking such a favor of anybody else; but we thought that, perhaps, you would do it for us." Amused, and yet touched by their perfect confidence in his good-will, Mr. May said to the mother, "It is too damp for your daughter to go into the garden until every thing is ready; but if you will come with me I will try to oblige you." They selected a spot between two currant-bushes, and Mr. May took a spade and made a grave large enough to contain the basket and its contents. Then he went for the daughter, and escorted her to the place. After "the funeral," Mr. May was thanked most profusely, and the women returned home. For some time afterwards the ladies of his own household kept threatening to put this sign on the front gate: "S. J. May, Undertaker for Cats."

GIVING AND TAKING FRANKNESS.

Mr. May was often invited to preach in "evangelical" churches; but instead of improving the opportunity to show that he was almost a Methodist, or almost a Presbyterian, he was accustomed to say: —

"The most important truths are those which relate to religion, and the best kindness we can show to each other is to impart our highest views of the Divine Character and of Human Duty. Therefore I shall tell you to-day what I believe to be the chief doctrines of the gospel; and I have also brought some doctrinal and practical tracts, which I shall be glad to have you take at the close of the service."

Sometimes he invited Orthodox ministers to occupy his pulpit, and he encouraged them to declare unto his people the whole counsel of God, as they understood it.

"Preach not what you think Unitarians wish to hear, but what you think they need to hear."

APPLAUDED IN CHURCH.

A distinguished clergyman was in Syracuse conducting revival meetings. He was announced to preach on the Justice of God in the Eternal Damnation of the Wicked. Mr. May wished to hear him, and gave up his own evening service, urging his people to go and ascertain what could be said in behalf of such a dreadful doctrine. In the course of his sermon the preacher gave a frightful picture of terrible suffering. The sufferer after millions of years of anguish kept exclaiming, "How long, O Lord! how long?" The answer kept coming from the throne of an inexorable God, "Eternally, eternally!" After the service, Mr. May met an acquaintance in the crowded vestibule, who said, "What do you think of that?" He answered in a very distinct voice, "I think we ought to ask our God, whose mercy endureth for ever, to pardon us for having listened in silence while our deluded brother blasphemed him." The next Sunday he replied to the sermon, telling a "packed" audience that he would rather be the victim of such infernal cruelty than to inflict it upon an immortal soul; for such a God was not a father, but a fiend. There was an outburst of loud and prolonged applause.

THE POWER OF KINDNESS.

At the time when Abby Folsom was so troublesome at antislavery conventions that sometimes she was carried out of the house on account of her violence, Mr. May was to preside at a meeting where she was present. He asked Miss Folsom privately if she thought she would be moved to speak, and obtained her promise to say only a few words. When she began there was great disturbance, and many insisted that she should not be heard. Mr. May told the assembly that Miss Folsom had the floor, and he would leave the chair if she was not sustained in her right to speak; adding, "I have promised her that she shall be heard, and she has promised me that she will be very brief." This restored order; and, after uttering a few sentences, Miss Folsom resumed her seat, very calm and very happy. In less time than it would have taken to carry her out, the business of the hour was resumed.

POLITICAL PREACHING.

During the Mexican War, a Democrat in Mr. May's congregation met him in the street, and said: "Some of us do not like what you have said of public affairs. We are very much displeased with you." Mr. May answered: "It is not the business of the minister to please the people, but to tell them what he thinks they ought to hear, whether it pleases them or not. I must preach to satisfy my conscience, not to gratify your tastes." The gentleman said it was an entirely new view of the subject, and he never complained afterwards.

HOW TO TURN AWAY WRATH.

Mr. May had a parishioner of intemperate habits, who was such a trial to his poor wife that the good woman went to her pastor and asked him, in her distress, if he thought it would be wrong to put an emetic in her husband's decanter, so as to give him a disrelish for spirituous liquors. Mr. May probably thought that the experiment might be worth trying; at all events, he did not tell the woman that it would be very sinful. She tried it; but the man became so ill that, in her fear, she made a full confession, even implicating Mr. May slightly. This infuriated her husband, who seldom met "the minister" afterwards without pouring out his hatred in the strongest terms. He would not listen to one word of explanation or expostulation on the part of his imagined enemy, who waited patiently for an opportunity to reassure him of his love.

Once, when Mrs. May had been quite sick, she went to ride with her husband, and they drove past the house of the intemperate man, who was working in his garden, in which he took great pride. Mrs. May coveted some of the fine melons, but thought she knew it would be a hopeless request if she should ask for one; yet Mr. May said, "I will see." So he guided the horse up to the fence; but the man had noticed their approach, and turned his back, while he bent over his work more diligently than before. Very soon a voice, so free from passion that he could hardly believe it came from the lips of one whom he had so often and so shamefully abused, said to him, in the kindest tones: "I have come to ask a great favor at your hands. If you will give me a melon for my sick wife, I will thank you. She has a great craving for melons. I know you have the best in town. Will you give me one for her?" The man was silent for some time, evidently struggling with himself. He had wanted to denounce Mr. May when he saw him approaching; but he was large-hearted, after all, and this direct appeal to his magnanimity thrilled him and subdued him. At last he said, gently, "I will bring some up to your house." "Oh, don't put yourself to so much trouble. We can take them in the carriage." "I prefer to bring them." He soon appeared at the manse with the best of every thing that his garden produced, refused all compensation, was at once reconciled to Mr. May, and gratefully accepted his assistance in overcoming his bad habit; afterwards regaining much of his former good standing.

THE FAMILY PLEDGE.

In one of his New England parishes, Mr. May offended an intemperate man by the plainness of his temperance preaching. The kindest treatment on the part of his minister could not make him yield. But when Mr. May was about to leave the place, he was rewarded for all his efforts and forbearance. The man asked him to come to his house at a certain time. When Mr. May got there, he found that a neat pledge had been prepared, with a tasteful frame, and room for all the family names. The man, explaining his determination, requested Mr. May first to offer prayer, which he did fervently. Then the father and mother signed first, of course, and then the children, in the order of their ages. The last was the baby, the father guiding the infant's fingers until its name was legibly traced. Then Mr. May most gladly appended his own name, as the witness of all.

HIS LOVE OF CHILDREN.

He never passed a child without a pleasant word. There was a magnetism about him which drew them to him. A friend, who was at the head of a large Reform School, says that whenever Mr. May visited him, which he sometimes did for several days, the boys all seemed to be acquainted with him at once. "They crowded right round him when he came into the play-ground, and were good boys, so long as he was among them at least. He did not lecture them, but showed them something new about their games, and took a little part in them."

Wishing to do the children of the "May School" some particular favor, as a mark of his appreciation of its name, he sent to Boston for a foot-ball; and a visitor at his house reports his setting off with the ball, and that, lame as he was, he went into the yard, taught the boys the rules of the game, and how to kick, entering into their first essays with the greatest merriment.

HIS GENIALITY.

As he moved through the streets, almost every person knew him; but, whether acquainted or not, he scarcely ever passed an individual without some kind of salutation. "I can't bear to go by and look as if I did not recognize a man's existence. It seems churlish. I bow to his humanity," he said. A gentleman who walked with him in Syracuse said, "Mr. May, I should think your head would be tired nodding."

THE IDEAL AND THE ACTUAL.

Twelve or fourteen years ago, Mr. May attended a meeting of the Western Conference at Alton. He met several Missourians, who saw him for the first time, and were won by his unmistakable sweetness of temper, even when engaged in the discussion of the slavery question. A lady who had known and loved Mr. May from her childhood was much amused when a gentleman from St. Louis said to her: "What a *change* has come over Mr. May! His voice has lost its harshness, and his face has no longer a fierce expression."

ASHAMED TO DIE.

On a certain Sunday, about ten years ago, Mr. May preached very acceptably in the morning, and a second service was announced for the afternoon. But at dinner his hostess persuaded him to eat a piece of her delicious mince pie, and he was soon so ill that it was impossible for him to preach again. Indeed, he suffered so much that his friends became alarmed, and sent for a physician. The doctor came, and found his patient in great pain. Instead of being utterly doleful, however, Mr. May looked up in his archest manner, and said, "Doctor, I am not afraid to die, but I am ashamed to die."

"THE LORD KNOWS I DO."

One day Mr. May found two stern-looking women at his front door. He invited them to walk in, with his usual cordiality; but they said, as if doubting their welcome, "We have come to you with a message from the Lord." "Then you *must* come in, for there is no one from whom I should be so glad to hear." After they were seated there was a long pause; but at last one of them said, "Mr. May, we have heard that you do not believe in the divinity of Jesus Christ." "You did not hear that from the Lord, for the Lord knows I do."

A MERITED REPROOF.

Mr. May was present at a High School Exhibition, and being shocked by some of the performances he addressed the teacher in the columns of a daily paper, as follows: —

SYRACUSE, Dec. 24, 1859.

MR. ——.

DEAR SIR, — I am very reluctant to censure any thing that you have advised or permitted. But the offence committed last evening, at the Exhibition of your High School, was too grave to be passed over in silence, and too public to be reproved only privately. For half an hour or more, your audience of two thousand persons, many of them young, were kept laughing at a very gross and immoral farce, all the more mischievous because so well performed. A lying knave, pretending to be a mesmeric doctor, in agreement with a foolish, naughty boy, practises upon the fears and the credulity of an old, doting father, in order to defeat his plan of sending the graceless youngster to a boarding-school.

I cannot imagine a worse lesson that you could have given the rising generation ; a lesson in trickery, lying, and filial impiety. There is already in our country so little reverence for age, and respect for parental authority, that an audience of our people is the last in the world before which such a farce should be introduced for the sake of fun.

A word to the wise is sufficient. I know you will see and acknowledge the worse than impropriety of which you have allowed your pupils to be guilty, and am sure nothing of the kind will again occur at the exhibition of our High School. Every true parent and good citizen must disapprove of it as much as I do.

Sincerely your friend, S. J. MAY.

A DEATH-BED REPENTANCE.

To be at Peace with God we must be at Peace with our Fellow-men.

"A few years after I had entered the ministry, I was summoned to the house of old Mr. B., a dying man, who was said to be in great distress of mind. I had no experience in such cases, and was therefore not a little distressed in my own mind to know how I ought to deal with him. I was but little acquainted with Mr. B. He was reported to be a strictly honest man, but ill-tempered, irascible, and very jealous of his rights, and therefore always in a quarrel with some of his neighbors, or with those for whom he worked. As I walked to his house, I earnestly bethought me what I should say to him. I inwardly prayed for help ; and the Comforter, *the spirit of truth*, came to my assistance. I resolved to deal frankly with him and tell him that his faults of temper were undoubtedly the source of his misery.

"On approaching his humble dwelling, I heard his groans and outcries for mercy. His daughter met me in the yard, and told me that he had lain all night thus bemoaning aloud his lost condition, and imploring forgiveness.

"As I took my seat by his bedside, the wretched man gave way to a paroxysm of despair, and seized my hand as a drowning man grasps any thing within his reach. So soon as he was calm enough to listen I said: 'Mr. B., this is all wrong, foolish, a waste of the little time that is probably left you. God is not well pleased with groans and shrieks of misery. Your unhappiness is owing to your faults of character, and the sins they have led you to commit. I am told that, although an honest man, you have been cross, quarrelsome, and at times very abusive in your language to those who had, or who you thought had, injured you. Now you cannot be at peace with God, until you are at peace with men; and how can you expect or with any propriety ask him to forgive you if you are cherishing in your heart resentment and ill-will towards those whom you consider your enemies. I do not think, Mr. B., you will die to-day or to-morrow: the doctor says you may live a week or more. Instead, therefore, of wasting your time, and disturbing your family by your groans and outcries, let me advise you to set about forgiving those who have injured you, and asking the pardon of such as you have injured.'

"The old man recovered himself, and went on awhile recounting the wrongs that had been done him by one, another, and another. 'Well,' said I, 'Mr. B., for all these things they are accountable, and of them they must repent, or suffer the consequences. If they are really as bad as you have described them, I should think you would pity them, and pray for their repentance and forgiveness. But it is your especial duty to think rather of the wrong you may have done to them in your anger; be sorry for that, and sincerely ask their pardon. Unburden your conscience, as far as you may, of the load that is upon it; make all the amends you can for the injury you have done to others in deed, word, or thought, and leave them, as you must, to take care of their own accounts with the Impartial Judge.' Mr. B. was much affected by my plain dealing, and soon made confession of many things that he knew had not been right in his treatment of those who had offended him; and at last said: 'Yes, I ought to. I will forgive all my enemies, and ask them to forgive me, all excepting Captain W. It seems as if I could not forgive him, he has so often wronged and abused me. I am afraid I should not forgive him if I said I did. And I know not how I can ask his pardon, while I feel he has treated me so much worse than I ever treated him.' 'Ah! Mr. B.,' I replied, 'Captain W. is the very one of all others with whom you must seek to be reconciled, for he is the one with whom it seems that you are most at enmity. Don't die, I pray, until you have forgiven him, and have been forgiven by him. I suppose the Captain is a hard, overbearing man. It is very probable that he has been unkind, ungenerous, unjust towards you. But that is his concern. He must answer for that. You have only to make amends for the wrongs you have done him. And if he sees that you are truly penitent, very probably his heart may be touched. He may be made conscious of his trespasses against you, and not only forgive, but ask to be forgiven. But whether the Captain shall be brought to a right state of heart or not, see to it that you do the work that is meet for the repentance required of you. Recall to your remembrance the harsh language you have used, the abusive, profanely abusive, epithets you have sometimes heaped upon him; and confess to him that nothing should have provoked you so to injure him and offend God.'

"Mr. B. was still more affected by my earnest appeal. Tears flowed freely down his rough cheeks. His bosom heaved with emotion. He covered his face. Presently he cried, 'Oh! pray with me, pray that I may have help!' I did pray fervently, for I felt deeply. I prayed that if the course I had marked out for the poor, unhappy, dying man was indeed the right one, he might be spared, guided, and strengthened by the Holy Spirit to pursue it.

"A day or two after the above interview, I was told that a marked change had come over Mr. B. He had ceased from his groanings, had become more considerate of his family, and of all who came to assist in nursing him. He was tender and affectionate, and often rapt in silent prayer. I was told he had sent for one and another of his neighbors and others with whom he had quarrelled, and made very humble confessions, and asked their forgiveness. Moreover it was said his penitence had melted the hearts of several who had done him wrong; and that his sick-room had been the scene of mutual acknowledgments and touching expressions of mutual forgiveness.

"Before a week had quite passed, I went again to see him. No outcries or groans saluted me as before on drawing near to his house. Quietness reigned around it. As I entered his room, the sweetest smile I had ever seen upon his face greeted me. He eagerly stretched out to me his trembling hand, and with tears of joy, which words could not express, he said: 'O Mr. May! I have done as you advised me, and I have found peace, sweet peace of mind. I sent for Mr. A. and Mr. D. and Mr. G. Others came, on hearing that I wished to see all with whom I had quarrelled. Each one has spoken kindly to me. Each one has assured me of his forgiveness. Some have made apologies for my violence, more than I could have made myself; and most of them have confessed that they too had done me wrong, and begged my pardon. I have had a happy week! I found it so good to forgive and be forgiven, that I felt last Tuesday as if I must see Captain W. He came, and it was the best of all. I told him I was unwilling to die without having confessed to him how sorry I was that we had quarrelled so much; how ashamed that I had so often abused him; and that I hoped he would forgive me. And, what do you think, Mr. May, the Captain would hardly wait for me to finish what I was saying before he took my hand and replied: "Mr. B., you have as much to forgive as I have. We have treated each other badly. I have been in some respects much more to blame than you have. I am glad you sent for me. I beg you to forgive me, as I do you heartily. And I pray

God to forgive both of us." His manner was very tender. He wept while he was speaking. I never knew the Captain had so much kindness.'

"After resting a little while, the dying man resumed: 'O Mr. May! I cannot tell you how much better I feel; such a load removed from my heart. I have forgiven my enemies, and they have forgiven me. I have more hope now that God will be merciful to me. I am not so afraid to die.'"

SLEEPING WITH A MADMAN.

Mr. May's temperament, into which entered so largely firmness and gentleness and sympathy, and his great personal courage, adapted him peculiarly to deal with the insane, over whom he always exercised a singular influence.

When quite a young man his character was put to a severe test, as the following anecdote shows. Near his father's house lived a highly respectable family, of whom the husband and father was subject to periodical insanity, which at times amounted to maniacal fury. At such times his wife and children lost all control of him, and were often obliged to retreat to remote parts of the house, and lock themselves in. Mr. May, of whom the gentleman was very fond when in his right mind, was one evening informed by a messenger that he was in one of his fits of insanity, and that the family were helpless, and locked into the attic. He hastened over to their home, and found the maniac in full possession, roaming furiously through the rooms, mixing complaints of his family for deserting him with threats of violence against them. Mr.

May succeeded in calming him, and urged him to go to bed and try to sleep.

"How can I sleep, Sam?" said the poor man, pathetically. "My wife and children have hidden away; and I am so lonesome, I couldn't sleep if I went to bed." "Do try," urged Mr. May. "Will you go and sleep with me, Sam?" "Of course I will," was the prompt response: "only you must promise me you will keep quiet, and not get up till morning." "I will promise." "Give me your word of honor, Mr. ——." "I give you my word of honor, Sam, I won't get up till morning."

Mr. May kept his part of this strange compact, and actually went to rest in the same bed with the lunatic, and fell asleep. During the night, however, he awoke, and found his companion gone. He arose instantly, and in his night-clothes set out to find him. Groping his way downstairs, he discovered him in the dining-room, evidently excited again, and engaged in whetting the carving-knife upon its steel. Mr. May, who knew that his characteristic trait was truthfulness and pride in his honor as a gentleman, advanced immediately to him, and sternly said:—

"Mr. ——, I thought you were a man of your word!" "And who says I am not a man of my word?" roared out the madman, starting up to confront him. "*I* say so!" said Mr. May, boldly. "You have just broken your word to me. You promised on your honor that you would stay abed till morning; and here you are downstairs in the middle of the night."

The right chord was touched. The poor lunatic melted at once. "Did I, Sam?" he quietly answered; "then I forgot it. Oh, forgive me! my head is in such a whirl!" He consented to return, and they actually resumed their partnership of the bed. In the morning reason had in some measure returned; and Mr. May, on awaking, found his companion dressed, and somewhat sadly waiting for him to arouse.

KEEPING HIS PROMISE TO A LUNATIC.

Another instance of his resolution was his treatment of a gentleman of Syracuse, who, though not of his parish, had such implicit confidence in his fidelity and courage that he intrusted to him the secret of a conscious tendency to insanity, which he feared he could not permanently control. "I want you to promise me solemnly, Mr. May, that if it comes to that, and you hear that I have lost my reason, you will come here and take me, whether I consent or not, and carry me to the Utica asylum." Finding him in earnest, Mr. May gave his pledge as requested. Some years elapsed. At length a severe affliction developed the dreaded tendency. Mr. May, hearing that the gentleman had lost his reason, took a carriage and drove to his door, and going in told him he had come, as agreed, to carry him to the asylum. The lunatic refused, and became somewhat furious. Mr. May pleaded with him to consent, urging the superior treatment he would receive, and the danger to his family, should he be allowed to stay at home. At length, finding he would not yield, he said: "Mr. ——, I am here by agreement with yourself. You asked me to come, and, whether you consented or not, take you to the asylum, if ever you became insane. I promised to do so, and I shall certainly keep my promise. I shall have to do it by force if you will not go voluntarily. Now do not distress us all by resisting; but come, as I ask you to." Such persuasions induced him at length to get into the carriage. But, arriving at the depot, the old spirit of insanity revived, and he began to protest against going into the cars. Again Mr. May said: "My friend, you must. It was our agreement. I should have to have you carried in if you refused to walk. Now come, don't make a scene, but take my arm, and let us walk in together, and let no one see there is any thing the matter." The lunatic once more yielded, and they arrived at the asylum after a quiet ride of two or three hours.

MR. MAY'S ROMAN CATHOLIC CANE.

Some years ago an effort having been made by citizens of Syracuse to found a City Hospital, which project failed through the impracticability of obtaining proper nurses for such an establishment, Mr. May proposed at the meeting in which this conclusion was reached that they should call upon the Sisters of Charity to undertake the work. He urged their well-known skill and devotion, and had ascertained that they would take charge of a hospital and conduct it on strictly non-sectarian principles so far as the admission of patients was concerned. The anti-Catholic sentiment, however, proved too strong; and his suggestion was finally voted down, to his great disappointment, by a decided majority.

Some time after this scheme had been thus abandoned in despair, there arrived in the city two or three Sisters of Charity, charged with the duty of doing what the citizens had given up. They began practically, hiring a small house, and putting in one or two beds, for which occupants were readily found. At the same time they exerted themselves to increase the extent of their accommodations. Hearing of Mr. May's action in the former case, they called on him, and were assured of his readiness to co-operate with them, provided they would conduct their hospital on non-sectarian principles. They agreed to this, and received the active assistance of Mr. May and other public-spirited Protestants; the effort resulting in the establishment of St. Mary's Hospital. It now contains some fifty beds, has an efficient corps of the well-trained and devoted Sisters as nurses, and is well provided with all needed appurtenances. It is partly supported by the city, is wholly free to all patients without regard to religion, and is admirably conducted. Mr. May was deeply interested in its success. He became well acquainted with the Mother Superior, for whose ability and devotion he entertained the highest respect, and advised cordially with her and others interested. In how gratifying a manner his sentiments and efforts were appreciated, we take great pleasure in exhibiting in the incident we now record.

The hospital being well under way, a Fair was held for its benefit, and was very successful. Many Protestants attended, but by far the largest portion of its patrons were Roman Catholics. A gold-headed cane having been offered to be given by vote to a clergyman of the city, it was actually assigned to Mr. May by a large majority, although his principal rival was a much-respected Catholic priest. As this result was really determined by the votes of the Catholics, the event became a pleasing instance of that good-will among Christians which Mr. May so much loved. But more was to follow. It was arranged to present the cane to him publicly, at a Festival to be held at the hospital, in celebration of its assured establishment. When the evening came a large concourse of Catholics and Protestants filled all available parts of the building. A prominent Catholic gentleman, presenting the cane, addressed Mr. May in terms which it would be gratifying to reproduce here, warmly acknowledging his interest in the undertaking from the beginning, and offering him grateful assurances of the respect which his Catholic fellow-citizens felt for him. Mr. May, much affected, accepted the gift, responding in cordial terms to the address which had been made; and in friendly festivity terminated an occasion which was, perhaps, unique in the relations of the two great portions of the Christian Church.

CHAPTER XIX.

PERSONAL TRAITS AND HOME LIFE.

Personal Appearance. — Manners. — His Mirthfulness. — Energy. — Food. — Temperance. — Physical and Moral Courage. — His Aversion to Riches and Luxury — Utilitarian. — Neatness. — Invited Criticism. — His Literary Habits. — Humor. — Doctrinal Duel. — How he usually spent the Day. — His Domestic Virtues. — Never Irritable or Impatient. — Craved Manifestations of Affection. — A Wise and Fond Father. — Mrs. May.

IN person Mr. May was of middle stature, straight and well-proportioned, rather slender when a young man, but becoming stout, although not corpulent, in later years. His complexion was fair, with a fresh color; his hair, which was very fine and silky, was black, never more than slightly sprinkled with gray, to which his beard turned at sixty; his eyes brown, the pupils small, the lids a little drooping, and with an indescribable twinkle of genial good-nature about them; the nose and mouth were large, but shapely, the expression of the latter decided and firm. His countenance was singularly expressive from its great mobility, reflecting changes of feeling readily. "When I first met him, at twenty-seven years of age," says an old friend, "I thought him the handsomest man I had ever seen."

The likeness which accompanies this volume, regarded as fair, but not excellent, by his friends, is from a photograph taken but three months before his death. It gives, perhaps, something of the sweetness of his countenance, but partially lacks the masculine strength which underlay its expression. Nothing could exceed the sweetness of his smile or the contagious heartiness of his laugh. His voice was remarkably powerful and searching, but perfectly smooth, very musical, and well modulated. Theodore Parker said of it, "God made that voice on purpose to pronounce the Beatitudes." He sang delightfully, with great expression and the highest enjoyment, both sacred and secular music; being very fond especially of English ballads, of which he knew a great many. One of his classmates tells us that a college party "was never thought complete if they could not get May in to sing." His manners were of exceeding grace and dignity. He retained a good deal of the style of the old school, and in formal intercourse was courtly and almost precise. But his unbounded geniality relieved his bearing of all stiffness, and in familiar society made him easy and informal. Yet even in the most intimate relations there was a considerate politeness in his behavior, which he never relaxed or forgot. He greatly disliked the neglect of courtesy which he thought characterized, to some extent, our recent times. He was emphatically well-bred. Manners were morals with him, and the disregard of the little amenities of behavior in domestic and private life always tried his feelings and offended his taste. "It is so easy to say a pleasant word," he used to urge. "A little act of attention is worth more than a real service." He carried these principles into his treatment of the poor and humble, and it was one secret of his influence with them and their delight in him. A man, he held, is, as a man, entitled to courtesy as much as to justice; and he was scrupulously attentive to all the dictates of politeness among the humblest of the objects of his charity. "It does them more good to be treated with respect than to have food or clothing given to them," he used to say.

He showed towards servants and laboring people a sympathetic friendliness which hardly seemed condescension, and which made them devoted to him. In his own family they always attended to his wants with an enthusiasm of loyalty; and a lady tells us that, when he called at her house, her servant was always greatly disappointed if any one else went to the door to let him in. He taught his family to encourage the self-respect of such persons by their mode of speaking to them; and, except domestics, they were always addressed as "Mr." or "Mrs.," and not by nicknames.

His entrance into a room was delightfully gracious, and his presence among a circle of friends was a guarantee of sociability and merriment. "He was one of the most mirthful men I ever knew," says one who was long familiar with him. His fund of stories and personal anecdotes was almost inexhaustible, and he told them with the greatest glee and with a large share of dramatic effect. His habit of thought was, however, essentially sober, although cheerful. Mirth and humor he loved, but he was highly sensitive to levity or irreverence. Even wit he rather feared, often saying he was glad he was not a witty man, it was so hard to use wit without abusing it. The scathing satire of his friends, Horace Mann and Theodore Parker, he always spoke of with almost a shudder.

Although delicate in youth, Mr. May inherited from his parents a robust constitution, and enjoyed superior health throughout his life. His capacity of endurance was very great, as the variety of his activities implies; but this depended largely also on his equability of temperament, and the unqualified heartiness with which he took up every thing he had to do. No energy was wanted in overcoming the friction of disinclination to duty. He was in every thing hearty. He enjoyed life, meeting it cheerily, and taking it up earnestly and joyously. "There is one life, of little importance to other people, perhaps, but which *I* take a supreme interest in: I mean my own," he was fond of saying.

He was no ascetic. He was a generous eater, fond of good cheer, and liking to see a bounteous table; although in his personal habits he was extremely simple, always contented with what was set before him, and never making any suggestion for the gratification of his own appetite or taste at his own table. His wife used to say it was of no use to cook for him, he could not tell what he had eaten. The one thing he loved better than all others was boiled rice, on which, when interrupted in the midst of composing a sermon, he would often dine exclusively. He was very fond of tea, and used to jest at this taste and his temperance principles at once, by calling himself a "*tea*-totaller." He liked also the taste of wine, and always said he should enjoy wine and the sociability to which it contributes, if he could use it conscientiously. But having in early manhood adopted the principle of total abstinence, it became so deeply rooted in his conscience that it always pained him to see intoxicating beverages convivially or freely used. He could hardly excuse it, that men, to gratify themselves, should risk making weaker brothers offend.[1] It was difficult to persuade him in

[1] This sentiment, and the frankness with which Mr. May was able to utter his convictions, are both illustrated in the following letter. He had been invited, by the committee of gentlemen charged with arranging the festivities of St. Patrick's Day, to attend the dinner. The compliment to him as a Protestant clergyman was highly acceptable; but he felt unable to attend, and declined, for the reasons expressed in the letter: —

SYRACUSE, March 17, 1853.

MESSRS. D. MCCARTHY AND OTHERS.

GENTLEMEN, — I am much obliged to you for your invitation to the proposed celebration of St. Patrick's Day. I should be very happy to express, by accepting your invitation, my kind regards for that portion of my fellow-citizens who have come directly, or by descent, from Ireland.

But I see so much poverty, wretchedness, and crime following from the use of intoxicating drinks, that I abhor the sight and smell of them; and cannot consent to give my countenance to them, no, not for an hour, except it may be in the chamber of sickness, under the direction of a discreet physician.

If any people on earth need these artificial stimulants less than others, it seems to me they are the Irish. Our Creator seems to have bestowed upon that branch of his human family a large share of *animal* spirits, — of buoyancy and light-heartedness. I know

age to take wine as a means of strength, although he always conceded its utility to the old or infirm. But, when he took it, he fell into the old decorums so naturally, that his family were accustomed to tell him that he "should not drink healths in a medicine."

He united to his generous and well-knit physique a high degree of physical and moral courage. He used to tell a story of his grandmother, a lady of Revolutionary times, who, when a robber was getting into her window at night, sprang from bed, seized him by the shoulders, and pushed him out upon the ground, saying, as she did so, "You rascal, you'll wake my husband!" The same heroine, hearing one speak of fear, exclaimed, "Fear! What is fear? I don't know what the word means." Her grandson was endowed with a portion

not what else has sustained them under the load of accumulated wrongs which they have been compelled to suffer.

In a country like ours, with such spirits as they have, nothing can prevent them from obtaining at once the comforts of life, and rising in due time to affluence and honor, *if they will let ardent spirits alone.* But the use of intoxicating drinks perpetuates their shiftlessness, excites them to quarrelling, to disturbances of the peace, and violations of right, wholly foreign to their natural kindness and good humor.

If the celebration this evening was to be without wine, or any kind of ardent spirits, it would give me pleasure to attend it; but I cannot willingly subject myself to the pain and the shame of seeing men (for a momentary gratification) swallowing that which I know may commence in them, or perpetuate, an indulgence that leads to poverty, woe, and crime.

Would to God that the Irishmen of Syracuse would to-night instal Father Mathew as their Patron Saint, and for ever after live in accordance with his principles.

Respectfully. SAMUEL J. MAY.

of her character, as some of the anecdotes we elsewhere narrate exhibit. The phrenologist Fowler, not knowing who he was, examined Mr. May's head, and declared it was the head of a military man; and, when informed of the principles and character of his subject, maintained that he was nevertheless correct, as, according to his system, Mr. May had courage, firmness, decision, order, and other military qualities, largely developed. An active Abolitionist in 1835 certainly needed all these. In college he was, in fact, drill-sergeant of the college battalion, at that time celebrated for the elegance of their evolutions. He was, however, never prone, we believe, to athletic achievements or exposures, was timid and awkward with horses, and dizzy upon great elevations.

He never shrank from any call of duty, but was disinclined to taking any needless risks. Similarly, although generous and charitable almost to prodigality, he had a great aversion to waste. This sentiment made him possibly a little unjust in his aversion to riches and the luxury attendant on them. He could not look upon the palaces of the wealthy without remembering the squalor of the poor. Ostentation in dress, architecture, or equipage, always offended him; partly from the reason we have just mentioned, partly from a natural simplicity and practicality of mind which were very characteristic of him. These latter qualities made him, though extremely fond of music, thoroughly dislike such as was of a florid or operatic character. He disliked and disapproved much of the modern church music, and seldom enjoyed the "Vesper Services" of late years used in many churches. The same traits of character seem to reappear in the emphases of his theology and the tenor of his preaching, which were always and characteristically practical. He valued things for the use they subserved. Mere beauty he probably did not adequately appreciate. His taste in poetry was guided almost wholly by his moral sentiments rather than by æsthetic sensibility. He could scarcely endure Browning or Tennyson, but delighted in a ballad or sonnet of Wordsworth, and was profoundly stirred by a moral lyric of Whittier. Fiction he enjoyed almost not at all. His wife told him he read a novel as if it were a treatise of theology. He admired the grand in nature or art, from the reverential tendency of his mind, and an object like Mont Blanc or St. Peter's profoundly affected him; but he was not in general acutely sensitive to the quieter and subtler forms of natural or artistic beauty. He would value the portrait of a friend, or some champion of the right, or a picture like one of Mrs. Fry reading to prisoners, which always hung in his study, the gift of his friend, President White, more than any mere work of art. He was, however, sensitive to personal beauty, although incapable of comparing it to high moral qualities.

Neatness and order he valued highly, and practised habitually. His longest manuscript was, although he wrote with great rapidity, legible and elegant to the end. He abhorred bad handwriting, and thought it almost wrong, and certainly of questionable civility, to impose it on a correspondent. He was not, however, very systematic, although his sense of duty made him thorough in the discharge of every task. Any thing ill done offended him.

He liked to feel that his own public efforts were creditably performed, and always asked his wife and children on return from church how they had liked his sermon. But he never betrayed any thing of personal ambition, and was extremely modest in his estimate of his gifts and actual services. He accepted criticism of his conduct, views, or style, with perfect candor and good will, and was genuinely satisfied to be shown where either might be improved. During the earlier portion of his Syracuse ministry, he lived near the church; and the sociable manners of his people led to the habit of a large number following him home after service on Sunday evening, to talk over the suggestions of the day. Very earnest debate often sprang up, in which Mr. May's views and his style were extensively criticised. He bore his own part frankly, but one who was usually present says, "It never occurred to me to hesitate in saying any thing, as if Mr. May would care if I disputed or criticised him."

Mr. May was essentially a moralist and philanthropist. He valued greatly, therefore, the substance of doctrine, but not much the details of speculation or scholarship. Hence he was not a profound student or a systematic reader, although his habits might have been different in this respect, had his time been less broken and consumed in benevolent activities. His daily routine found him, however, always in his study, and he never seemed so happy as when he could command quiet hours there. Entries often occur in his diary to this effect: "A quiet morning with my books, which I enjoyed exceedingly." He retired to his study immediately after breakfast, often saying as he went in, "Now I *do* hope no one will come to interrupt me." But he could hardly say "No" to any caller, even on his busiest morning. Living, latterly, at some distance from the centre of town, he made that an excuse to himself for letting in those who came; and so at dinner-time it was almost customary for him to enter the dining-room with the half-pathetic remark, "There, my morning has been all spoiled again." The ladies of his household were always on the alert to protect him from these intrusions, and would plead with him to let them say he was engaged, but his kindness of heart constantly defeated their vigilance. An outer door, opposite the principal entrance, opened immediately into the study; and if Mr. May heard the bell, and there was the least delay, they were pretty certain to find that he had opened this before they reached the other. He was always very contrite, but never reformed in this respect, although he confessed that he often impaired thus the quality and finish of his literary work. Finally the study door became well known to all that needed him; and the unfortunate of all colors, tribes, and religions, with agents, missionaries, and reformers, seemed to go to it by instinct. He was patient with them to the last degree, hearing every story out, and showing himself incapable of brusqueness or irritability with a human being. He detected imposture with more skill than his compassion left him credit for, yet probably his judgment was often overborne by his indulgent sympathy and pity. His sense of humor also relieved the tedium of these innumerable inflictions; and he had many a hearty laugh at the oddities of such visitors, and at his own sufferings. The grave respect with which he would discuss the whims of some poor fanatic like his long-time friend, "the Prophet of the Everlasting Covenant," was admirable. And it was not hollow either; for his quick sympathy made him love to gratify the poor visionary on whom every one else would, he knew, turn the cold shoulder.

One story illustrating this patience is worth telling here. An aged believer in the Trinitarian theology had convinced himself that he could exhibit to Mr. May his doctrinal errors by a sort of Socratic method, and requested him to appoint a time when he would be willing to submit to it. His plan was this: The discussion was to be in writing as to the main points, although limited conversation was to be permitted, if necessary, in arriving at them. Each disputant was to be allowed a second, who was to remain wholly silent unless appealed to. Mr. May consented to every proposition, and with a trace of glee invited a friend of similar temper to act upon his side. At the appointed hour the aged apostle appeared at Mr. May's study-door, with his second, and a huge pile of manuscript. A table was provided, at which all parties took their places with pens and paper, and total silence reigned. The disciple of Socrates was intensely grave; Mr. May and his second with some difficulty restraining their sense of the grim humor of the occasion. The duel began with a shot from the aged Calvinist. He wrote and passed to Mr. May this question: No. 1, "Do you believe the Bible?" Mr. May inquired, "Do you mean to ask if I believe every word in the Bible to be true, or whether I believe in its general historical and doctrinal purport, and accept its spirit?" The old gentleman reflected and replied, "The latter." Mr. May thereupon wrote as his answer, "I do." It was now, by the terms of the agreement, Mr. May's turn to write a question. He wrote, "Do you believe the Bible to be true and correct in every particular, or do you concede the existence of some defects, interpolations, mistranslations, and inconsistencies of narrative?" Becoming evidently a little perplexed, his opponent presently wrote his reply: "I admit the existence of some such defects." It was now time for question No. 2. All waited in solemn quiet for it to be written. The old gentleman reflected long, fumbled and studied his MS. He had evidently expected Mr. May to give some sort of negative answer to his first question, and the affirmative reply had thrown his line of battle into disorder. At length he rose, and with considerable candor said: "Mr. May, I have been in error. Your views are evidently different from what I had imagined. I supposed you did not believe in the Bible. I thank you for your courtesy; but, if you please, I will withdraw from this discussion." "Certainly," replied Mr. May: "I am only glad if it has shown you that you had misjudged my position. You will certainly want, however, to understand Unitarian views better, and I wish you would accept from me some of our publications." The old gentleman assented, and Mr. May proceeded to select a considerable number of tracts from the supply he kept always on hand. They were graciously accepted, and the apostle of Calvinism prepared to depart. Before taking his leave, however, he said, solemnly, "Mr May, I have only one more favor to ask; and that is, that what we have just written may be consigned to the flames." Mr. May at once gathered up all the leaves and scraps which had been employed, and threw them into the fire; and then, very gravely, with his MS. and his second, the proposed agent of his conversion withdrew, carrying quite a body of Unitarian literature under his arm. When he was fairly out of hearing, Mr. May (as his second in this duel tells us) leaned back in his chair and actually shook with laughter, till the tears ran down his cheeks.

We have elsewhere remarked that Mr. May, although devoted to many benevolent reforms, and incessant in private charity, remained always characteristically a parish minister. This sphere he loved unreservedly, and felt to be his chosen field of permanent service. His habits of life, which were very uniform, conformed to this, and were always those of a pastor. The morning, as we have already said, was passed in his study, reading or writing, unless interrupted; the afternoon he devoted to parish visits and to charitable or other active offices. After dinner he dressed, and with his cane, a constant companion, set out for town. His cheery voice was always heard, before he started, calling up to his wife a good-by, asking her commissions, and indicating his probable programme for the afternoon. His parish being widely scattered, and his engagements outside it being so varied, he was apt to be absent from tea and to return only during the evening; an infringement upon his home life which he always regretted, but which the distance of his home from the centre of town made almost unavoidable. Returning, he enjoyed reading awhile aloud from the papers, or, when time permitted, some article from a magazine or passages from books which were interesting him. He retired by ten or half-past ten, and was almost instantly asleep. Six or seven hours was all he cared to sleep. He used to say his best thoughts came to him at dawn; and he wrote much before breakfast.

He loved to see his family all together at the breakfast-table, and depended on its being a social and cheerful meal. His own good health made him always fresh and ready with hearty greetings and interest in all the doings of the day before and plans for the day to come. A great part of his life he conducted a simple religious service before leaving the breakfast-table, and was always fervent and happy in it. But he preferred to omit this rather than to persevere in it through any kind of disturbance, or when all were not in the mood for it. He always inclined to read from the New Testament. One winter, however, all his family being absent except Mrs. May, he read through at this hour the Prophets and a large part of the historical books of the Old Testament, expressly to refresh his memory and hers. He afterwards wrote to his son that he had been astonished to find how large a portion of the Old Testament was practically valueless. He had really forgotten, he said, how much of it is unintelligible, uninteresting, and remote from the concerns of modern life. "What a pity," he exclaimed, "that instead of spending money and pains to reprint and circulate such material, we cannot, instead, make familiar chosen passages, from whatever source, which should really be inspiring and suggestive."

We do not desire to eulogize in writing of Mr. May, but we should not satisfy the grateful feelings of his family if we failed to place on record here the loveliness of his bearing in his home. He practised no virtue abroad which was not fully paralleled in his most private life. Devoted affection, unselfishness, thoughtfulness, responsiveness, cheerfulness, were his unvarying characteristics, and they made a sunshine throughout his house. As the head of his family, he loved respect, but exacted no peculiar attention to his individual wants or tastes. He seemed to have no selfish wishes, and certainly had neither moods nor whims. His serenity, born not more of temperament than of principle, was uniform. The fret of daily life seemed scarcely to touch him. "It is a literal truth," says one of his children, "that I *never* in my life heard my father utter an irritable or impatient word." He bore interruption of his own pursuits with complete patience, and entered instantly and heartily into the interests or wishes of the youngest of his family. He liked to be admitted to the confidence of his children, and, when he could command leisure, to participate in their pursuits. He craved manifestations of affection: a pleasant word, a smile, or loving act, touched him tenderly. He loved to be cordially greeted and to be caressed. He used to say, when one was paying him any little personal attention, "How I love to be *muched!*" *i.e.*, made much of. One of those who waited on him in his last illness writes, "He was the only man who ever when sick deserved the name of 'patient.'"

He was earnest to gratify his children's tastes, and to secure them any enjoyment on which they set their hearts, but, above all, to provide them every possible opportunity of education. On his own gratification or comfort he spent neither money nor thought; but for them he would sacrifice every thing. Never enjoying a large salary, it was not easy to give them the advantages he wished. But he strained every nerve to keep them at good schools, and to provide them the privileges of more advanced training. A principal reason with him for removing to Syracuse was, he often remarked, the expectation of securing his children a better education and a better start in life, as well as of keeping them about him as they grew up.

It was always a pleasure to him to see his family all together and happy. The noise of children's play never disturbed him, he used to say, so long as their voices were happy. When engaged himself, if he passed through the family sitting-room, there was always a beaming smile of satisfaction on his countenance. In every success of his children he took a loving pride; always visiting their schools frequently, and often examining them at home, to observe their progress in their studies. But his affection was always governed by principle; and he was so much opposed to false methods of stimulating pupils, that, when one of his children who attended an advanced school where no ranking system existed, received the approval of the instructors so peculiarly that they proposed to confer a special rank, Mr. May requested them not to do so.

Mr. May's married life, ended on earth by the death of his beloved wife in 1865, extended over a period of forty years. Mrs. May was the daughter of Peter Coffin, a highly respected merchant of Portsmouth, N.H., who removed, in middle life, to Boston. Lucretia Flagge Coffin, who became Mrs. May, was distinguished in youth for her great beauty of person; of a singularly bright mind, a vivacious and sensitive temperament, earnest for mental culture, strict in moral principle, of strong religious feelings, and actively though quietly benevolent. She was a most devoted wife and mother, a diligent housekeeper with the traditions of New England, a skilful and gentle nurse, and a constant reader and student. Of her intellectual thirst and the attainments to which it led her, Mr. May was fondly proud. She was a good historian; read French habitually throughout her life; and in her last years took up Italian and learnt it, unaided, well enough to pursue the principal Italian poets with fluency and enjoyment. The best modern literature of our own language she closely followed, while the older English writers she knew almost by heart. With the books of her husband's library she was almost more conversant than himself. She was a daily student of the Bible, which she usually read in French, and was quite extensively acquainted with Scripture literature. On questions of criticism Mr. May often appealed to her with great confidence and respect. During the earlier portion of their married life she was his constant companion in the arduous duties which then devolved, especially in a country parish, on the minister and his wife. From these she was debarred in later life, by the impaired condition of her health; but her private charities and domestic activity never ceased. She was a warm and cordial personal friend, lively in familiar society; while the poor and unfortunate who came within the reach of her benevolence had no kinder word of gratitude for her husband than for her.

Generous and self-denying to an extreme, she was judicious in practical affairs, and a better manager than her husband, who always said that the worldly embarrassments in which his somewhat uncontrollable generosity involved him would usually have been escaped if he had consulted her. The home was always a place of refuge for passing unfortunates, and was familiar with the tread of almost every man or woman who has contributed conspicuously to American reforms. Among these latter, Mrs. May, always a painstaking hostess, had many particular friends. Of those we are now at liberty to name, Theodore Parker and Wendell Phillips were, perhaps, the chief. But in the equal hospitality with which she treated the various and innumerable guests whom her husband's sympathies and temper brought to their home, the humblest shared as fully as the most illustrious.

The union of these two was marked by a deep and unchanging mutual affection and tenderness. The domestic and personal sacrifices to which a career like Mr. May's exposed them, she shared with perfect acquiescence; and her husband watched with devoted sympathy over the ill-health which in her later years afflicted her, and which a less unselfish and more popular course than his might in some measure have prevented.

On the occasion of her death Mr. May wrote, among others of similar tenor, the following letters, in which his respect and affection for his wife are faithfully shown: —

SYRACUSE, May 8, 1865.

MY DEAR FRIEND, — My day of sorrow has come. The dear wife with whom I have lived in love forty years has left me. I rejoice for her sake, but grieve, oh! how sorely, for my own. She has been a sufferer in the flesh for thirteen years, crippled in her ability to be as useful to others as she longed to be. The good she did to those she had it in her power to befriend showed how much she would have done for very many more, if her ability had been equal to her desire.

But her pure, timid, compassionate, conscientious spirit has now left the poor body in which she suffered so much, and has entered, I believe, into a more glorious body, in which she will be able to go upward and onward in that career of improvement which she longed for, without encountering the impediments that here beset her path.

In accordance with her often expressed wish, her funeral is to be quite private; and I wish that you would be with us at the time, and speak to us the words that shall seem to you fitting, and offer such prayer as the spirit of sympathy with our human infirmities and confidence in the Divine wisdom and love may inspire.

Yours truly, SAM'L J. MAY.

MR. C. D. B. MILLS.

SYRACUSE, May 18, 1865.

DEAR BUCKINGHAM, — Your very tender letter of the 11th was the first of many that have come to me since the death of my precious wife. If earthly friends can uphold me, I am sure I shall not fall; and I feel also that the almighty arm of the Heavenly Father is supporting me.

I did not know that so many who sympathize with me in my bereavement knew so well how much I have lost.

You, and others who have written me, speak of my dear wife very discriminately. She was not only bright, yea, often brilliant, but she was perfectly sincere, single-hearted, and pure as an infant. Her respect for the true and the right was profound. Her thirst for knowledge was insatiable. Her pursuit of it was diligent, and often urged her beyond her strength. She delighted in the conversation of intelligent persons; and one of the many pleasures that have been granted her during her latter days was a long visit, the last of March, from her special favorite, Wendell Phillips. She enjoyed him to the utmost; and a sweet letter, just received from him, assures me that the pleasure was mutual.

. . . .

We buried her body on Wednesday at 5 P.M., by the side of her darling grand-daughter. Mr. Mills officiated, and said most beautifully all that the occasion required. Give my love to your wife.

Truly, affectionately yours, SAM'L J. MAY.

CHAPTER XX.

CLOSING YEARS.

President of the Board of Education. — Instrumental in procuring the Abolition of Corporal Punishment. — A New School-house named for him. — Chosen President of the Alumni of Cambridge Divinity School. — His Interest in the National Conference of Unitarian Churches. — States his Theological Opinions. — Regrets that Women were not invited to the First Conference. — Fraternal Feeling towards Universalists. — Resigns his Pastorate. — Prizes the Letters sent to him. — Takes Great Pleasure in noting the Harvest in Windham County, Conn., from the Seed which he sowed there long before. — His "Preferences." — His Views of the Bible.

MR. MAY'S interest in public affairs was never more deep and lively than during the last ten years of his earthly life. When his fellow-citizens manifested their appreciation of his worth, if not also their regret for some of the indignities to which he had been subjected on account of his fidelity to principles which they finally accepted, by choosing him President of the Board of Education, he entered upon the duties of his honorable position with earnestness and diligence. The schools of Syracuse derived great benefit from his experience as a teacher and his life-long observation of the best methods of instruction.

His influence in behalf of the abolition of corporal punishment was very great, and his face was never more radiant than when he told of the success of such experiments as that of appealing to the hopes rather than the fears of pupils. "We are saved by hope," was one of his favorite texts; and he believed, with all his heart, in the duty of judicious encouragement.

In one of the Syracuse schools the teacher adopted a plan of having a medal to be awarded to the class which should make the most creditable progress from time to time. This class chose from its own number a boy who should be the medal-bearer. The most indolent and mischievous boy in the school soon began to feel his obligations to his classmates, paying more attention to his lessons, and being less frequently reproved for misconduct. His class gained the medal; and his classmates, of their own accord, chose him medal-bearer, to reward him for the efforts he had so evidently made to improve in his deportment and scholarship. The reformed boy was completely overcome by this generous tribute.

This story afforded Mr. May unbounded pleasure, and he was fond of citing it as an illustration of the latent nobility in the human breast. He took an honest pride in the new May school-house which was named for him.

Honored in his own immediate country, this faithful prophet was also revered throughout the length and breadth of the land. His presence at any gathering in the East or the West added to the happiness of the whole assembly. His election as President of the Alumni of the Cambridge Divinity School was only one of many expressions of reverence and love for him in his old age.

With all his love of manly independence and his respect for individual convictions, Mr. May was such a lover of his kind, that he longed for associated action whenever it could be obtained without any sacrifice of principle. Therefore he was pleased when the call for the convention which organized the National Conference of Unitarian Churches was issued. His opinions at this time are well expressed in a letter to Rev. Edgar Buckingham.

SYRACUSE, Feb. 8, 1865.

DEAR BUCKINGHAM, — Your wise and witty epistle of the 1st reached me on the morning of the 2d, and prompted me to reply to you immediately. But I thought it better to wait until after we should have seen what the committee would propose for the Convention to do.

The programme is better than I expected, and yet indefinite, just as is the condition of our denomination. And yet, though I foresee not what will be done, nor indeed very clearly what it will be best to do, I think it advisable to hold the Convention. If it shall be, as I trust it will be, largely attended, and by churches and ministers of every variety of Unitarian, liberal, and rationalistic belief, by supernaturalists and anti-supernaturalists, it will serve one good purpose, at least: it will make us better acquainted with each other, and with the unsettled state of our ecclesiastical body.

I hope the Convention will be enabled to define simply and clearly who ought to be considered professed Christians and who real Christians, and at the same time allow that many may be dear children of God who are not Christians; that purity of heart and righteousness of life alone can make any one acceptable to the Heavenly Father; and that if any men do attain that purity and righteousness without the aid of Jesus Christ, they will still be accepted by him and by God.

It seems to me self-evident that the acknowledgment of Christ's authority as a teacher of divine truth and a leader of salvation is indispensable to the Christian name and to any standing in the Christian Church, but that such acknowledgment alone will not entitle any one to consider himself, or to be regarded by others, as a true Christian, if he is conscious of suffering any impure desires or unholy purposes to dwell in his bosom, or is seen by others to be a worker of iniquity. And, on the other hand, if a man is conscious of pure desires and upright intentions, of earnestly aspiring to know and to do the will of God, he may look up as much as any other man may, with expectation of the Divine approbation; and if his Christian neighbors see in his life the evidences of his piety and benevolence, they should accept him as worthy of their fellowship, although he may never have heard the name of Christ, or may have failed to be convinced that he was a teacher sent from God. Please let me know how much of this statement you are ready to indorse.

For my own part, I am a supernaturalist, or what others would so call. I believe that Jesus worked miracles. I believe that he raised dead men to life, and that he himself arose from the tomb in which his lifeless body had been buried. But I do not believe that his miracles are the most important things that he did, nor does he seem to me so to have regarded them. I believe that he was, or will be, more than any other man, the *Saviour of the world*, because he inculcated the principles of true righteousness, the righteousness of God, more clearly and forcibly than any other teacher had done; and because he illustrated those principles and manifested their power in his own life and death.

I believe that Jesus of Nazareth was the best teacher of true religion that ever yet has lived; and that, as a Christian minister, it is my duty to persuade all whom I can influence to put themselves under his instruction and guidance; to learn of him and imbibe his spirit, as the surest way to salvation.

And I believe that when men shall have become holy as Christ was holy, miracles will no longer seem supernatural to them, and that some of them may do even greater works than Jesus did. Do you agree with me so far? It is my intention to attend the Convention, and to take along with me the two best men I can get to go. Why have not women been invited? God made man dual, and it is not wise nor safe for us to be singular in our attention to any of the great concerns of life. I wish we could have such women as Frances Power Cobbe and L. Maria Child and Lucretia Mott with us. I am sure their counsels would aid us as much as those of any men we shall have there. The emancipation and enfranchisement of women is the great work to be done before the human race can do and become what the Creator intended them to be and do.

Are not the Universalists to be invited to the Convention? They ought to be recognized by us, cordially and gratefully, as a most valuable part of the body of liberal Christians. They have borne a most faithful and persistent testimony against the greatest of all the abominable doctrines of the orthodox theology; and the brightest, the kingly Starr, in our Unitarian constellation, was one of their number.

Yours truly and affectionately,

SAMUEL J. MAY.

He seems to have attached a special value to the letters which were written in acknowledgment of copies of his "Brief Account of my Ministry," preached when he was seventy years old. These cordial notes from Samuel E. Sewall, Francis G. Shaw, Charles Eliot Norton, Adin Ballou, Maria W. Chapman, John H. Heywood, John W. Chadwick, and many others, were carefully preserved. We found them in a package which also contained other papers that must have been very precious to him, including a fine letter from Sister Hieronymo, who seems to have been at the head of St. Mary's Hospital, at Rochester, N. Y. Under the date of February 20th, 1867, she writes to her "esteemed friend," expressing her faith in his sincere regard for her, and her knowledge of the deep interest that he had ever taken in establishments which had for their end "the alleviation of suffering humanity," invoking his assistance. There must have been a beautiful sympathy between the Roman Catholic Sister of Charity and the Protestant Brother of Mercy. Her letter closes, "Yours in Christ."

He took much satisfaction in observing the harvest which had sprung up from the good seed which he sowed in Windham County, Conn., many years before; and it was with great delight that he saw, in 1865 or 1866, that his old county gave a large majority in favor of giving the ballot to colored men, when all the other counties of the State gave majorities against the righteous measure.

On the 19th of July, 1869, Mr. May gratified a daughter of his old friend and classmate, Dr. J. P. Spooner, of Dorchester, by writing in her Book of Preferences that his favorite flower was the Pond Lily; his favorite color, Light Blue; his favorite musical composition, "The Last Rose of Summer;" his favorite painting, Johnson's "Drummer Boy;" his favorite dissipation, Russian Backgammon; his favorite virtue,

Charity; his particular aversion, Cant; the animal that he liked best, a Little Child; his favorite prose-writers, Dr. Channing and Theodore Parker; his favorite poets, Whittier and J. R. Lowell; his favorite preacher, Edward E. Hale; his favorite singer, Miss Wheaton, now Mrs. Morgan; his favorite male character in history, Jesus of Nazareth; his favorite female character, Mary L. Ware; that he would prefer to spend the summer in Massachusetts, and to live in the United States; that he would be satisfied with as much money as he could spend wisely; that, in his opinion, a man should marry at twenty-five, and a woman at twenty-two; and that the journey that he should prefer to take would be a trip to California.

About six weeks before his death, Mr. May addressed the following letter to the editor of a paper which had contained an erroneous account of his views of the Bible:—

To the Editor of the "Syracuse Journal."

I have just read in your daily "Journal" of last Saturday a very meagre and, in several particulars, inaccurate report of the semi-annual meeting in Utica, last week, of "The Central New York Conference of Liberal Christians." I am sure that, if a full *verbatim* report of all that was said in the discussions at that meeting could be laid before your readers, they would receive a very different impression from that which the statements in your paper of the 13th must have made.

The most important subject discussed by us was the one proposed by Mr. Gerrit Smith: "What is True Religion? and What are its Requirements?" All the speakers, if we except, perhaps, Rev. Mr. Jewell, of Rome, agreed that true religion is the harmonious development of our moral nature, in accordance with the laws of God inscribed by him upon our hearts. We can all partake in some humble measure of the Divine nature, and the true religion is that which leads us to unfold that divinity and keep ourselves in harmony with it. Jesus Christ, the highest, best teacher of religion, continually appealed to the sense of the right, the true, the good, which he knew must be latent, if not patent, in all his hearers. Many of his instructions were given in parables, from which they were left to draw the intended lessons by their own discernment.

It was insisted by several of the speakers at our meeting — especially by Mr. Smith, Mr. Mills, and myself — that the Christian world has been misled into the greatest errors by assuming, the Roman Catholics that the Pope, and the Protestants that the Bible, is the highest authority in matters of theology and religion. To assert and maintain the infallibility of the Bible is as absurd and dangerous as to assert and maintain the infallibility of the man who occupies the papal chair.

I repeat what I said at Utica. "The Bible is, I believe, the best of books. In it we find the highest, the sublimest moral and religious precepts, and the most glorious revelations of the character of God and of the nature and destiny of man. But it is not all true, not all of equal value and authority. There are in it many words that could never have come by inspiration of the pure, benevolent, and holy God. There are in it things which I am not willing my children should ever read. Indeed, I have often wished that we had an expurgated Bible."

In another part of our discussion I said: "It seems to me necessary, in the first place, to define what Christianity, the true religion, is. It is not to be learnt equally from all parts of the Bible; from the words and acts of the writers and distinguished personages in the Old Testament as well as the New. Jesus Christ is the best teacher of Christianity, which

I revere as the truest, highest manifestation of religion ever yet made to man. We should learn it of him. We should study his life and character even more than his words. Christ was the impersonation of Christianity. We should contemplate his conduct in all the various scenes of his ministry, until we feel the influence of his spirit, and realize that what he was we should aspire and strive and pray to become.

Respectfully yours, SAMUEL J. MAY.

SYRACUSE, May 16, 1871.

Rev. C. D. B. Mills writes to us:—

"In his last sickness I saw him several times. He seemed not to be apprehensive that he was nearing the end of his earthly career, at least he was deeply preoccupied with plans of future work, and so probably hardly thought of any interruption at hand. His mind was clear. The desire to do some things that lay immediately before him was very strong, but there was the same calm poise, and the peace that had habitually marked all his life. Once he said he hoped he should live two or three years longer to accomplish some work that appeared to him of high importance. 'In the fall,' said he, 'I purpose to offer to our Society a series of Lectures on the History of the Bible, that very valuable, least apprehended, and most idolized Book.' He was very anxious to state himself more fully upon this point of the true character and just apprehension of the Bible, as his views had been made the subject of attack and gross misrepresentation by a Baptist preacher of Syracuse, at the very commencement of his sickness.

"On another occasion, referring to his past life, he remarked that on review he now saw he had committed some mistakes, that there were things in the history he would fain wish were otherwise. 'But in purpose I have wrought for Truth; I have sought to do for humanity.' Referring to the views that he was coming more and more firmly to hold regarding authority, the historic in religion and the ideal standards, he said : 'In large part alone, and at some personal cost to myself, I have worked my way along to light and liberty. I see more and more clearly, feel increasingly sure, that I come here to the solid ground, the bed rock. I stand on it firmly and with full assurance. The past I cannot regard with regret, or view my life as a failure. It has realized, has netted something : it is in a fair degree accomplishment and success. The course I have pursued is vindicated to my best judgment, and I feel that all is and shall be well.'

" This was the substance of what he said : I cannot reproduce the exact language."

CHAPTER XXI.

DEATH AND BURIAL.

HIS LAST DAY ON EARTH. — PRESIDENT WHITE'S VISIT. — FAITH IN IMMORTALITY. — IMPRESSION MADE BY HIS DEATH. — FUNERAL SERVICES.

MR. MAY'S death was quite sudden. In the spring of 1871 he planned a visit to New England of considerable length, but severe illness prevented his leaving home. At the close of June, however, he felt much better, and began to look forward again to seeing his Eastern friends once more. On Saturday, the 1st of July, he was remarkably bright and hopeful, spending several hours in most animated conversation with those who called upon him. To one person he made cordial mention of James Freeman Clarke's book on "Ten Great Religions," then recently published, and spoke at length of its great merits, with frank allusions to what he considered some limitations and defects. In the afternoon a visit from President White, of Cornell University, gave him much pleasure. He was delighted to learn that a generous man had offered the University a very liberal gift, upon the condition that young women should have the same advantages as young men in that institution. Mr. May promised to give the college his portrait of Prudence Crandall if this should be consummated;[1] and he parted with Mr. White in the most cheerful and affectionate manner. Indeed, what proved to be their last words on earth to each other were overflowing with joy and hope. President White said that, in view of the rapid advances of great causes which Mr. May had so much at heart, he must consent to live at least thirty years longer, to enjoy the triumphs of truth and right. As President White left the room, Mr. May called after him, "Andrew, you must let me off with twenty years," and received the playful reply, "No: we really cannot spare you for thirty years." [2]

About ten o'clock in the evening he became very ill. As his strength ebbed away, he manifested a desire that his daughter should kiss him, and then, with a farewell smile, his spirit took its upward flight.

On Sunday morning, his old church being closed on account of Mr. Calthrop's vacation, many of his parishioners were in Rev. Mr. Mundy's congregation, and the announcement of his death from the pulpit was so startling that the services were interrupted by the sobbings of the bereaved people. The whole community were deeply impressed. Colored people at once put on

[1] Mr. May had already presented to this University his large and valuable collection of books and pamphlets relating to the anti-slavery contest.

[2] This characteristic playfulness did not indicate any lack of his habitual earnestness. His sincerity was such that he could always be spontaneous. In another mood, not long before, alluding to the uncertainty of his recovery, he uttered these remarkable but equally characteristic words: *"If I die, I may have a clearer vision, but I cannot have a surer faith."*

mourning badges, as they had done when Mr. Lincoln died. The daily papers contained long and glowing tributes to his worth, some of the heartiest expressions coming from the Democratic organ.

On the days between his death and burial, the house of his son-in-law, Mr. Alfred Wilkinson, with whom he had lived, was visited by many friends from far and near who wished to look once more upon his face. Gerrit Smith came from Peterboro, notwithstanding his own illness, and also wrote: "Mr. May was the most Christ-like man that I ever knew. He made Christ his pattern; and how successfully, was proved by his never-failing gentleness, meekness, and sweetness. Heaven is more desirable to me now that my dear May is there."

On the morning of Thursday, July 6th, there was a private service at Mr. Wilkinson's house. Rev. Frederic Frothingham read appropriate passages of Scripture, Rev. W. P. Tilden prayed, and Mr. A. Bronson Alcott made an address of indescribable beauty, delicacy, and tenderness. At ten o'clock the body was removed to the church. Not long afterwards the household reassembled to listen to the reminiscences of Mr. George B. Emerson, Rev. W. P. Tilden, and others. Mr. Emerson spoke of his early and ever-growing love for Mr. May, of their college life, and of the delightful Sunday evenings which he had spent with him at Colonel May's house in Boston. Mr. Emerson believes that in going to Brooklyn, Conn., and declining calls to other places, Mr. May was governed by the consideration that in worldly goods it was the poorest parish, and least likely to obtain a desirable pastor.

After the precious dust had been placed in the familiar church which was exquisitely decorated, before the pulpit from which he had spoken so many bold and loving words, it was visited by a great number of persons. "The casket rested upon a base of clematis and evergreens. On the lid lay a 'shock of wheat fully ripe and fit for the Master's use.' Over the centre rested a crown of lilies, roses, and ivy: at the foot lay a wreath of clematis and geraniums." "All sorts and conditions of men" seemed to be attracted to the spot. Among those who came and went were members of every denomination and political party. Protestant Daughters of Mercy stood beside Roman Catholic Sisters of Charity; and Indians, with "persons of African descent," were near the fairest women and the chief men of the city.

Just before the time appointed for the public service, a violent rain-storm came; but the people were too much in earnest to be hindered by it. Until the doors were opened, there was a crowd in front of the church, which was soon densely packed. Twenty-one clergymen were present, including a Jewish rabbi. The President of the Board of Education and other members of the Board, with many teachers, came. The Mayor, the member of Congress, the Superintendent of the Asylum for the Feeble Minded, and other prominent citizens, including at least one Roman Catholic, were pall-bearers. Rev. Mr. Calthrop prayed. Thomas J. Mumford read selections from the Bible. Rev. C. D. B. Mills, of Syracuse, delivered an eloquent address, in the course of which he said: "In the last century the hut of a noted Indian, Logan, chief of the Cayugas, is said to have been recognized by his brethren as they passed it, by the inscription: 'Here lives the friend of the white man.' But upon the door of that unpretending house standing upon yonder hill-slope might have been inscribed through all these years, 'Here dwells the friend of all men!'" Mr. Garrison followed with an admirable delineation of Mr. May's character, including a most apt quotation of Wordsworth's "Happy Warrior." Bishop Loguen, of the African Methodist Episcopal Church, a noble-looking man of gigantic stature, then spoke very tenderly of this friend of himself and his people. Rev. W. P. Tilden read excellent notes from Rev. Charles Lowe and Rev. R. R. Shippen, who acknowledged Mr. May's great services to the Unitarian cause; and Mr. Tilden added his own tribute of personal gratitude. After prayer by Rev. F. Frothingham, "Nearer, my God, to Thee," was sung, and the services at the church were closed with a benediction.

Hundreds followed the body to Oakwood Cemetery, two miles away. Along the route we noticed flags at half-mast over little houses which seemed to be homes of colored people. When we passed citizens on the street, they stood with uncovered heads until the procession had gone by. Upon reaching the grave, the Sunday-school children, who had been unable to get into the church, were formed in two lines, and sang a hymn:—

"In that sweet by-and-by,
By-and-by we shall meet
On that beautiful shore."

Rev. Mr. Calthrop spoke of the grand lessons of Mr. May's life, and called upon the young men present to heed them. President Andrew D. White, of Cornell University, said:—

"Here lies before us all that was mortal of the best man, the most truly *Christian* man, I have ever known; the purest, the sweetest; the fullest of faith, hope, and charity; the most like the Master.

"When the Sermon on the Mount was read this afternoon, it seemed prophetic of the man. It was *not* 'Blessed are the pure in heart, who accept the Thirty-nine Articles;' *not* 'Blessed are the peacemakers, who subscribe to the decrees of the Council of Trent;' *not* 'Blessed are ye when men shall revile you, provided ye agree to the Westminster Catechism.' No. The blessings of that greatest of utterances since the world began were without human tests, and they fell upon our friend in full measure, and his life was the radiant witness of them, and we all saw them.

"Had our Lord come upon this earth again, and into these streets, any time in these thirty years, he was sure of one follower. Came he as black man, or red man, or the most wretched of white men; came he in rags or sores, this, our dear friend, would have followed him, no matter what weapons, carnal or spiritual, were hurled at the procession.

"I account it among the greatest of blessings that it was given me to know this man; and I shall always rejoice that in the last afternoon of his life I spent a most delightful hour with him, and bore away his blessing."

He was followed by Thomas J. Mumford, Rev. C. D. B. Mills, and Rev. E. W. Mundy. After the casket was lowered, the Sunday-school children, one by one, dropped flowers and tears into the grave. This ended the touching service; but the people still lingered, as if reluctant to leave the spot.[1] Although night was at hand, it was some time before the cemetery was deserted.

1 His little grandchildren coming up to cast in their flowers, a common impulse to follow their example seemed to run through the throng of older friends; and perhaps the most affecting incident of the day was the eagerness with which they crowded forward to express in this personal way their love for Mr. May. Any thing like a flower, even a leaf from a tree, was enough; and before the earth covered it the casket was already hidden out of sight.

Cambridge: Press of John Wilson and Son.

ROBERTS BROTHERS' PUBLICATIONS.

THE ROSE-GARDEN. By the author of "Unawares." "*Tout comprendre c'est tout pardonner.*" 16mo, neat cloth. Price $1.50.

Extracts from some of the many favorable notices of "The Rose-Garden."

"I have been reading "The Rose-Garden" with real delight. It is a perfect gem of a summer story." —*Extract from the letter of a talented lady.*

"It is very long since we have met with a story more thoroughly deserving of praise, from whatever point of view it may be regarded, than the work before us. The writer's skill in delineation of character is very far beyond that of most novelists of the day; and this skill is shown, not in elaborate and pre-Raphaelite attempts at description, but in the few but telling touches that show the true artist. It is, indeed, a rare gift to have the power of writing a domestic story which, while it could not possibly have any influence except for good on the most pure-minded and unsophisticated English girl into whose hands it might fall, shows great knowledge of the world, and is healthily exciting.

"We could not reasonably expect to be taken to a rose garden without falling in with a thorn or two; and the most that we can say, and at the same time the least that we ought to say, of this delightful story, is that it is in every way worthy of its well-chosen title." — *The London Illustrated Review.*

"She has some rare and charming qualities which ought to place her among our favorite writers. There is no reason why, with careful self-culture and diligence, she shall not be one of the popular novelists of her time." — *Saturday Review.*

"One of the recent issues from the press of Roberts Brothers bears the pretty title of "The Rose-Garden;" and in one sense it is not inappropriate, for it is read with a quiet enjoyment that leaves a pleasant fragrance in the memory. The plot is simple and natural, and each character has such marked individuality that its life moves in a real way. The book is an illustration of the keen unhappiness, the nervous uneasiness, that come out of falsehood, or are the ten-tongued offspring of its mute brother, — silent deception. Mrs. Opie has dealt with white lies and black: this author, with a fine and subtle skill, develops the mischievous power of a gray lie." — *Courier.*

"It is not often that we have the pleasure of reading such a pleasant story as "The Rose-Garden." The title-page informs us that it is by the author of "Unawares," a book that we do not remember, yet one that must be delightful reading, if it is as good as this. The story is simple and pure, and marked by delicate characterization. It describes French country life charmingly; but the thought that runs through the whole book, and lifts it up to something higher than a mere story, is given in the sentence, "To understand all is to pardon all." The author shows how a weak and timid nature may be led into faults that cause most grievous consequences, and yet how powerful an agent of good is a deep affection." — *Louisville Courier-Journal.*

Sold everywhere. Mailed, postpaid, by the publishers,

ROBERTS BROTHERS, *Boston.*

www.ingramcontent.com/pod-product-compliance
Lightning Source LLC
LaVergne TN
LVHW020229110826
845151LV00003B/865

* 9 7 8 1 4 2 5 5 3 0 9 6 9 *